MOVING
DIVERSITY
FORWARD

HOW TO GO FROM
WELL-MEANING TO WELL-DOING

AMERICAN BAR ASSOCIATION

Center for Racial & Ethnic Diversity
General Practice, Solo & Small Firm Division

Cover design by Elmarie Jara/ABA Publishing.
Cartoons by Jerry Craft

Printed in the United States of America.

21 20   15 14

Library of Congress Cataloging-in-Publication Data

Myers, Verna.
  Beyond diversity : moving from well-being to well-doing / by Verna Myers.—1st ed.
    p. cm.
  Includes bibliographical references and index.
  ISBN 978-1-61438-006-1
  1. Law firms—United States—Personnel management. 2. Diversity in the workplace—United States. I. Title.
  KF300.M94 2011
  340.068'3—dc23

                                                    2011027965

Contents

Chapter 7
Are You Sure He's Our Waiter? I Think He's the Band Leader: How Is Your Lens Shaping What You See?

Chapter 8
He's Black. What Do You Mean He Can't Dance? Check for Your Biases When Things Get Bumpy

Chapter 9
Dancing with Peggy McIntosh: Breaking the Thirteen Deadly Habits of Workplace Oppression

Chapter 10
White People Have Always Been Center Stage: Understanding White Privilege and Other Forms of Unearned Privilege

Dedication

To Trés, the light of my life.
To Albert and Cora, my foundation.
And to Famane, my rock.

I have a bias which leads me to
believe that no problem of human
relations is ever insoluble.

Ralph Bunche

Acknowledgments

This book is a miracle to me: something I talked about doing for years has now come into being. So my gratitude begins with my Creator, who has gifted, guided, and graced me beyond my imagination. I am also grateful to my parents for providing me with a firm foundation of love, faith, courage, and integrity. Thanks to the Biggers, the Camerons, and the Myers for their unconditional love, support, and grace. I am also thankful to all my ancestors, whose endurance, sacrifice, hard work, and unyielding belief in justice have made it possible for me to realize my dreams.

I would also like to thank all my clients, diversity professionals, and colleagues who have engaged, challenged, and supported me over the years. In particular, I am grateful for the many men and women of every background who have shared their painful and promising stories with me in the hope that, by doing so, our workplaces and lives would more open, respectful, and inclusive of others.

Early on, there were several individuals whose encouragement and downright insistence got me to sit down and write this book. Thanks to the open-hearted Becky Shuster, who walked and talked with me one night about how we could write a book together drawing on our deep friendship that crosses racial, cultural, class, and religious boundaries. We haven't written that book yet, but that conversation made me think I had something worth writing. Great thanks also to the wonderful Ralph Jordan, who challenged me to finish the book. My office manager, Carol Centrella, willed this book into existence with her sweet and nurturing belief in the importance of what I had to say and her amazingly hard work on behalf of Vernā Myers Consulting Group (VMCG). My deep appreciation goes to Martha Fields, my book coach. Her enthusiasm, her commitment to supporting the writings of women of color, and some real deadlines made it possible for me to complete the manuscript in six months. Thanks for helping a sister out!

Some supergenerous friends and colleagues walked me through many versions of this book. I am thankful to my good friend Martha Eddison Sieniewicz for lending her enormous writing and editing talent to my work over the years and her feedback at the beginning stages of this book. I think she came up with the "being asked to dance" metaphor. I also have to thank Arnie Kanter, my mentor and friend who proudly refers to himself as a BOWN (bald, old white man). His perspective and advice have been invaluable for the book and my career. Thanks to Lane Vanderslice for challenging me about how to tell the truth with power and possibility. Bless you. Thanks also to the brilliant and outrageously witty Theresa Cropper, diversity director extraordinaire, who read an early draft and gave me the thumbs-up, which meant so much to me. I appreciate Todd Shuster, Eliisa Frazier, and my classmate Amelia Zalcman from the publishing world for giving me positive feedback on earlier chapters and suggestions about content, structure, and publishing. Thanks to the really busy people who took time to read the manuscript and offer valuable feedback on the book: Keith Early, Bill Freidman, Patty Keenan, Lauren Rikleen, Susanne Zimmer, and Jim Concannon.

There has been no greater blessing during this process than my editor, Stuart Horwitz (Book Architecture). Stuart, thanks for believing my heart, hearing my voice, and reminding me that "unity is the highest good." His genius and humor gave me great encouragement and created clarity and structure for the book. I am forever indebted. I also have to thank Karen Byrne at Book Architecture for pitching in at the last minute to help me make my first deadline! I truly appreciate all the care, support, and encouragement from the very beginning to the end by the publishing and marketing team at the ABA. It was such a pleasure working with Rick Paszkiet, Sandra Rogers, and Kelly Keane. Cie Armstead and the Diversity Center championed the book idea from its inception and enthusiastically supported me throughout the process. Thanks also for all the enthusiasm and support of Laura Farber, chair of the General Practice, Solo and Small Firm Division. Andrea Harris of Lachina Publishing was also incredibly flexible and helpful with the book layout.

Thanks to all the writers who encouraged and guided me through this process. I really appreciate Monica Parker, who began two years ago convincing me to write, included me in her book, and answered all my questions about undertaking this task. Susanne Goldstein, first-time writer, and Steve Shapiro, a veteran, have been so helpful and generous with their time, information, and inspiration. I am also so thankful to the smart and industrious Debbie Epstein Henry, another first-time writer, for her willingness to share all she knows. Many thanks to my new friend and writer, Debby Irving, who is writing a book called *Waking Up White*. Her eagerness to share her journey and support mine has been validating in so many ways. I am forever grateful to Liz Walker, my sister in Christ and cycling, for her encouragement and for sharing the incomparable Stuart Horwitz with me. I know it is just a matter of time before we are reading her amazing memoir.

So many thanks to my cool white friends (new and old) and colleagues who came to my house to participate in focus groups and share their experiences and thoughts about racial inclusion. Thanks to Mary Clark; Barbara Deck; Anna H. Lifson; Chris Miller; André Perrault; John Rabinowitz; Elizabeth Rettig; Doug Reynolds; Lindsay Rosenfeld; Comma Williams; Brina Waldoks; and my other cultural informants—Jesse Levandov, Paul Marcus of Community Change, Georgiana Melendez, and Maria Melendez. Thanks to my heart and true friend, Janis Robinson, who hosted my first, pre-book release party in Chicago with a fabulous group of black professional women. I am grateful for these very accomplished women who gave me their time and reassuring feedback.

I relied heavily on a team of folks to do the hardest work on the book. J. Corey Harris was on top of any request I made for materials, research, and the organization of focus groups. Judy Rakowsky, and Wendy Weiss also did great work researching and editing. Jillian Hubbard did a fabulous job getting the manuscript out for folks to read and review. Thanks to Ellen Lubell, my lawyer, who read the manuscript and made me cry when she told me that she could feel the love in these pages. Hats off to my new friend and brilliant cartoonist, Jerry Craft. He took my words and our experiences as black professionals and worked late into the night, turning them into comics that made me laugh out loud. Thanks to Michael Myers, Sr. for the many books and movies on racial issues we have discussed over the years and for adding to our resource guide.

So much of what I have learned on the issue of racial diversity and organizational change comes from amazing thinkers and writers whose intelligence, kindness, and generosity inspire and challenge me. For enhancing my work and sharing their ideas with me, I would like to thank Valerie Batts, Mahzarin Banaji, Lani Guinier, Peggy

McIntosh, Charles Ogletree, Scott Page, David Thomas, Cornell West, Mark Warren, and David Wilkins.

Thanks to my VMCG family for all their dedication to the work of creating equal opportunity and fairness in our world. Barbara, Bill, Comma, Doug F., Doug R., Jane, Kay, Laurie, Marguerite, Tricia, and Yvonne—thanks for all your patience and understanding during this time. Kay and Doug, we've come a long way. Thanks for allowing me to use your stories; your lives and your commitment to the cause of social and racial justice has always buoyed me and helped VMCG become what it is.

Thanks to the Birthday Sisters in Boston and all over the country—especially my prayer partner, Sheila Hubbard—who root for me, make me laugh, keep me honest, and pray for me.

Finally, there have been many white people—mentors, teachers, and friends—who have played an active role in creating success in my life. Some are named above. In addition, I want to thank Flora Davidson, Ken Erickson, Ester Fuchs, Scott Harshbarger, Anne Ellen Hornidge, Richard Pious, Christine Royer, Steve Shay, and Kathleen Sullivan. All of these people helped me know that what I am saying in this book is possible.

About the Author

Vernā Myers, Esq., principal of Vernā Myers Consulting Group, LLC (VMCG), is a nationally recognized expert on diversity and inclusion within law firms, law departments, and law schools. Ms. Myers is a dynamic speaker and creative advisor in support of creating inclusive environments and improving the recruitment, retention, and advancement of underrepresented groups. VMCG has collaborated with over 90 legal clients to effect sustainable organizational change by conducting cultural assessments, developing comprehensive strategic diversity action plans, and facilitating compelling and interactive workshops in the U.S. and around the globe. A highly  sought-after speaker at numerous conferences worldwide, Ms. Myers sponsors her own successful annual Opus Conference on Race and Ethnicity in Large Law Firms.

In 2010, Pepper Hamilton LLP awarded Ms. Myers its Diversity Champion award. In 2009 she was chosen as one of The Network Journal's "25 Influential Black Women in Business," and in 2008, one of The Massachusetts Lawyers Weekly's "Diversity Heroes."

Prior to establishing VMCG, Ms. Myers was the first executive director of The Boston Law Firm Group, a consortium of firms committed to increasing racial/ethnic diversity. She served as deputy chief of staff for the attorney general of Massachusetts (1997–99), where she executed a comprehensive diversity and inclusion initiative: increasing minority recruitment; conducting diversity and sexual harassment trainings; and performing outreach to the state's diverse population. Ms. Myers practiced corporate and real estate law in Boston for six years at Testa, Hurwitz & Thibeault, LLP and Fitch, Wiley, Richlin & Tourse, LLP.

Ms. Myers graduated from Harvard Law School and received a bachelor of arts, magna cum laude, from Barnard College, Columbia University. She lives in Newton, Massachussetts and is originally from Baltimore, Maryland.

About the Artist

Jerry Craft is the creator of the award-winning *Mama's Boyz* comic strip (www .mamasboyz.com, distributed by King Features Syndicate since 1995). One of the few syndicated African-American cartoonists, Jerry has published three books. *Mama's Boyz: The Big Picture,* won a S'Indie Award for Best Children's Book. He has illustrated seven additional books, comic books, and board games.

Introduction

The idea for this book grew out of two conversations, one with a client and one with a friend. Let me start with the conversation that I had with a client, a white managing partner of a large, prestigious law firm. I was sitting down to discuss his firm's diversity challenges and recent initiatives and I asked him why he thought, that despite all their efforts, the firm had not promoted a black attorney to partnership in twenty years. He explained to me that his firm had made great strides over the years with minority recruitment, but that the retention of black attorneys was a real problem. He thought one problem was that their black attorneys had been lured away: by other firms, the firm's clients, the government, and other attractive opportunities. Then he quickly added, "But we have also had some spectacular failures with black attorneys. They just don't seem to do as well here."

When I asked him if he thought black attorneys—those who left on their own volition, and those who were asked to leave—may have encountered any barriers to their success at the firm, he earnestly expressed his belief that the firm was an absolute meritocracy: there were no impediments to anyone's advancement. "This is a firm where people succeed or fail on their merits." In our conversation, he used phrases like "we have dipped down" and "bent over backwards" for black attorneys and finally concluded, "Maybe we aren't hiring the right people." Whatever the cause, he explained that the present situation was unacceptable; and yet, the firm was at its wit's end about what could be done to fix the problem. That is why he had hired me, a diversity consultant.

In the spirit of honesty, I have to admit that for a long time in my consulting career, I did not quite believe my clients when they told me that they didn't know what to do. I could not understand why they were perplexed by increasing numbers of people of color coming into their institutions hopeful but exiting quickly thereafter, disillusioned and disengaged. Sometimes, to illustrate what one problem might be, I would bring up a director's offensive comment or exclusive behavior, and the response from my client would be, "But I'm sure that is not what she meant." Or I would point to the failure of an influential partner to take a senior black associate in his practice group under his wing and the response would be, "Yes, but that partner doesn't mentor anyone." When I would suggest that maybe a certain system or practice lent itself to bias and could disadvantage blacks and other people of color, I would get quizzical looks and the comment, "It's difficult for anyone to succeed here; how is that a race issue?" In addition, many white people within my workshops would tell me that they didn't know what to say or what to do in certain work situations involving a person of color, or they were afraid to broach an issue with a black person.

After hearing these sentiments over and over again, I formed my theories about why these people, who solve complex problems all day long, were at such a loss when it came to relating across race. I have to tell you that none of my suppositions were very flattering. To me, it seemed that the problems, the issues, and certainly the "dos" and "don'ts" were obvious. If I knew the thinking of my clients, their behavior, and the organizations resulting from their behavior were shaped by their own cultural values, life experience and racism, why didn't they understand that? I know "racism" feels like a harsh charge; it is, especially for many of my clients who believe deeply in equality and fairness. When I use the term here, I am not talking about intentional racism, or people behaving out of racial animus. I am really referring to a more modern form of racism—unconscious biases and assumptions rooted in notions of racial superiority and inferiority that affect the way people behave and are embedded in the way organizations operate. This type of contemporary racism, sometimes called "aversive racism" or "implicit bias," is perpetuated by good, kind, well-meaning white people.[1] It is subtle and mostly unintentional, and yet it is as concerning as old-fashioned forms of intentional and conscious racism.

Then one day, I had the second of two conversations that prompted me to write this book. My white friend, Gene, is quite progressive and is married to a black woman from South Africa with whom he has a son. We were speaking frankly about something that I wrote about white people and race relations, and he said, "All the things you say about how white people get it wrong are true, but when I hear these things, I get depressed. It would be great if you would go a step further and tell white people what they can do to improve how they relate to black people. White people need some hope that they can improve the diversity in their organizations and their relationships."

Initially, I argued with Gene. I informed him of how his request felt for me as a black person: "Why is it always us?" I said. "Why is it that the 'out group' has to teach the 'in group' basic respectfulness and awareness? As black people, we're exhausted by life generally, trying to make it in the majority world, making you all feel comfortable with us and now you are asking us to do your work for you." It isn't just the mental fatigue and psychological toll, of course. Trying to manage all this wears us out physically as well. You can look at the recent studies that show that the internal organs of black people are older than whites their same age, even when they have the same income and education level and the same level of health insurance coverage. The only way that scientists can explain this phenomenon is that black people are under more stress than their white peers.[2]

I pleaded with Gene over the telephone, "Can't you all work as hard to understand us as we have in order to understand you?" We have studied hard to succeed in predominately white institutions, schools, and communities. We know the lingo, the jokes, the habits, the history and the nicknames, of the majority group. Then I remembered that some white people can't see that there is a system out there that is hard for black people to navigate successfully and fit into. It is a system individual white people didn't create, but that reflects and benefits them. However, many black people see this system clearly, and we work hard to put our individual best forward, but we feel constantly snared: not only by individual racism, but also by structural racism.

I continued making my case, "Believe it or not, most black people believe in meritocracy, too; we just want to be a part of it. We want white people to help break down the barriers that keep so many black people existing along the walls of the dance floors of their organizations, rather than getting out in the middle of the floor and dancing." I explained that black people, like anyone else, want to be part of the lifeblood of the organization and regarded as valuable and indispensable.

Gene continued with his plea for real concrete steps. I kept trying to hear what he was saying because of our relationship and my respect for him. Then it came to me. What if I believed him? What if I took my white friends and clients at face value, took their word for it? What would that mean? After all, as a diversity consultant, I am always telling people to "try on" others' ideas and beliefs. I reasoned to myself: my friend is brilliant, educated at Columbia, one of the best schools in the world; he became a partner in a large prestigious law firm; and he is now living in a multi-cultural family. Yet, he is telling me that he knows good and kind white people who need help if they are going to build the bridges necessary to create real opportunities and deeper relationships with black folks. What if I believed that there are many white people who want to engage with, invest in, and support black people—to "dance with black folks"—in their personal and professional lives. Whether I like it or not, they need to be guided and encouraged.

Then Gene said, "Vernā, you do this in your workshops all the time. You not only raise people's awareness about race and other diversity issues, but somehow you tell smart and powerful white men—who think they know everything—what they can do better. They listen because you do it in a way that gives them some confidence that they can get there. Just write about what you do in your workshops."

So, I decided to respond to my friend's request. My hope is that he is right about my ability to shed light. I am optimistic that white readers will take the examples of the big and small action steps I offer and feel a combination of informed hope and deep responsibility. This is not a book about inviting black people to the party; that has already been done. It is intended to be a resource for the white people who are willing to go outside their comfort zones, to ask black folks to join them on the dance floor of inclusion, where power and opportunity are shared and where black people are expected to be full participants on every level, in all facets, and in the deepest respects.

Diversity Is Being Invited to the Party; Inclusion Is Being Asked to Dance

Dance Lessons for this Chapter:

☑ The difference between Diversity and Inclusion

☑ You can't change without changing

☑ What Inclusion requires from organizations and individuals

I always open my diversity workshops by introducing myself as a "recovering attorney." I don't know who coined that term, but it describes me perfectly. I practiced law for six years, but for more than eighteen years of my professional life I have been advising organizations on issues of diversity and inclusion. My work has been about helping institutions—founded, shaped, owned, and dominated for a long time by white men—to create more welcoming and supportive work environments for everyone, especially people of color, women, and, more recently, those in the lesbian, gay, bisexual, transgender (LGBT), and disability communities. I have also worked to encourage and help open-minded and caring white people to go beyond the superficial and distanced relationships that sometimes exist between black and white people at work, in our neighborhoods, in our schools, and in other areas where we come together.

As a diversity consultant, my clients have ranged from the largest and most prestigious law firms in the country, to mid-size and small firms, educational institutions, major corporations, and non-profits. Everywhere that I have consulted, I encounter good, well-meaning, smart, bright, affluent white people who ask me to tell them what they could do to increase diversity in their workplaces, their kids' schools, their board of directors, their faculties, etc. Many of them are motivated by their own moral code, their own sense of what is fair. Diversity is simply the "right thing to do." Others want to be the employer of choice, to attract talented individuals of every background, especially millennials, who may be more interested in working in a diverse environment. Some are looking for diversity to bring new skills, competencies, and networks to their organizations; some are compelled by gaining access to different markets in different parts of the country and the world. Recently, law firms have stepped up their emphasis on diversity because many of their clients have begun insisting on it. Some of these clients are presenting cases in front of diverse groups of jurors and/or are trying to make sure the legal advice they receive includes a diverse set of perspectives. I have also worked with people who believe that diversity fosters a more creative, innovative, and effective organization.

However, I have discovered that most often when they say "diversity," it is a code word for "race"; and by race, they mean "black or African American." When they say, "We can't find any 'qualified diverse candidates,'" they usually mean, "We can't find black people who meet our 'standards.'" When it comes to recruiting for diversity, what they don't realize is they are looking for black people in the wrong places. They are searching for them in the same neighborhoods, organizations, schools, and networks from which the white candidates have come. They have limited their search to the places they know and trust and are unaware of the vibrant and diverse networks existing outside of their experience.

Sometimes, even when I offer information about other possible places to recruit, I hear, "We interviewed (or hired) one person from there, and we weren't very impressed, so we aren't going to try that again." They view unqualified white candidates as individuals, but black prospects become representative of their whole group. The unconscious racism that I mentioned earlier and that we will talk about extensively in this book causes them to question and undervalue these other resources and candidates who might emerge from such networks.

> So I have to remind some white managers that "hoping" race is not a factor in a workplace issue with a black person is not an effective management strategy. I tell them, "You can't assume race, but you can't hide from it either."

Some of my clients, who may have figured out the recruitment piece, get stuck on how to handle the racial issues that may emerge now that they have hired black people into their organization. A manager will ask me how she should approach a situation involving an African American employee. When I ask her if she has considered the possibility that race may be influencing the dynamic, her reaction is usually, "Well, I hope not." So I have to remind some white managers that "hoping" race is not a factor in a workplace issue with a black person is not an effective management strategy. I tell them, "You can't assume race, but you can't hide from it either."

Why Black and White?

My clients are also concerned about increasing the representation and retention of other historically excluded groups, such as LGBT individuals, Asians, Latinos, multiracial individuals, and women. For several reasons, however, I have chosen to focus this book on issues between black and white people and the retention and advancement of blacks in predominately white institutions. First, I want to address the diversity area where most of my clients have made minimal progress, especially given how long black people (at least black men) have been working in the corporate arena. While my clients seem more optimistic about the success of their diversity efforts with regard to other underrepresented groups, they know they have a problem with retaining and advancing black people. In some industries, such as in the legal field, many are genuinely concerned that they may be actually losing ground when it comes to blacks.[3]

Many of my clients believe that their ability to bring in and advance black people is the real litmus test for their diversity efforts.

They feel a responsibility, given all the struggles that have been fought by black, white, and other people to create racial equity, to continue until we see black people as a group thriving in these environments. My clients see that even though there has been some forward movement integrating and advancing black people within their organizations, there are still perplexing problems that seem to make it impossible for them to retain a critical mass of black individuals at the managerial and executive levels. Even at this time in the history of the United States, when we have a black President, a black Attorney General, black megastars, and well-paid athletes and entertainers, the corporate workplace still seems to resist the changes that would better integrate, cultivate, and elevate black talent.

I have also chosen to focus on the black and white issue because I think it is emblematic of the many other important problems regarding other marginalized groups in the workplace and in our society. Despite what some of my clients believe, I know that the environment for other underrepresented groups is not as rosy as they perceive, and from what I have been able to see, it isn't just a "matter of time."

The number of white women thriving in corporate America has increased greatly in the last 30 years, but the maternal wall is still extremely difficult to surmount and gender bias continues to impede women's access to the very top of corporate institutions. I have seen little evidence that most women are able to advance without being willing and able to imitate men and embrace a male model of success. Asians (as large and diverse as that grouping is in itself), unlike blacks who feel like everything they do is overly scrutinized, wrestle with not being seen at all—some have said they are the "invisible minority." Latinos are severely underrepresented in many industries and graduate schools, and subgroups like Mexicans and Puerto Ricans encounter some of the same obstacles as African Americans. Plenty of gay employees are closeted or careful about in whom they confide because they worry that their identity may make building and sustaining relationships more difficult. Individuals with physical disabilities are rarely seen in the many institutions I advise.

You will see that, throughout the book, I have used examples and stories that include all types of diversity. It is hard not to draw the many parallels between blacks and other racial and ethnic groups and other traditionally excluded groups. Their experiences are shaped and limited by the same barriers that blacks confront: the "isms" (racism, sexism, heterosexism, elitism, etc.), lack of awareness, discomfort with difference, stereotypes and bias, and systems and practices that reinforce those already in positions of power and exclude others who have been regarded as "less than" or outside the norm. I have watched individuals in these groups, just like blacks, expend great energy trying to "fit in," by minimizing their differences in order to succeed and to make others comfortable with them.

The issues confronting blacks and other marginalized groups converge a great deal; yet, I believe there are issues unique to black people that make it hard for many of them to thrive in majority white institutions. I wanted to be able to talk about and offer solutions to those distinct hurdles. My hope is that if we can untie this knot of black and white issues through awareness, knowledge, skill, and action, it will help create institutions of inclusion for all groups.

Lastly, I have narrowed the discussion to black and white because I am black.[4] As a black person, I can speak with the most authority about my experience working and consulting in the corporate environment and living in the United States of America. That is not to say that my experience is every black person's experience. I do believe that many black people share a cultural background and have a common experience with regard to racial prejudice in this country. However, black people are not a monolithic group; they are individuals, and they also have various group identities.[5] I imagine that if you are a black person reading this book or if you are picturing a certain black person, many of my descriptions of black culture or issues encountered by blacks will resonate with you. However, it also may be true that the racial identification and life experiences put forth in this book are very different than you have known or seen. I think this underscores the heterogeneity that exists among blacks. For white readers, remembering to regard each black person as an individual, not just as a member of a racial group, will be extremely important to keep in mind as you seek to be more proactive in creating inclusion across racial lines.

Also, for white readers who may be accustomed to seeing themselves and being regarded by others as individuals, the challenge will be to explore your identity as a member of a racial group that shares some common experiences, cultural patterns, and issues.[6] If you are a white person or you are picturing a certain white person when reading this book, you may find descriptions of white people here that you cannot relate to personally. There will be other times when you will see yourself or the white people you know right in the center of these pages. Feel free to ignore what seems foreign and focus on the situations that ring true.

We cannot correct for racism by ignoring race.

All people—black, white, and individuals of all races and ethnicities—get to define for themselves the group or groups to which they belong and whether race or ethnicity is relevant to how they identify at all. I am also very aware that there is really only one race—the human race. There are no subspecies of humans; humans are 99.9% identical genetically.[7] What we call race in our society is not biological. It is a rather modern, social construct that assigned superiority and inferiority to groups based on physical characteristics.[8] *However, while race isn't real, racism is.* Centuries of declaring the white race as superior and embedding and supporting that hierarchy through laws, policies, and practices has and continues to have a huge influence on black people's access to opportunity and life outcomes. We cannot correct for racism by ignoring race.

Diversity vs. Inclusion

My goal is to help well-meaning white people, like my clients, erase the impact of racism. I am talking not only about eliminating barriers in the workplace; I want to give conscious and caring white people, like my friends, the skills to cultivate rich, rewarding, and meaningful relationships across race.

I think most of my clients and friends would agree with these goals. However, as I have discovered after working hard in this area for many years, diversity, at least in the way we have thought about the idea up until now, can only take us so far toward these objectives.

Our diversity efforts have been focused on identifying underrepresented groups and bringing them into the workplace. Organizations will bring out their one or two black executives for all to see in the same way that some very kind white people I know will proudly share that they have black friends (or a black friend). However, the real question is not how many black friends or colleagues you have but the substance of the experience the black person is having in the friendship or the organization.

Diversity is about quantity. Inclusion is about quality. I learned this when I was executive director of the Boston Law Firm Group (now called the Boston Lawyers Group). As a consortium of large law firms in Boston, we initially aimed all our efforts at outreach and recruitment of attorneys of color, and we saw the numbers increase tremendously. Then we noticed them stagnate and even decline; all the people we invited in the front door were leaving out the back! We used to think that diversity was a goal in itself until we discovered that unless the environment, the friendship, the neighborhood, and the workplace are inviting, fair, and respectful, diversity is not going to thrive.

It's not that black people are helpless. It's not that we don't have our own dance steps to learn as well. However, I see us coming to a party where center stage is occupied and controlled by white leaders, managers, teachers, and politicians. So, even when we work hard to put our faith in meritocracy, learn the rules, master the norms, and sometimes adopt different ways of dancing outside of our comfort zone to better connect with white people who are uneasy with us, we still encounter barriers to genuine inclusion. What do they say? "It takes two to tango"? In the workplace, we eliminated legal barriers to racial discrimination, which was a crucial step, but it is not enough. We removed roadblocks, but we did not build bridges of true understanding. A similar situation occurred with fair housing laws—they allowed black people to move in, but then white people moved out.[9] So, many black and white people have never had a real opportunity to get to know each other as individuals, to live and play next to each other. We also neglected the tough conversations needed to reconcile after so many years of racial bigotry and to process what we learned and needed to unlearn.

In my own social circles, I see how hard it is for white people to fully understand how much distance black people travel to create connection and how important they are, as white people, to bridging the gap that remains. I had girlfriends in a book club graciously open their homes to me, but refused to show up at my house the night I hosted because they were afraid to come to my mostly black and working class neighborhood. I just waited in my lovely home with wine, cheese, and crackers, and they never showed. When I moved to an affluent, predominately white neighborhood, white parents just assumed that my child was from the Boston voluntary busing program (METCO) where children of color from Boston are bused to predominately white schools to better integrate them. I have watched them kindly invite METCO kids to sleepovers at their beautiful homes in our tree-lined community but refuse to allow their boys to go to play football in the predominately black and brown Boston city neighborhoods where these same METCO students live.

> *What I have noticed is that trying to be nice often stands in the way of creating real inclusion. It prevents action or creates a situation where black people are ignored or coddled, rather than engaged and challenged.*

Most of the white people in my community and the workplaces where I consult are well intentioned, but they continue to be ineffective partners in the dance of inclusion. Some of them feel guilty and ashamed about the past and present predicament of black people, and they try too hard to be "nice" to black people, or they don't know when and if they should confront black people about a problem or issue. What I have noticed is that trying to be nice often stands in the way of creating real inclusion. It prevents action or creates a situation where black people are ignored or coddled, rather than engaged and challenged.

Without knowing it, a nice white supervisor or teacher is setting some black employee or student up for failure because she can't bring herself to deliver the critical feedback the black employee or student needs to improve. This niceness is also typified by white people who hire black folks who are wholly unqualified for the job. It is a misguided, sentimental attempt to "help" the black person and to support the organization's "diversity" goals. It may seem counterintuitive, but this kind of behavior is based on an assumption that black people are inferior. When you don't hold people to standards of excellence, deep down you are indicating that you don't think you can find talented black people to meet your standards. The goal of diversity should be to fully integrate and utilize talented black folks. However, the aim becomes hiring people for the color of their skin, rather than for what they can bring to the organization—which is the true value of diversity. I will talk more specifically about these tendencies and how they implicate unconscious bias in Chapter Eleven.

Even when I know white managers who explicitly view African Americans as their equals, I observe them avoiding investing in, mentoring, or building meaningful relationships with blacks. Sometimes, they tell me that they worry they will say the wrong thing or not be able to identify with their black colleagues and supervisees. They view encounters with black people as risky. They worry they will be accused of being a racist and/or sued. ***They prefer to stay at a distance rather than make mistakes, when, in actuality, the distance itself is often a far more serious injury.***

"Which one do you suppose is the alpha?"

On the other side of the coin are the white folks who require more from black people, not less. It is hard to observe hiring committees (comprised only of white people) pass over black candidates who are quite capable but who do not possess that look, fit, or veneer—the right unthreatening, polished, and "whitened" tone, diction, and appearance that some whites seem to require before they can see a black candidate's competency or potential.

As we will see later in our discussion in Chapter Eleven on in-group favoritism, we are all guilty of being more attracted to and favorable toward people who are like us. So, some white supervisors, unbeknownst to them, are looking for themselves in a black candidate. It is as if they want the candidate to be black but act and even look like them. It reminds me of a cartoon where two men in suits are trying to decide which of the professionally dressed women waiting outside the office door they will hire. One of the men asks the other, "Which one do you suppose is the alpha?" In other words, they are staring at women, but they are really looking for a man.

How many times have successful black people heard a white person say either cheerfully or in an absentminded fashion, "I don't think of you as black person." Gay folks and women hear the same type of comments: To a gay person, "When I look at you, I don't see a lesbian." Or to a woman, "You are more of a man than I am." Even when such a comment is meant as a compliment, embedded in it is a revealing negative stereotype. Most black people don't appreciate being considered the exception to their race; they want to be regarded as proof positive that blacks are as good as anyone else. Of course, other blacks prefer to be regarded only as individuals, not representatives of any group or confirmation of any stereotype, be it positive or negative.

Real change in the inclusion of black people in our institutions will not happen unless we are willing to reexamine our ideas about merit. There are so many obstacles for blacks to overcome that are not about what they bring as individuals in the way of talent but about who sees that talent and chooses to help direct and develop it. How does the culture of our organizations—the unspoken rules and norms—impact the newcomers? Who will help translate these hidden ways of operating for groups, like blacks, who have been traditionally excluded from these environments? One problem is the paucity of black role models available to black people to translate and demystify the culture and point out the pitfalls.

We fail to acknowledge that so many of the opportunities in a meritocracy are shaped by the comfort level that white decision makers have with people who are most like them and by the discomfort and lack of identity and predictability they have with those who are not like them. Black people often encounter negative stereotypes about their intellectual capacity, their work ethic, and their deportment. So whereas there are a few black individuals who have had great success in majority white institutions, this lack of comfort and identification and negative stereotyping on the part of some whites make it much harder for blacks as a group to thrive. They are less success-ful attracting mentors and sponsors who have the power to positively influence their careers. There are some black people who seem to clear certain of these hurdles only to discover as they move up the ladder that they are excluded from the most exciting, rewarding, and lucrative opportunities within the institution. They are not invited on the important committees, tapped for leadership roles, or chosen as the beneficiaries of business that is being handed out or handed down. This isn't because they are not qualified; it is because they are not preferred or are invisible to those who make these decisions.

Blacks also have to contend with the racism and sexism (for black women) from vendors, clients, judges, decision makers, and secretaries outside their workplace. I wish I could have a dollar for every black man who was refused entry to his own down-town office building by the weekend security guard or parking garage attendant; or for every black female associate in a law firm who has been asked politely by a visiting cli-ent for rubber bands or coffee because she is mistaken for a secretary; or for the black lawyer with briefcase in hand who has been yelled at by courtroom officers because he is sitting in the attorney area since, of course, he must be the defendant.

After all the resources spent and goodwill extended, many white people, in exas-peration, ask me why we haven't gotten further in racial understanding or increasing the diversity in our workplaces and lives. Sometimes, they don't like my response. I tell them what I have come to believe. Not enough white people have done their work: the work of seeing the barriers to true meritocracy, the work of putting themselves in the shoes of black people to learn more about their experiences and perceptions, the work of understanding how being white has shaped their worldview and self-percep-tions, and the work of gaining the skills of deciphering and managing cross-racial and cultural dynamics. That's a lot of work, but without it you cannot create fundamental change in your sphere of influence.

The real question isn't, "Why haven't we seen a change in diversity?" The actual questions are these: "Do we want real change?" "What does change mean?" "Why should we want to change?" Here's what I mean: I have been invited to many work-places to conduct internal assessments of an organization's diversity strengths and weaknesses. Often, when I present the analysis of how the firm's culture, informal processes, and policies (usually its formal policies are great) undermine its diversity goals, the firm's response is, "You did an excellent job describing our culture, and we are upset to hear that some women, people of color, and LGBT individuals are having a difficult time here, but we couldn't possibly change that—it is the way we have always done things." In other words, the firm's leaders are not going to change the organization's culture or the way they do things because it has worked well for them so far. They tell me, "We are the best at what we do in our industry." I smile and conclude, *"So you are committed to diversity, and you want to be more diverse, but you don't want to change anything?"* Those in power assume that to welcome change would risk their success or, at least, what they have defined as success.

Diversity Is Being Invited to the Party; Inclusion Is Being Asked to Dance

In order to become more diverse, you have to want to change. An organization cannot expect to cultivate difference if it is bent on perpetuating its present culture, one that reflects narrow and monocultural thinking and values, not because people are bad or evil but because they have developed their culture based on who created and led the organization in the past. You can bring people from different backgrounds into a culture like this, but you will never reach inclusion. You will never know the power of difference unless you allow the organization to evolve to appreciate the new views, cultures, ideas, and networks that different people can offer and then find the ways that these diverse contributions can strengthen the institution as a whole and further its goals.

Inclusion requires us to reconsider things such as

⇨ how to make space for different styles of communicating and relating;

⇨ the different ways contributions can be made and valued;

⇨ the benefit of not only competition but also cooperation;

⇨ the various ways that people of different backgrounds, cultures, and perspectives are motivated;

⇨ how work allocation, mentoring, and evaluation systems may be biased toward those who are most like the people in decision-making roles;

⇨ how the quality of collegial relationships influences individual professional development and collective success;

⇨ what commitment to work and family looks like; and

⇨ how to operate outside our comfort zones.

Inclusion requires an organization to revise policies and practices that have a disproportionately negative impact on those who are not white and male, and to find ways to provide the supports to offset the unique barriers experienced by women and people of color in the work environment. As I tell my clients, the bottom line is, *"One can't get change without changing."* The same is true in our personal lives.

What transforms a majority white corporation or law firm into a multicultural organization? It is not only about inviting in people who are different from the leadership, it is also about engaging with them honestly, investing in their success, and acknowledging that white privilege might be an obstacle. It is the difference between saying you believe in diversity and actually doing something about it. It is about getting down to the real dance.

The dance of inclusion asks us to

⇨ learn the history and culture of groups different from your own;

⇨ participate in communities and activities where black people are the majority;

⇨ appreciate European culture and the way it has shaped your worldview about others;

⇨ learn how much you don't know and the reasons why you don't know,

⇨ reveal what you don't know;

⇨ let go of the need to know everything and be the authority;

⇨ overcome the fear of being wrong;

⇨ make some mistakes; welcome correction as an opportunity for learning and for deepening relationships; and

⇨ operate outside your comfort zone.

There are big steps, too, such as creating and changing policies and procedures, sponsoring studies, establishing foundations, and supporting pipeline initiatives that will increase awareness, interaction, motivation, and opportunity. Every white person can find something big or small to do to advance the ball. There are many white people who are already active and making a difference. I know because they have made a difference in my life. However, we need more individuals in the dominant group who want real change and who believe that they can do something to make it happen.

Dance partners for racial inclusion

⇨ are active;

⇨ change their old dance moves;

⇨ share their knowledge and resources with black people;

⇨ proactively build relationships with black people;

⇨ seek out and identify opportunities for black folks; and

⇨ allow black folks to lead them and teach them.

In other words, inclusion requires white people who are willing to look around their professional and personal dance floors to see the black people standing along the walls of their organizations, communities, sacred places, schools, gyms, and clubs and ask them to dance.

Let's get this party started!

Endnotes

1. See the excellent work of Gaertner and Dovidio on aversive racism, especially, S. L. Gaertner and J. F. Dovidio, *Understanding and Addressing Contemporary Racism: From Aversive Racism to the Common Ingroup Identity Model*, 61 J. Social Issues 615 (2005) *and* J. F. Dovidio and S. L. Gaertner, *Affirmative Action, Unintentional Racial Biases, and Intergroup Relations*, 52 J. Social Issues 51 (1996). Also look at John F. Dovidio, *On the Nature of Contemporary Prejudice: The Third Wave*, 57 J. Social Issues 829 (2001).

2. D. R. Williams, *Race, Socioeconomic Status, and Health: The Added Effects of Racism and Discrimination*, 896 Ann. N.Y. Acad. Sci. 173 (1999). ("This paper analyzes the myriad ways in which race and socioeconomic status (SES) combine to affect health. The research found, on many occasions, racial differences persist even at 'equivalent' levels of SES. Racism is an added burden for non-dominant populations. Individual and institutional discrimination, along with the stigma of inferiority, negatively affect health by restricting socioeconomic opportunities and mobility. The research also found that racism can directly affect health in multiple ways such as racial bias in medical care, the stress of discrimination and the societal stigma of inferiority can have a negative impact on health.")

3. The National Association for Legal Professionals (NALP) found a decline in the number of minority lawyers between 2009 and 2010, especially among associates. Among all employers listed in the 2010–2011 NALP Directory of Legal Employers, just 6.16% of partners were minorities. African Americans comprised only 1.7% of partners with variation by cities. Atlanta has the highest percentage of black partners, followed by Washington, D.C., Baltimore, and New Orleans. For a closer look at these statistics see NALP findings on women and minorities in law firms by race and ethnicity, accessed Apr. 15, 2011, http://www.nalp.org/jan2011wom_min#table1.

4. I should also take this time to say what I mean when I use the word "black." For me "black" refers to those of African descent from the United States, Canada, England, the Caribbean, South America, wherever; the word covers the whole diaspora. "African American," for me, is a narrower classification, a subset of the black group. African Americans are the descendents of African slaves who were brought to America. I am African American. I like being called "black," but others might prefer African American, which is fine for me as well because I definitely identify with being American. African Americans or black people are also part of what I refer to as "people of color"—those of African, Asian, Latino or Hispanic, and Native American descent.

5. In a recently written book, Eugene Robinson, Disintegration: The Splintering of Black America (Doubleday 2010), he suggests that there is no one black community. Instead, there are four sub-communities: the Transcendent—those who are of the elite class, like Oprah Winfrey; the Mainstream middle class—the majority of black Americans; the Emergent—immigrants from Africa and the Caribbean; and the Abandoned—a large group of the underclass that is growing in the rural parts of the South and inner cities.

6. I use the word "white" to refer to people who have Eastern and Western European ancestry. More recently, the term "European American" has been used to denote "white." Some people also use the word "caucasian." Some whites prefer to be called by their country or origin, such as Irish American or Italian American.

7. *What Is Race?: Is Race for Real?*, http://www.pbs.org/race/001_WhatIsRace/001_00-home .htm and http://www.pbs.org/race/001_WhatIsRace/001_00-home.htm (last accessed Apr. 17, 2011).

8. The PBS series, *Race: The Power of Illusion*, http://www.pbs.org/race/000_General/000_00-Home.htm, gives a wonderfully comprehensive explanation regarding the theory of race, race as a social and political idea vs. a biological fact, and the power of race and racism on life outcomes. This is a three-part series that offers a discussion guide and background readings on genetics, history, and society.

9. Actually, in 1999 some studies argue the biggest contributing factor to neighborhoods transitioning to all black neighborhoods is white avoidance—white people living in all white neighborhoods who, when they move, are not willing to live in integrated neighborhoods—rather than white flight—white people moving out of neighborhoods when black people move in. L. Quillan, *Migration and the Maintenance of Racial Segregation*, Center for Demography and Ecology, University of Wisconsin Working Paper No 98-29.

I Think I'm a Pretty Good Dance Partner: Is This Book for Me?

Dance Lessons for this Chapter:

☑ How to determine if this book is for you

☑ What motivates people to learn the dance of inclusion

☑ What stage of this journey you may be in on the raod to racial inclusion

☑ What kind of dance partner you are now

If you are a white person who wants to be a good dance partner in promoting racial inclusion, one of your first steps involves challenging how you have come to see the world around you. I know that no one gives up one's worldview and the comfort that it brings easily. One does it for a good reason or because there is no other choice. This book is for individuals who can see a good reason to delve more deeply when it comes to race, even if it causes some internal and external rumbling, discomfort, or embarrassment. These are people of all ages, from different communities, professions, life experiences, and places in the country. They have different motivations for taking the plunge. Here are some of the types of people and reasons that I have seen. Are any of these you?

⇨ You are a white baby boomer compelled by your belief in justice and racial equity. It is a moral thing for you. You are frustrated by the persistent absence of a critical mass of black people in so many of the influential institutions and communities of which you are a part.

⇨ You are the director of human resources in your organization, and every day you see talented African Americans leaving your company. You want to find a way to help your leaders see their unconscious biases and become more aware of their behavior. You want to stop having to spend so much of your time dealing with the fallout of racial misunderstanding between black and white employees.

⇨ You are a CEO, partner, or director in a professional service firm or a general counsel who sees racial diversity as an economic and creative engine that will enhance your bottom line—attracting the "best and brightest" from every background will allow you to be more competitive in new and diverse markets.

17

⇨ You are a young white person involved in social causes and working closely in the black communities that you want to help improve. You worry about how to gain the trust of the black people you are trying to assist.

⇨ You are a young adult who confides in me that you just moved into a neighborhood undergoing gentrification and you don't know how to feel or what to do about being one of the "whites" who are sharing space with and sometimes displacing the long-time, poorer black residents there.

⇨ You are a teacher, a nurse, a doctor, or a director of a community development organization in an under-resourced neighborhood, and you are wondering why the disturbing racial disparities between blacks and whites seem to remain.

⇨ You are a leader of a non-profit, a governmental agency, or a school, and you are motivated by your organization's mission of justice and fairness; the communities in which you operate have become more racially and ethnically diverse, and you are trying to figure out how to stay relevant and better serve your growing client base.

This book is also for those for whom racial difference has appeared unexpectedly at their backdoor in the form of a black person—a new supervisor, son-in-law, grandchildren, client, or even their President—and there is no choice. It is also for people who have voluntarily befriended a black person, are curious about certain things, but don't want to say the wrong thing and ruin the budding relationship. On the deepest level, this book is for white folks who are beginning to acknowledge the cost of being white in America—the consequences of not knowing and rarely being taught or exposed to the history and contributions of African Americans and other people of color. These are the white people who feel the price of whiteness—the guilt, the pressure to know all things, the homogenization of the culture of their own ancestors, the worship of the individual at the expense of community, and the isolation from the majority of color populations in U.S. cities and the world. *These white people have figured out that it is in their enlightened self-interest to build meaningful, genuine relationships with blacks and other people of color as peers—not as people to be pitied, feared, ignored or assisted, but as people who are essential to know and have in their lives.*

We Are All on a Journey—What Stage of the Journey Are You In?

Whenever I come into a diversity workshop, I encounter people who, despite their belief in racial equality, are all over the map when it comes to their racial and cultural awareness and skills. At Vernā Myers Consulting Group (VMCG), we tell our participants, "We are all on a journey when it comes to learning about these issues and no one has completely arrived," including the consultants. As I reveal aspects of my own journey in the chapters that follow, you will see why we say, "including the consultants." I have written this book for folks who know they have some distance to travel and have decided they want to be a better partner on the dance floor of inclusion. Now, this isn't *So You Think You Can Dance* or anything like that. It's not a competition. You're not being judged, but I want to help you mark where you are on the journey right now. In other words, what kind of dance partner are you today? Below, I have described different stages of the journey in which you might find yourself at the beginning of this book. If you know where you are starting, you can aim more specifically at where you want to go, and you can celebrate the distance traveled by the time you finish this book.

"Aware and Ready to Dance" Stage

This book is for people who have reached the stage where they already have a heightened awareness about racial exclusion and are looking for more ways to be proactive participants in creating inclusion. They are people who

- ⇨ believe that the election of President Obama meant that we as Americans are still capable of great things, of doing the right thing—of throwing off our demons; these people also know that his election did not usher in a post-racial America or solve the problem of race in our county.
- ⇨ are worried that if well-intentioned white people don't rise up and get articulate and skilled about race and racial inequity, some other, not so well-intentioned, whites will succeed in reversing the racial progress that we have made as a country.
- ⇨ recognize that the well-dressed black man in the elevator is Greg, the company's only black vice president, but want to find the "right" thing to say and do to make up for those women who seem to be clutching their purses, fearful that he will steal them.
- ⇨ assume that the black people in their workplaces are just as bright as they are and want to learn how to confront their white peers who assume that the smallest mistake a black person makes is proof positive that "standards were lowered."
- ⇨ don't assume they or anyone else is owed a spot in a private educational institution based on standardized test scores—especially since studies show they are poor predictors of a student's ultimate success in the institution and beyond.
- ⇨ admire how far some blacks have come to get where they are, and wonder if they could have done as well given the same life circumstances.
- ⇨ are growing uncomfortable with the homogeneity of their lives and institutions and see the vitality and brilliance of difference—as one older white partner in a law firm said to me: "I've done white guys for a while now; it's getting a little tired."
- ⇨ just hired a promising, enthusiastic, bright black woman and want to see her grow and succeed.
- ⇨ know Uncle Jack is being bigoted when he complains bitterly about how little John's spot at Princeton went to some unqualified black person or shares even more blatant examples of racial prejudice or ignorance, but who don't quite know how to express their conflicting opinion to Uncle Jack in a powerful way.
- ⇨ have a black grandchild and want to see him or her develop self-confidence and feel included within his majority white family.
- ⇨ have white children, nieces, nephews, and grandchildren and want to know how to talk to them about racism and their responsibility to help eradicate it.
- ⇨ find themselves in charge of an institution, unit, department, committee, board, or school or in some position of influence and see that they have the power to create a multi-cultural and inclusive environment, but feel they need more awareness, knowledge, or skills to implement the necessary changes.

⇨ have done lots of work on their own racism but want to reinforce what they've learned, encourage other white people to take the journey, and find ways to bring their black neighbors, colleagues, and employees to the dance floor with them.

"Cool Moves but Still in Need of School" Stage

This book is also for the naturally cool, fun white people who get along with everybody. However, they are in the stage where, if they want to go beyond cool to deep, they need more information to better understand the unique history, experiences, and issues that influence the lives of many black people. These are people who

⇨ know and feel at ease with black people for a lot of reasons but are still wary of talking about the issue of race when there are black people in the room whom they don't know and who don't know them.

⇨ have a vague sense and perhaps some evidence that racism impacts their interactions with black people, but aren't sure how.

⇨ don't deny they see color but sometimes are unaware of what that difference means; for example, when the only black person in a restaurant other than their dining companion is the wait staff.

⇨ are willing, like some of my friends, to admit that they are sometimes baffled by what I ask of them—to see me as an individual and at the same time to respect just how much I am connected to and shaped by my racial identity; when I started getting involved in the black student organization in college, my best friend, who was white, asked, "Why do you have to do all that black stuff?" I said, "'Cause I'm black."

⇨ notice that a person is black and try to tell them what that should mean: "Hey, you're black, so I know you like rap music," or "You're black; why aren't you sitting with your folks?"

⇨ have had enough exposure to middle class blacks that they know we, just like all people, come in different shapes, sizes, personalities, experiences, and pathologies, however, they still keep unconscious stereotypes about working class and poor blacks.

⇨ have the courage to take the conversations deeper and want to know how to recover from a mistake, but wonder why some black individuals can get so upset when white folks make the slightest blunder.

⇨ wonder, but are afraid to ask, why some blacks give their kids such weird names that start with "La" or end with "isha."

"Oh, Was that Your Foot?" Stage

Also, it occurs to me that this book might be for the very wonderful, liberal, white people who don't know they are still on the journey; they think they have arrived. These are people who don't know what they don't know, so they are stepping on black people's toes and have no idea they are doing it. They are sometimes referred to as "naïve offenders." These are people who

⇒ have been known to say things like, "I don't see color" or "I don't think of myself as a white person." I don't know how to break it to you, but most black people notice that you are white. It's okay to be white and to acknowledge that you are white. It is okay to acknowledge that I am black. To do otherwise may seem to deny or ignore our distinct experiences. However, knowing when and when not to recognize race as relevant in a dynamic or conversation takes time to understand and learn. Many of us like being black, and we don't want you to ignore it, we just don't want you to use it against us. An older white woman partner who had survived for a long time in her law firm's white male-dominated culture once explained, "We used to say, 'Don't treat us differently because we are women,' but what we really should have been saying is, 'Don't treat us badly because we are women—we are different.'"

⇒ think of black people as exotic or novel sexual objects; it was so weird hearing people going on and on about First Lady Michelle Obama's arms rather than her smarts and professional accomplishments.

⇒ play that game where they refuse to mention someone's race when they are describing a person to me even though they know I will be meeting him for the first time in a crowded restaurant. It's okay to mention that someone is black in this situation—it is an important physical detail. After all, if I am in a Boston restaurant, and you tell me that the person I am meeting is black, I can eliminate most of the people in the place.

⇒ in the most random fashion, interject something like "my son/brother/sister's son/uncle is married to a black woman" or "one of my best friends/colleagues/neighbors is a black man" into a conversation with every black person they meet.

⇒ feel the need to use what they consider black slang when they meet a black person: "What's up man/brotha?" A black associate in a firm once told me that a white, more junior associate who did not know her called her on the phone and said, "'Sup, playa?" (translated: "What's up, player?"). The black associate told me she thought, "I don't talk like that. What would make her think she could talk to me that way, especially in a business setting where I am her superior?"

'Sup, playa?

"I'm Not Dancing" Stage

Finally, I think it might also be helpful to be frank about those for whom I did not write this book. This book is not for those who have decided not to get on the pathway to responsibility and action on issues of racial justice and inclusion. They are the people who

⇨ are intentionally racist. I don't have time to convince them to change their beliefs and value system when there are others who see the penalty that racism exacts on all of us.

⇨ refuse to examine their understanding of meritocracy.

⇨ are unwilling to be "destabilized" by new information—learning that all of us have either been taught or have caught (just by growing up in our society) racist attitudes is embarrassing. It is initially overwhelming to find out, as a white person, that you have worked hard in life, but much of what you have been able to achieve is due to the fact that a system of power and privilege, which you had no part in creating, favors people with white skin and European heritage.

⇨ think that black people should "just get over it." Black people would love to, but we will need your understanding.

⇨ believe that black people are naturally violent, or believe other negative stereotypes about black people.

⇨ don't want to live next to a black family or have their child marry a black person.

⇨ can't see the many contributions that black people have made to this country.

⇨ believe black culture is inferior to theirs.

⇨ have no interest in learning more about the history and contributions of blacks and other non-European groups.

⇨ think that black people are responsible for much of what ails our country.

No matter what stage you find yourself in, my hope is that after you finish this book you will return to this chapter to see where you are: if you have moved, answered any questions, or emerged as someone different along the journey. By the way—if you found yourself in the "I'm Not Dancing" stage and you want to move out of it—I welcome you. Whether you are in the "Aware and Ready to Dance," the "Cool Moves But Still in Need of School," or the "Oh, Was That Your Foot?" stage, there is work to do. I find there are always layers and layers of awareness and more areas of action that we must challenge ourselves and others to take.

However, be careful. Taking steps to increase racial inclusion is a lifelong journey; it doesn't happen overnight, so don't expect perfection. Action is what we are after here. It is what distinguishes diversity from inclusion and turns well-meaning into well-doing. Action is what will allow us to realize new and enriching relationships, more creative and relevant organizations, and a more just society for everyone. So, do I think you can dance? Absolutely!

3

I Know the Cha Cha; Isn't That Like the Charleston? Aren't We All the Same?

Dance Lessons for this Chapter:

- ☑ How black and white people are both alike and different
- ☑ Why being color-blind does not lead us to inclusion
- ☑ Ways to deepen your relationships across race
- ☑ The benefits of racial and cultural inclusion
- ☑ How to explore your racial/cultural background and how it will help you to be a better dance partner

My life adventures as a black woman in America, my experiences as a racial minority in majority white law firms, my work as a diversity consultant, and my many personal relationships with people from different racial and ethnic backgrounds have provided numerous observations and stories (both painful and promising) about the complex dance of race relations. Even with all that I have learned, I was a little wary about writing a book for white people, for two reasons. First, in my work as a diversity consultant, I have found that it is a good idea to have racially mixed consulting and facilitation teams, because white trainers can speak about whiteness and white racism in ways that I cannot. In addition, I believe that in order for blacks and whites to make progress toward genuine conversation and relationships, white people will need to do intra-group work and learn from each other, instead of relying exclusively on people of color to increase their awareness, explain cultural differences, and teach them the skills of inclusion.

Yet somehow, as a black woman, I have been able to bring something to the conversation of race that white people can hear in a way that motivates, rather than disheartens them. Perhaps my life circumstances, appearance, personality, training, and faith are what allow me to present these ideas in a package that well-meaning, educated white people find welcoming, non-threatening, and still challenging. I am similar enough to many of my white friends and clients that they recognize and feel comfortable with me. In most cases, we speak the same language. I do worry that I may be the "preferred" type of black person, and that I may be preventing white people from seeing and embracing the entirety of the black experience, which isn't always—and for good reason—as even-tempered, open to, and trusting of white people.

A white friend recently asked if I had considered the personal cost of my work—speaking as an African American with white audiences everyday about the difficult issues of race. She asked if I had to give up, change, or suppress myself in any way, in order to do the work I do and to get to where I am at this stage of my professional life. It was a good question. I know I have struggled in the corporate world, like many black people (and lots of other people who don't quite fit the corporate norm), to decide which racially offensive behaviors I will respond to or choose to ignore. I have made conscious calculations about what to change or hide about my culture and background, in order to be accepted. Yet, it has been easier for me than for some, and I have tried to use my facility in these environments to create places where black people and others don't have to pay too high of a price to succeed.

Being in the Minority Is a Noticeable Difference

I do move quite comfortably in white circles; nevertheless, I have a different background than most of my white clients and friends. My upbringing and experiences as a black woman in this country have given me a different perspective about and experience with race. My native language is not quite the same as the one that I use to navigate the white world and I believe I scan and assess the world differently than most of my white friends.

Let me give you an example. This past summer, I rode my bike in a huge fundraiser with two white women, whom I absolutely adore. We went from Sturbridge to Cape Cod, Massachusetts, pedaling 192 miles over two days, with over 6,000 other riders, and I counted five black cyclists, three of them black women; two Asian women; and maybe two riders whom I could identify as Latino. My point? I counted! I am sure my white girlfriends did not. Not only did I count, I searched. I would spot a brownish arm or leg of a cyclist ahead of me and get a little excited; but when I got closer to discover I was wrong, my heart would sink a bit. I can hear some white people saying, "Oh, that's so sad. But why should it matter how many people of any race or ethnicity there were? Were people being mean or unwelcoming toward you?"

On one level, of course, it doesn't matter. I was accompanied by friends, and I was among thousands of like-minded, similarly motivated (some would say crazy) people riding more kilometers on a bike than many people are willing to drive. It is a real feel-good time, and everyone is on a high. On another level, I do wonder how a white American would feel if the numbers were reversed: 5,997 people of color and three white people sprinkled among a weekend of roads, hills, towns and rest stops. *People don't need to be mean to you for you to feel like you don't belong.*

When I am the only black person at a party or event, I notice it; I'm used to it, but I don't prefer it. It is not my ideal setting and yet my predicament is usually invisible to the majority of people there. Most don't notice the absence of people of color, especially before I arrive. They don't reflect on the myriad personal and social factors that led to the party being segregated. Even if they are able to notice, they are too scared to acknowledge the situation. However, I have grown comfortable talking out loud about what is different for me as a black person. I have learned ways to bring up

racial issues in a manner that most people can hear and not feel blamed. Sometimes I use humor. As I tell my white friends, "Don't you think the host should pay me a fee for integrating this party? You know we live in Boston; this could be a profitable business for me." They usually laugh, look around, and notice the reality that hit me in the face the moment I arrived.

But Aren't We All the Same?

Often at work, and sometimes in their communities and schools, black people are in settings where most of their dance partners are white. This is their daily reality, but it is not one that many white people fully appreciate. In workshops, I have had many white people say, "Aren't we all the same? All this talk about difference—don't you think that's the problem?" While at the same time, people of color insist, "We are so different; we can't even begin to talk about it." Several years ago, black people started saying, *"It's a black thing. You just wouldn't understand."* The slogan became so popular, it made it onto T-shirts, travel cups, pens, mugs, even teddy bears.

I believe that all human beings are the same in many ways, especially concerning our basic needs and desires. Here are some of the ways.

What We as Human Beings Have in Common

We have the desire to
- be well;
- be free from suffering;
- be loved;
- have food, shelter, and clothing;
- be happy;
- enjoy the fruits of our labor;
- be respected;
- be treated fairly;
- engage in meaningful work;
- experience genuine relationships; and
- have all these things for our loved ones.

I could go on, but I think you get the point. These are fundamental and essential commonalities. Affirming these universal needs reminds me of how connected we all are and what we are fighting for when it comes to racial inclusion. At the same time, I also believe in recognizing, understanding, and embracing our differences—rather than trying to downplay them. Even if we look at the list above, I notice that people have a very different understanding of these desires and different approaches to securing them. For example, some people believe that they deserve the things on the list above, whereas others see the presence of these things in their lives as gifts for which they are grateful. Some believe having what one needs is enough, whereas others believe that one should try to obtain as much as one can. Some are focused only on obtaining these things for themselves, whereas others feel it is their responsibility to ensure that their larger community's needs are met and are willing to sacrifice what they have to make that possible. These differences in understanding and approach are influenced by our culture, our worldviews, and our life experiences, and they are important to examine and affirm as well. They change how we behave and how we relate to and judge others.

Valerie Batts, the president of Visions, Inc.—a cutting-edge multicultural consulting firm—calls this idea "Both/And" thinking, and it is one of the hardest concepts to teach my clients. ***Diversity is about both commonalities and differences, not "Either/ Or."*** To build inclusion, we have to learn to acknowledge and work with multiple and, sometimes, seemingly conflicting realities. The truth is that the "Both/And" is not where the conflict arises; it is in the "Either/Or" where we insist that one person's reality is the right one, and there is only one correct way to understand differences. Somehow, noticing that we are both the same and different makes me want to keep talking, across racial differences, rather than squaring off in my corner fighting about who's right. The "Both/And" concept almost magically frees me to understand how race influences not only my worldview but also the perspectives of my white friends, who will say, "Yes, you are the only black person here, but you know we all love you." Both things are true: I feel *both* uncomfortable being severely outnumbered in a party *and*, blissful being there nevertheless because I am encircled by my caring friends, who happen to be white. I am glad my friends have taken this initial step toward integrating their lives and, at the same time, sad about the barriers that remain to prevent them from hosting a more diverse gathering.

Why Being Color-Blind Can't Get Us to Inclusion

One barrier is what most white people were taught to believe about how to be fair to black people—justice equals color-blindness. I have my doubts about whether people can actually be color-blind, but maybe it is possible. I don't want to argue that point. I do know it is absolutely true that many white people are blind to the impact of color. If my friends remain color-blind, I will forever be the only black person at the party, and they will have no appreciation for the impact that this repeated experience has on me. Being the only black person at a social event is not the biggest deal in the world, and I don't want my white friends to stop inviting me to their events! After all, when it comes to a party, I am free to accept the invitation or not, to come and go as I please.

The real problem with color-blindness, as it has been taught, is that it leads to inaction.

However, if you think about how this type of underrepresentation plays out at work, in the classroom, on a committee, or in a community day after day, you can imagine the isolation that many black people feel and how it affects their sense of belonging. Sometimes, when I am the only black person at an event, boardroom, or office, I can see all the beliefs, behaviors, and systems that have conspired to prevent, create, and perpetuate my "lonely only"[1] status. I have written this book so that these beliefs, behaviors, and systems can become as apparent to my white clients, colleagues, and friends, and together we can take steps to make the changes that allow racial inclusion to be nourished in our communities and organizations.

The real problem with color-blindness, as it has been taught, is that it leads to inaction. If you ascribe to it, you are not required to notice that race is a dimension that may be making a difference in people's lives. When Martin Luther King, Jr., spoke so eloquently about black people being judged by the content of their character, not the color of their skin, he wasn't saying to dismiss a black person's race. He was warning us not to dismiss the worth of a black person because of his race. The real test of fairness is not about ignoring that a person is black. It is about seeing that a person is black and still being able to regard her as an individual, rather than a set of assumptions and stereotypes.

Some folks nevertheless insist that noticing and talking about differences is counterproductive. I might agree if we were starting from an absolutely clean slate—one with no history, no racial disparities, and no present-day experiences with racism. However, in a world where there are so many unacknowledged beliefs, behaviors, and invisible systems that serve to categorize some groups as culturally superior to others, it is intellectually disingenuous to ignore difference in the name of creating unity and harmony.

Tim Wise, a well-known white educator and anti-racism activist, discusses many of the problems with adhering to the color-blind approach in his book, *Color Blind: The Rise of Post-Racial Politics and the Retreat from Racial Equity*. He explains how color-blindness can make racial fairness harder to attain on the personal and institutional level:

> ... Implicit racial biases (which often exist side-by-side with an outwardly non-racist demeanor and persona) frequently influence the way we view and treat others. But colorblindness, by discouraging discussions of racial matters and presuming that the best practice is to ignore the realities of racism, makes it more difficult to challenge those biases, and thus increases the likelihood of discrimination. ... Colorblindness can perpetuate and even deepen systemic racism. ... Encouraging individuals and institutions to downplay the role of race and racism in the lives of the public will only impede the ability to respond to the needs of that public.[2]

By the way, I know that moving away from the idea of color blindness means we are changing the script that many well-intentioned white people have been following about how to bridge racial boundaries. However, the United States has been on a journey of its own, learning just what it takes to reverse centuries of oppression and exclusion. We have moved from passing antidiscrimination laws to campaigns of racial tolerance to celebrating different aspects of our cultures (e.g., music, dress, foods, and holidays) to the idea of inclusion. Some of us have also begun to realize that beyond inclusion is the idea of cultural competency—the ability to understand different cultural dynamics and also to utilize differences to enhance our lives and communities.

U. S. Journey Toward Racial Justice

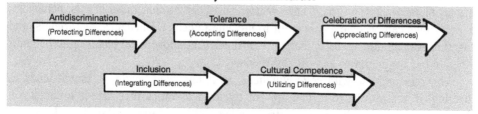

Inclusion Is Not Only the Right Thing to Do; It's the Rich Thing to Do

Among the reasons the color-blind approach doesn't help us reach inclusion is that it means we don't get to notice what is so interesting and exciting about bringing racial and cultural differences into our organizations and communities. I work to improve racial inclusion in the environments in which we work and live because I know how enriching difference can be—the energy, the intellectual stimulation, the innovation, and the personal growth and satisfaction. I would like more people, especially those in dominant groups, to experience the power of racial, ethnic, cultural, and other types of diversity as I have, and not to disregard it. It is a loss to all of us personally and professionally when individuals and groups are underrepresented or are discouraged from expressing their different ideas, skills, and ways of doing things.

In his book *Covering*, Professor Kenji Yoshino of Yale Law School explains that while organizations may appear to welcome diversity, what they signal through their behaviors and rules is that people different from the norm are welcome but only if they behave like the majority group and adopt its values, language, and culture.[3] These organizations want people from different backgrounds to "cover" the things that make them different. This attitude is a hidden threat to the civil rights of these individuals because they are not allowed to express their difference without negative repercussions (e.g., firing, lack of promotion).[4] His argument is underscoring the difference between diversity and inclusion. In order to embrace inclusion, the white majority will need to find ways to welcome the part of difference that makes them uncomfortable or is not like what has been deemed superior. Difference does require more of us. Being out of one's comfort zone, having to learn new things, not knowing what to expect or how to act is not easy, but the information and skills needed to appreciate difference can be learned, and the rewards make the work well worth it.

It has been hard to convince some of the white people I advise about the rewards of cultivating difference within their workplace and the reasons we don't always want to adopt sameness as the "be-all" and "end-all." I understand why this is a difficult concept for them to fully appreciate. If one has never been educated in a school or worked in an organization where multi-culturalism is practiced, it may be hard to imagine that there is a better and richer way of relating and working.

However, much research has been done regarding the power of diversity. Most recently, in his book *The Difference*, Professor Scott Page uses mathematical calculations to prove that a group of people with different skills and perspectives are able to find better solutions and make more accurate predictions than a group with homogeneous skill sets and perspectives—even if the members of the second group score higher on individual ability tests.[5] I've had the opportunity to work with Professor Page on several occasions, and he often explains that different skills and perspectives are so important to problem solving and making predictions because people who think the same get stuck in the same places. However, he also warns that bringing difference together only works if people appreciate and respect their differences and can learn to get along. This is why diversity alone is not enough; it is why we have to learn the skills of inclusion.

David Wilkins, a Harvard Law School professor who studies the legal profession and speaks all over the world about the state and future of law firms, believes that law firms could benefit greatly from the perspectives and skills of people of color and women. Professor Wilkins explains:

> Law firms ought not to be content with the status quo because it is unlikely to be a winning strategy overall as we move forward in the new millennium. Innovation rarely comes from the established players because they're the ones who are most comfortable with the status quo. New ideas almost always come from the outside—from people who come from the outside, see the inside clearly enough to understand it, but yet have a new perspective. And there, I think, women and minorities can make a difference. And when you add the global dimension and expansion that firms are doing, they've got to figure out how to integrate people from different places, cultures, and worlds. Minorities have figured out how to integrate; they have had to

be bi-cultural. They already have those cultural integration skills that will be valuable to these firms.[6]

I believe Professors Page and Wilkins are correct, but unless a white individual has had positive, seminal experiences with a black person, "Diversity is our Strength," is nothing more than a nice platitude. Unless having access to different perspectives and skills made an appreciable difference in his or her world, he or she might think like one white partner who said to me on a break from our awareness workshop, "I can see how Jews are valuable and women too, but what do blacks offer? How are we better off?" I took a deep breath. I appreciated his earnestness and honesty. I knew he was saying out loud what many people think.

I know that it's hard for whites who haven't had much exposure to black people, given all the negative stereotypes and racism, to view them as valuable assets. You might see their value if you, as a white person, avoided a major mistake in a labor and employment case when a black associate with a different life experience pointed out a key issue that would have been extremely damaging at the jury trial if someone hadn't caught it beforehand. In that situation, you would become immediately curious and interested in what else this person might know and see that you don't. Unless you've had a life-changing experience—devoting your life to an anti-racism initiative with black people, or worked closely with a black person who has become like family to you—it's much harder to know the value of racial diversity in your life and work.

A friend of mine adopted black children years ago, and he explains his experience this way: "Before we adopted our children, we thought of ourselves as good, 60s-style liberals. But by being the parents of these kids, we have 'become black.' We see race quite differently now. We have had many experiences that I cannot explain in any way other than racism." He admitted to me that he has discovered that much of his success in life and his sense of being right with the world are not due only to his demeanor, hard work, and talent, but also to the respect afforded him in the world because he is a white man. Fathers understandably work hard to create security for and bequeath opportunity to their children. He told me that "it is terrible as a father to know that I can't protect my kids from racism." My friend has made a self-discovery while at the same time realizing, ultimately, that he cannot bestow his whiteness on his children. They are in the same family, they are the same; but their racial differences make a profound difference.

The type of revelations that come from being in close relationships with black people may be painful and upsetting, but they are imperative for any white person who is trying to create racial equity and inclusion. In a strange way, while they are negative, they are also valuable because they provide you with more information, a broader worldview, and a deeper empathy—all useful tools in the dance of inclusion. So how do you gain access to both the positive and enlightening experiences that I have been describing so that you can better appreciate racial difference?

Deepen Your Experiences across Race

In the chart on the next page are some ways that you might begin to seek out more opportunities to deepen your exposure and connection to black people. However, I want to caution you about your approach to this whole thing. You are not on an assignment;

Deepen Your Experiences Across Race: Finding Seminal Experiences

1. At work and outside of work, look at the relationships with black people that you now have, or look around for the black people who are in your orbit.
   ~ On what level are you sharing?
   ~ When you converse with them, what do you talk about?
   ~ Do you know what they are doing in their lives and what they care about?
   ~ Are you sharing your life with them, the things that you truly care about?
   ~ Is race a subject that you discuss?
   ~ Begin to attend to deepening your connection and see where it leads. Don't push.
   ~ Read the rest of this book so that you know the "dos" and "don'ts."
   ~ Do the self-awareness work that provides the tools to interact effectively and respectfully.

2. If you are leading a committee, initiative, or department, think about finding a black co-leader with whom you can work on the project.

3. Volunteer to be a sponsor of the black employee resource group at work and spend time getting to know the members of the affinity group.

4. If you are a mentor to a black person at work, consider developing a two-way relationship, where you learn as much from your mentee as the mentee learns from you—construct the time you spend together so each of you shares views, perspectives, and experiences. Involve your mentee in things you enjoy; participate in the events and activities in which your mentee is involved.

5. Increase your exposure to different cultures—attend black churches; book talks with black authors, writers from other backgrounds, or white writers who examine issues related to black history and experience; events with black musicians and artists; and other events, especially where you will be in the minority. Reach out to the black people you encounter there.

6. Participate in a multi-day workshop with black people from your community, place of worship, or job.

7. Get involved in anti-racism work, where you are rolling up your sleeves and working in collaboration with and/or directed by black people (e.g., health disparities, criminal justice, educational reform). You can get involved in the YWCA in your area—the YWCA's mission is to empower women and eliminate racism. You could also search the Internet for the phrases "racism," "anti-racism," "ending racism," or "racial dialogues," in your city or a city near you.

8. Make connections with other white people who are participating in intra-group (white people with white people) dialogues about race or those working on anti-racism initiatives to learn more from them about how white people can improve race relations. You will gain confidence and encouragement about building cross-racial relationships in a safe environment, and you may meet the black people to whom white members in these groups are connected.

this is not a project or an anthropological experiment. It is important not to try too hard, but to have a sincere desire, an open mind, and the willingness to put yourself in situations where black people are more likely to be in the majority or in leadership. This is about changing YOUR life. You are looking to be changed, not to change someone else.

Explore and Share Your Cultural Diversity

One benefit of having a deeper (rather than more superficial) relationship with a black person is that it allows you to explore your differences in a way that feels safe. There will be enough commonalities and connections in the relationship that there is room to notice and talk about some of the significant differences in culture, background, manner, and perspective that exist between you and the black person. Sometimes, I have found that when certain white people insist that "we are all the same," it is because they are afraid to look at how racial and ethnic differences unfairly disadvantage some and advantage others. However, other times, the resistance is due to the fact that they don't know and haven't experienced how exciting it is to explore and share one's cultural diversity and learn about the diversity of others. In one of my favorite workshop exercises, called "Exploring Our Cultural Diversity," we ask participants in small groups to share the answers to these questions within their small groups:

Exploring Our Cultural Diversity Questions

⇨ What is your race, your ethnicity, your socioeconomic class (now and growing up), your religion, your gender? (Feel free to share any other identities you consider important.)

⇨ What types of diversity have there been in the various stages of your life?

⇨ What do you like about your cultural background?

⇨ What do you find difficult or what don't you like about your cultural background?

Initially, many people are intimidated by the exercise, but once people get started telling their stories, individuals of every background love it. They learn so much about themselves and others. They hear stories that challenge the assumptions they were keeping about other participants without even knowing it. For many, it is the first time that they have had the opportunity to share honestly and proudly about their backgrounds in a diverse group. Even groups of people who have worked together for a long time remark how little they knew about each other and how much more connected they feel after the exercise. The connection serves to create more team cohesion, more trust, less strife, and more openness, which facilitates the opportunity to address issues directly. This in turn, increases productivity and efficiency as a group.

What is your story, your background? There are a number of white people who say in my workshops, "I don't have a culture. I'm just plain, normal 'white toast.'" Some even go as far as saying, "I feel jealous sometimes of ethnic minorities because they have so many interesting things about their cultures." Be assured, everyone has a cultural background: messages, values, and behaviors that have informed their upbringing and shaped who they are. We will talk more about this in later chapters. "Normal" is already language that reinforces the notion that there is an "in group," a "right group." If you are "normal," what are others? Abnormal? In fact, many people who think of themselves today as just "normal" were ethnic minorities at one point in this country. Both white people who were ethnic minorities in their communities and people of color talk about hiding their homemade lunch from other kids at school, because their ethnic food was so different and they wanted the "normal" food, like peanut butter and apple pie. They were embarrassed then, but now they are sad that they don't know how to cook their families' traditional cuisine. People also share how they realized that, as small children, teachers and/or parents discouraged them from speaking their native language, and now they regret not being able to speak that language or teach it to their children. Some have lost the story of their ancestors' struggles before and after coming to the United States, because it was not talked about at home.

In these comments, I see that many whites have lost their culture because of the need to assimilate, to "melt" into the pot of America. Many of them have lost customs, languages, and connections to the country of their ancestors in exchange for a chance to survive, blend in, and have the American dream. These groups have been able to do this because of their white skin. Some may even have indigenous or African heritage, but have given up their connection to those cultures and identities in order to access opportunities in the U.S. Blacks have made real efforts to blend, but, for many, the visibility of our physical features and the racist beliefs and behaviors of many whites have made that extremely difficult.

Actually, I have known both the experiences of assimilation and racism in my life. I have been the beneficiary of the great American equalizer: a good education. However, I have seen so many members of my family and my community experience a different America, where the dream of equal opportunity has been denied, despite their hard work and talent. It is the "Both/And" of my life experience that motivates me to do the work I do as a diversity consultant. I have watched our country make strides toward racial equity and then retrench, over and over again. I hope to encourage more white Americans to work harder to make good on our country's ideals for everyone. If you want to make a difference in continuing to move our communities and organizations toward racial inclusion as a white person, it will be important for you to examine how your background has influenced who you are. You will also need to take a keen interest in learning about the backgrounds and cultures of others. This is how seminal experiences begin to take shape. In workshops, I will usually model the Cultural Sharing exercise before I ask others to do so. So, I will do the same here. Below is what I might say if I did a quick cultural sharing:

> I am a black, single, Christian, straight, able-bodied woman. I emerged from a working class family on the west side of Baltimore, fortified and propelled by the incredible sacrifices of my selfless parents. Like many people in the United States, I grew up in a homogeneous neighborhood. Everyone was black and Christian, although we were families of different socioeconomic and educational levels. I happened to be in the right place at the right time when the government decided to fund recreation centers with swimming pools in black neighborhoods, summer jobs,

enrichment camps, and open enrollment to "magnet" schools.

As a middle schooler, I took three city buses (the 51 to the 13 to the 6), with my friend Julie away from my neighborhood every morning of the week, to access integrated and better-quality schools, and to meet—for the first time—white people whose lives, houses, customs, foods, and language were quite different from my own. My dad and my brother were quite skeptical of my new world and wanted little to do with it. In fact, my brother warned that I was becoming a hippie.

What made a good college education possible were scholarships, an emphasis on grades rather than test scores, Pell grants, and an incredibly articulate, older white woman from Barnard College named Christine Royer. Ms. Royer met me at my high school's counseling office, liked my spark and promised my mom she would take care of me in the mean streets of New York City (it was the late 1970s). I only applied to one college; I didn't know any better. Thank God I got in.

I met and befriended so many different kinds of people in college: Jews, gay people, people born outside the United States, Chicanos, Asians, even biracial and middle class black people. (I had never really met black kids whose parents were professors and had siblings who also went to elite colleges. Based on my experience, I thought only one child per black family was given that chance and I was it for my family.) All this exposure expanded my world, and made me want more diversity. At the same time, I discovered racism in college—in the expectations of some professors, the comments of some students, and deeply entrenched in the institution.

My parents had never mentioned racism; I thought it was over, a thing of the 1960s. It was in college that I realized, for the first time, that I was a black person. Before that time, I always thought of myself as "Vernā," an individual. My race became a salient factor in my identity because there were so few black students and professors, and because institutional racism was hard to ignore.

I was formally educated in the most elite schools in America, which means overwhelmingly white schools. No one in my family, including me, had ever heard of the Ivy League or Seven Sisters before I attended Barnard. When I told my father that I was accepted into Harvard Law School, he said, "Isn't that further up north? I thought you were coming back home."

I now live in an affluent, mostly white neighborhood in a culturally diverse town, just outside of Boston. I moved there to access good schools for my child. I have many friends of all backgrounds. I'm the proud mom of a beautiful 6'4" black man.

I love being black because black people are resilient, faithful, resourceful, brilliant, funny, cool, talented, and hard working. What I don't like about being black is that some people think we are intellectually and/or culturally inferior. I also don't like the fact that racism has taken such a toll on some black people that they limit their aspirations and those of other blacks.

Questions for Further Exploration

⇨   How does my background influence my sense of comfort with others from different backgrounds, especially black people?

⇨   What messages did I get growing up about other groups about black people and white people?

⇨   Where did I get them? Which of those messages do I still hold to? Which have I let go? Why? How?

⇨   How does my background help me understand racial issues?

⇨   How might my cultural background make it more difficult for me to see and feel motivated to create more racial opportunity for a black person at my job?

If I look at my background, it is a mixed picture. For the most part, it has turned out well. From the moment I boarded the bus on the corner of my street to cross town for an educational opportunity, I became a bicultural person—learning how to navigate in both the educated, elite, white world and the working class black world. I still remember, as a young person, trying to reckon with the stark contrast of my daily pilgrimage. The difference between my neighborhood and where I went to school caused profound confusion. Once I jumped on the No. 6 bus, the third bus on my route, with every mile, the streets looked cleaner, the houses grew bigger, the grass was literally greener, and, of course, the faces were whiter. It makes me think about how many different routes people have taken in their lives to arrive at the same place.

We all pretend to be the same at work, but our journeys have been quite different. I went to predominately white schools, forged genuine friendships with white friends, and was mentored by some amazing white professors. I feel comfortable relating to white people as peers. However, I observe many folks in my family who did not leave Baltimore and/or have not had my educational experience and don't connect as easily across race. Of course, there are costs to being someone who learned early on to cross boundaries—you have lots of stamps on your passport, but where is home?

What I am asking you to do is to think deeply about your own cultural journey, the costs and the benefits. In the box above are some additional questions for you to explore further. Maybe you will want to take the time to write them down and/or ask a friend or colleague to participate in the exercise with you, so you can compare notes.

The answers to all these questions are always quite revealing, and asking the questions means that you are thinking, learning, and acknowledging the impact of race and other identities on how you perceive the world, and how you are perceived by the world. More than perceptions, the answers to these questions shape your behaviors and interactions. This level of consciousness holds so much more promise for changing our present predicament than color-blindness does. ***It is hard to fix something you cannot see, or something you choose to pretend not to see.***

Endnotes

1. I first heard this term used by Theresa Perkins, the amazingly talented Director of Diversity at Perkins Coie LLP, and I thought it described perfectly the position in which many blacks find themselves in majority white settings.

2. Tim Wise, COLOR BLIND: THE RISE OF POST-RACIAL POLITICS AND THE RETREAT FROM RACIAL EQUITY (City Lights 2010), 18 and 19.

3. Kenjii Yoshino, COVERING: THE HIDDEN ASSAULT ON OUR CIVIL RIGHTS (Random House 2006).

4. *Id.*, 26.

5. Scott Page, THE DIFFERENCE: HOW THE POWER OF DIVERSITY CREATES BETTER GROUPS, FIRMS, SCHOOLS, AND SOCIETIES (Princeton University Press 2007).

6. Interview with David Wilkins, San Diego, California, Apr. 2, 2010.

4

With the Right Music, You Can Get Anyone on the Dance Floor: What Messages Are You Sending About Who's Included?

Dance Lessons for this Chapter:

☑ How organizations and communities can create inclusive processes to communicate and demonstrate inclusion

☑ Small personal steps that you can take to create more inclusion at work, in your community, at school, and elsewhere

☑ The phenomenon of "stereotype threat" and how it can negatively impact the performance of black people at work

In 2003, I returned to my law school for a conference celebrating fifty years of women at Harvard Law School. Now that you know a little about my background, you can imagine that the august halls of Harvard are a long way from my black community in Baltimore. As I listened to a panel of older women from the class of 1953, the first group of women to attend Harvard Law School, I realized they had traveled a long road as well. There was one story they told that really struck me because of how clearly it illuminated the difference between diversity and inclusion. I was all prepared to hear war stories about the sexism they encountered as they crossed the gender line, but I was completely surprised when the panelists told the audience that when they arrived at the ivy halls of the law school, there were no bathrooms for the women![1] As smart law school students, they argued to school administrators that requiring them to walk to Harvard Square (a good ten- to fifteen-minute walk) to use the restroom was unfair, since their male counterparts did not have to do the same. How would they make it to their classes on time? What would they do if they had to use the restroom during class or a test? The men at Harvard decided they had a point, and they installed a toilet in the janitor's closet in the basement of a large classroom building. That is where these fantastically brilliant women were relegated to go to the bathroom.

In 1953, Harvard Law School had gender diversity, but I would argue they didn't have gender inclusion. As we have discussed, diversity is about who is represented in the organization, whereas inclusion speaks more to who is respected, expected, and integrated into an institution. Diversity may be the conscious message that your organization or community is sending, but the lack of inclusion can be communicated easily and sometimes unconsciously. In the Harvard Law School example, without something as basic as a bathroom, would it be crazy for those women to conclude that the powers that be didn't want them to be there? At the least, they might imagine that the institution did not understand, respect, or see them. *To be seen, respected, and understood is fundamental to feeling included.*

Inclusion Is Not About Intelligence

Why didn't the really brilliant men who had been debating for decades about whether to discontinue discriminating against women provide bathrooms for their newly invited female students? Do you think it was intentional? I doubt it. Being good at creating inclusion for others unlike you is not about intelligence, at least not how we think of intellect. The brightest people can be clueless when it comes to promoting a sense of belonging and connection for others. That's because being smart about inclusion means becoming aware of the views outside your experience and expertise, in other words, outside your intelligence.

The work of Howard Gardner argues that cognitive intelligence, the type of capabilities we measure by IQ tests, is only one kind of intelligence. The capacity to understand the intentions, motivations, and desires of other people, what Gardner identified as interpersonal intelligence, is another equally important form of intellect.[2] Daniel Goleman also identified an intelligence he called social intelligence—understanding the perspectives of others, sensing and having empathy for their emotions, and taking an active interest in their concerns.[3] No matter what your cognitive intelligence, these social or interpersonal capabilities are what we need to promote inclusion. You have to concern yourself with the perspectives and needs of others. However, this is more difficult when the others are different from you in a significant way. It is made more complex when you are a member of the dominant group or "in-group" within an institution. Those in the "in-group" are like fish in the water of the organization or community. The culture and practices of the organization or community are so reflective of how the dominant group thinks and operates, it becomes hard for them to see that others may not be experiencing the environment the same way they are.

If you are reading this book, you want to know if you are doing something that may make a black person feel unseen and excluded in your communities, relationships, and workplaces. You want to stop doing those things and start being intentionally inclusive. In this chapter, you will find my best suggestions for making sure that when the black people to whom you have extended an invitation arrive at your home, school, boardroom, or office, they receive a clear message that they are welcome, visible, and valuable. These are the steps you can take to make sure you won't forget the bathrooms. They are the actions that help you realize when you should be bringing new music to the dance.

So how do you gain more awareness about who's struggling to survive in the environment that seems friendly and familiar to you? One way is to develop inclusive processes where the perspectives of others, especially newcomers, are solicited, respected, and integrated into how the environment operates. The administrators of the Harvard

Law School may have prepared for the first class of women students in 1953, but I am almost certain that they did not include the newly accepted women students in the process. Even if they had talked to other traditionally male-only schools that had already accepted women, it seems to me that those schools might have told them, "Oh, and don't forget the bathrooms." If they had decided to have a little focus group of women, with the actual students, or maybe with some other women to inquire if there were any issues or concerns they should anticipate, it seems more likely that group would have identified the restroom issue. Or it may have happened that at a breakfast or lunch meeting of the focus group of women where tea, coffee, or water was served, a woman would raise her hand and say, "Excuse me, where is the ladies' room?" Immediately the blinders would have been removed. This is the benefit of inclusion—we learn what we don't know and what we can't know without being exposed to the perspectives and experiences of others different from ourselves.

Processes that Will Help You Communicate and Demonstrate Inclusion

If your place of worship is about to develop a relationship with a predominately black church, your firm is working hard on increasing the racial ethnic diversity of its incoming employees, or your school has a number of new black families enrolling this year, what is your plan for inclusion? How are you going to get the information you need to anticipate what, if anything, needs to change about the way you are accustomed to doing things? Remember you can't think of many of these things by yourself. Your intelligence and intention will not be enough. The fish does not notice the water.

Here are some suggestions for processes that can help:

⇨ *Ask for input from others.* Are there other administrators, program coordinators, parents, presidents, or directors in other institutions who have been successful at creating more racial inclusion in other institutions? Remember to ask specifically about any dance steps they made or what they wished they would have known before they invited their new dance partners onto the floor.

⇨ *Think about when you first came to the organization or neighborhood.* Did you feel welcome? If so, what made you feel welcome? Were you aware of any particular identity of your own when you arrived (e.g. age, accent, geography, immigrant status, socioeconomic class, religion, prior employment, school affiliation, sexual orientation, gender, disability)? If so, how did you feel? Despite your present in-group status, these questions might help you remember it wasn't always that way and may give you a concrete idea of what "to do" or "not to do" with others who are orienting to the new environment.

⇨ *Consult others in your institution who may have been "swimming upstream" at one point in the organization's history.* What groups of people used to be underrepresented in your institution because of religion, ethnicity, age, or language? They may have insight about what made them feel included when they entered, or what they wished had been done to make them feel more accepted and integrated.

⇨ *If you are involved in an organization, undertake a cultural audit or assessment.* Have a third party conduct confidential interviews, focus groups, and surveys of those in the organization to determine how they are experiencing the work-place. How are racial minorities faring? How are the company's policies and practices impacting racial minorities, as compared to whites in the environment? Ask white people about their experiences and opportunities too so that you can get a complete picture, and compare how your practices are affecting everyone.

⇨ *Be prepared to examine and change how you do things in response to the information that comes from your cultural assessment.* Once you have started this process and invited people to give you feedback on how the present environment supports and hinders inclusion, be prepared to make changes. As I mentioned in the first chapter, you can't say you want change and expect to get there without doing things differently.

⇨ *Invite the new or underrepresented group to be part of the orientation process.* What do they want to know? What do they need? How can you and the organization be responsive? How do you keep the communication open and flowing?

Small and Simple but Important Dance Steps You Can Take to Create Inclusion in Your Environment

Some people, especially at work, explain to me that they don't have time to be inclusive. They have too much work to do. What I hear from minority groups is that the smallest things can make them feel more or less included, respected, and valued in their organizations, schools, and communities. It is not that these individuals aren't going to make their own efforts to integrate and engage, it is just much easier, quicker, and more comfortable when those who are in the majority meet them halfway. One junior associate in a large law firm told me that it made a world of difference when a white partner invited him to lunch and said the simplest thing: "I hope you are thinking about sticking around; you are doing great work." It wasn't the lunch as much as the comment that made him think more seriously about committing to a future with the firm. Sometimes, people of color tell me they feel included when a white person seems to engage with them about or show a genuine interest in an event, activity, artist, movie, or book pertaining to black culture. It feels good to be able to share the self they don't often display at work and to feel that the white person regards their interests and culture as valuable.

When I was compiling the list below, I thought about what I have heard from other black people about what helps with inclusion, and I also thought of the many ways that my white colleagues and friends have made me feel connected and integrated when I am in a majority white environment. You may see things on this list below that you do already. That's great! Keep doing them. They make a difference. Now find one or two actions from the list that you don't do at present, but you could stretch to do. Commit to doing them and see what happens.

⇨ *Go up to and speak to people of color wherever you see them.* Approach them at your kid's school, at the grocery store, at the school concert, at the PTO meeting, on the soccer field, in the elevator, at a reception, in the lobby, on your floor, or when you see them sitting by themselves on the bleachers. You don't have to make a big deal of it, just make contact.

⇨ *Call people by the name they want to be called.* Many people don't like to be called by a nickname. Nicknames are given to you by people who are in your family or your friends. For many black people, naming them without their permission feels like you are taking a liberty that you have not earned. I see the naming problem more so with people of color also because some have non-traditional names (or spellings, like my own) that people are not sure how to pronounce. If a person has a name you don't know how to pronounce, ask them how to pronounce it, rather than not speaking to them or calling them by the wrong name. I find that people with uncommon names are happy to offer some useful mnemonic device to help you remember the correct pronunciation.

⇨ *When you engage in conversations with black people, share a little about yourself and also take time to listen to them.* Especially at the job, go beyond the discussion about work matters; if this is something you do with others, it seems weird when you don't do it with black people. If you see their eyes glazing over when you are speaking, it is a clue that maybe you should ask them a question about their interests, their vacation, the books they like, movies they saw, etc. Black and white people can have significant commonalities, but there are also cultural differences and realities that sometimes create two separate worlds. What TV shows we watch, what places we feel comfortable visiting, and what we do on the weekends can be quite different. This is all good and can be enriching if you know how to converse in a way that allows both the commonalities and the differences to surface.

⇨ *Expand your social circles to include more black people.* Get to know the parents of the black kids that your children are friends with. It is not enough that your children have black friends; attend dinners and events where you know there will be a racially mixed audience or a majority of black people.

⇨ *At work, instead of going with the same people to lunch, for coffee, or a drink, diversify the group of individuals with whom you spend time.* Even though you may not be intending to send a message of exclusion, the impact of having only white people in your social circle at work, especially if you are in a managerial position, is that you are not interested in developing cross-racial relationships.

⇨ *When you develop a mental list of colleagues to lead a project, head a committee, or even to promote, go back over that list and see if it comprises only white people or even only white males.* Then think again about the firm's goals of inclusion and the benefits that diverse perspectives might bring to the group as a whole, and expand that list to include talented men and women of color and representatives of other diverse groups.

⇨ *Pay attention to whom you generally include in telephone calls, meetings, emails, and communications.* Who are you missing? Why haven't you included a particular black individual? Was she outside your view? Are you treating her the same as or different from others? Are there some implicit biases you are not acknowledging? Even if you are treating her the same, is the impact on her the same as it is on others? Is there a problem with her performance, and is that why you haven't included her? Have you told her? If not, why not? It is hard for people to contribute or perform at their highest potential if they don't have the information they need or if they feel excluded. ***Benign neglect is not benign.***

⇨ *Invite a black person with whom you work, with whom you serve on a committee, or who teaches or coaches your kid for dinner.* Watch to make sure that you are not assuming that dinner should always be at your house or in your part of town; be willing to go to his or her home or community as well.

⇨ *Share with black neighbors, colleagues, supervisees, and friends, information about the inside politics, unspoken rules, resources, scholarships, discounts, relationships and organizations that can improve their lives.* Many black people are new to professional and business organizations and clubs. Sometimes this is because the clubs excluded black people or made it very difficult for them to join. (Also, the black middle class has its own clubs and affiliations, but they exist separately from the larger white society.) As a black working class woman, there was a whole world of resources and powerful affiliations that I knew nothing about or had no idea how to access. Also, I was often unaware of the ways things were done or how people think in organizations that are predominately white. My white friends, many of whom are professionals and whose parents and grandparents were professionals, often say, "You need to know about this group or you need to meet this person; I will introduce you." Or they will say, "Do you know how this works? I would be happy to tell you." I really appreciate when they do this.

⇨ *Point out and help your black colleagues and supervisees avoid potential pitfalls and problems.* Lend them your perspective and experience in a certain area. Promoting inclusion is not only about suggesting, "Why don't you try this?" It is also about warnings, such as, "That's probably not the best way to do that." I had a wonderful, smart, white male colleague who agreed to be my mentor and provide me with the "white man's view" on certain strategies I was attempting to implement in a majority white male organization. Of course, he couldn't speak for all white males, but he offered invaluable insight into perspectives that I could not have come to on my own.

⇨ *Don't dominate the conversation in a meeting or discussion.* Make sure you are hearing from black people in the room about what they think regarding a subject or project, especially if they are in the minority on the project or in the organization. If their contribution differs from the mainstream or dominant position, consider its value and reward their courage. This contribution from a different perspective may be very helpful to your organization or firm; it may develop an area or strategy that you and the firm had not considered thus far.

⇨ *If points are made from diverse perspectives of men and women of color, don't dismiss them, even in subtle ways.* If you don't see the value of the perspective immediately, consider politely probing by asking that person how he or she could develop that point or new insight to advance the objectives, strategies and advantages of your firm (or committee). If the insights differ greatly from the historically dominant approach, the rest of the group may need to have those points made more clearly so that they can give it more thought after the meeting. By the next meeting, consider developing it and incorporating it into the group/firm's plan, strategy, etc. When you are able to support the point made by that person of color every member of the committee will see the value of this contribution. You will enhance his or her status, further the firm's goals of inclusion, and allow everyone to see benefits from inclusion for the firm as a whole.

⇨ *If you are running a meeting, notice who's not talking when you ask, "Does anyone have anything to add?" or "Are there any questions?"* The silence may not mean there is nothing more to be said. Many black people, especially when they are not well represented in an environment, are reluctant to speak out. They may see the situation different from the majority, and they are unsure how much of an appetite there is for doing things differently from what has been over a long period of time. They don't want to be perceived as "troublemakers" or "not good team players." Employ different strategies to solicit opinion and ideas (e.g., employing round-robins where everyone takes a turn; using secret ballots; writing thoughts and questions on index cards anonymously; soliciting information before and after meetings in person and via telephone or email; creating a suggestion box). When new ideas are offered, make sure that you respond in a way that encourages more input.

Watch Out for Stereotype Threat and Learn How to Counter It

One of the reasons some black individuals don't speak up in meetings is that they are concerned that their questions or comments may be held against them.

Professor Claude Steele of Stanford University and his colleagues Joshua Aaronson and Steven Spencer have been studying for many years this worry and the incapacitating effect it has on some black students' performance in college. They call this phenomenon "stereotype threat," the threat of being viewed through the lens of a negative stereotype. This occurs when individuals of any race or gender fear they will perform in a way that will inadvertently reinforce a negative stereotype held by their evaluators. The anxiety or intimidation that is produced causes individuals to doubt and adjust their performance in a way that they would not if they were not worried.

They discovered the occurence when in an effort to improve the performance of black students at Stanford, they found that the differences in academic success between white and black students occurred even among black students who came to school with the same preparation (SAT and grades), parental income, and quality of education.[4]

Steele and Aaronson began testing the idea of stereotype threat using various experiments with a control condition (where a stereotype was evoked: e.g., inquire about test-takers' preference in sports and music; complete word fragments with stereotype-related words) and an experimental condition (where the threat of stereotype is reduced). In one experiment, they gave white and black students a difficult standardized test. Under the control condition, the test was presented as an examination of intelligence and preparation, but for the experimental condition, the students were told that the test was not about intelligence; instead testers explained they wanted to examine the psychology of verbal problem solving. They used the same test and equally talented students; everything was the same except what the students had been told before taking the test. The performance of white students did not change from the control to experimental condition. However, the black students "solved, on average, twice as many items on the test that was given under the experimental condition.

One of the interesting discoveries that Steele and his colleagues have made is that stereotype threat impacts the most conscientious and hardworking students most severely. Also, the anxiety is produced only when the task is challenging. Steele explains,

> What exposes students to the pressure of stereotype threat is not weaker academic identity and skills but stronger academic identity and skills. They may have long seen themselves as good students— better than most. But led into the domain by their strengths, they pay an extra tax on their investment—vigilant worry that their future will be compromised by society's perception and treatment of their group.[5]

Steele and his colleagues' work focuses on students; however, I think it is especially relevant for black individuals working in elite professions that are focused on solving difficult cognitive tasks in a high-pressure environment. These are also the environments where performance is being evaluated informally and formally by individuals who are mostly white. Cognitive achievement has a lot to do with motivation and expectations, but Steele's research shows that reducing stereotype threat is accomplished when black students trust that the tester is fair and not being influenced by negative stereotypes.[6] The power of race to diminish the performance and contributions of black people will continue unless we can find ways, as Steele and his colleagues have done in their experiments, to change how our society and work environments create stereotype threat.[7] Steele did find that two explicit steps helped to reduce stereotype threat and increased black students' trust of their white evaluators. If the evaluators told students they were using high standards and that the students' work led them to believe that the students could meet these standards (this suggests that you are not viewing them stereotypically), the students trusted that the critique of the evaluators was unbiased. This trust that was developed allowed the students to hear the critical feedback and they became more motivated than the other white students in the study to improve their work.

I believe that if white supervisors and managers in the workplace took these two steps—articulating high standards and indicating, where appropriate, their confidence in the black person's ability to achieve these standards—they would help more black direct reports to perform at their highest potential. What will this take? Obviously, one issue is to work hard to uncover and offset the biases and stereotyping that do actually exist. We will talk in detail about how we might do this in Chapters Eight. In addition, there are ways that some very well-meaning white people have worked with black supervisees that need to change. We will explore these old dance moves and the new steps we suggest instead in Chapter Eleven.

You might be thinking that Steele's suggestions and the two lists of steps that I have offered in this chapter are nice reminders, but they are just about having good manners, being a respectful person, relating effectively with others, and being a good manager. You might also notice that everyone, no matter what race or ethnicity they are, would appreciate being treated this way. I would agree with you wholeheartedly on both accounts. If you carry out these actions already with all types of people, don't change anything you are doing; this is ideal. But, if not, committing to these behaviors with a particular focus on blacks and other underrepresented groups within your environment will promote inclusion for these individuals who, for various reasons, do not as often enjoy such treatment from individuals in the in group. This is not due to intention, of course, but to a lack of attention to how we do what we do and the impact it has on others, especially those in the out groups. Bathrooms are not a big deal, until they are forgotten. "Hellos" are not momentous, unless you have been feeling invisible. "I'm sure you can do it" may seem like faint praise, unless you are full of anxiety about your supervisor's presumptions. So, can we agree? Even though there are big steps required to create more racial inclusion, small things matter, too. If we take the time to pay more attention to the smallest things, we can break down racial barriers and make real progress toward including racial diversity in our lives and organizations.

Endnotes

1. J. R. HOPE & K. SULLIVAN, PINSTRIPES & PEARLS: THE WOMEN OF THE HARVARD LAW SCHOOL CLASS OF '64 WHO FORGED AN OLD GIRL NETWORK AND PAVED THE WAY FOR FUTURE GENERATIONS 264 (Lisa Drew Books/Scribner 2003).

2. H. Gardner, *The Theory of Multiple Intelligences,* 37 ANN. DYSLEXIA 19-35 (1987); HOWARD GARDNER, MULTIPLE INTELLIGENCES: THE THEORY IN PRACTICE (Basic Books 1993); HOWARD GARDNER, FRAMES OF MIND: THE THEORY OF MULTIPLE INTELLIGENCES (Basic Books 1983; republished 1993).

3. DANIEL GOLEMAN, SOCIAL INTELLIGENCE: THE NEW SCIENCE OF HUMAN RELATIONSHIPS (Bantam 2006).

4. J. Aaronson, *The Threat of Stereotype,* ASCD EDUCATIONAL LEADERSHIP (2004).

5. C. M. Steele, *Thin Ice: Stereotype Threat and Black College Students,* ATLANTIC MONTHLY (1999), http://www.theatlantic.com/doc/199908/student-stereotype (accessed Jan. 24, 2011).

6. *Id.*

7. In Steele's recent book, *Whistling Vivaldi: And Other Clues to How Sterotypes Affect Us and What We Can Do,* Steele describes the many experiments he and others have conducted on stereotype threat and what they have learned from them about how to counter the threat and to minimize stereotype threat: (a) improve the number of people from the social category in the setting so that a critical mass is reached, (b) make it clear that you value diversity, (c) foster intergroup conversations and frame these as a learning experience; (d) allow the stereotyped individuals to use self-affirmations, and (e) help the stereotyped individuals to develop a narrative about the setting that explains their frustrations while projecting positive engagement and success in the setting.

5

So You Were a Little Offbeat; It Isn't the End of the Dance: How to Recover When You've Stepped on Your Dance Partner's Toes

Dance Lessons for this Chapter:

☑ The impossibility of perfection on the dance floor

☑ A new dance called S-A-M-E

☑ The difference between intent and impact

☑ The impact of micro-inequities on people of color

☑ The effect your missteps may have on a black person if you don't try to correct them

☑ Things you can do and say after you have made a misstep

Several years ago, I was walking down the streets of Boston with Earl—a blind gentleman—and his guide dog. He and I had become acquainted because, as the Deputy Chief of Staff for the Attorney General of Massachusetts, I was working with the disability community to improve the office's services and outreach. It was a beautiful day, and without thinking, I started to say, "Hey look! It's such a beautiful day, isn't it?" As the word "look" flew out of my mouth, I abruptly halted my speech and sort of swallowed the end of the sentence. Earl asked, "What did you say?" And I said, "Oh nothing." He asked again, "No, what were you saying?" So I 'fessed up by responding rather sheepishly, "I was going to say, 'Hey look, it's a beautiful day,' but then I realized you can't see it." He responded with a bit of a teasing in his tone, "First of all, I know that when you say 'Hey look,' you don't mean it literally." I remained quiet. Then he continued, "Just describe the day to me. Tell me what makes it beautiful; is it the sun, the sky, the trees?"

I think I apologized; I can't remember. What I will never forget was how stupid I felt. I was forgiven and schooled at the same time. I recognized my own sense of relief and gratitude once I was told what to do. I went on to describe the day, and that interaction led to a conversation about his background and how he lost his sight. The amazing thing about this awkward moment is that it turned into a wonderful conversation that I think we both appreciated. That interaction actually narrowed the gap between our differences and deepened our working relationship. What could have been a lasting wedge between us became an opening for understanding and connection.

Just because I am a good, well-meaning person doesn't mean that I know how to be respectful of difference in every situation. Yes, there are some basic guiding principles that we can apply. These are ways to prevent some obvious infractions and to stay open to learning; however, actual comfort and facility with difference comes through education and interaction. Sighted folks can be blind, too; it is hubris to think otherwise.

Do the S-A-M-E Dance

S = STOP: Stop Expecting and Pretending to Know
A = APOLOGIZE: Don't Hide Behind Your Intent
M = MISTAKES: It's Okay to Make Mistakes
E = ENGAGE: Start the Dance of Engagement

Sometimes you may find yourself saying the wrong thing to a black person, revealing your lack of awareness or saying something that has an impact you didn't intend. To counter this, I want to teach you the S-A-M-E dance. These are the steps that you can take to recover when you have trod upon your partner's toes and that might also help you avoid doing so the next time around. I call it S-A-M-E because, as I mentioned in the last chapter, we *both* have our differences *and* share the same fundamental human needs. Getting the S-A-M-E steps down helps to bridge our fallibilities and underscores our shared humanity. I'm pretty sure that most black folks will keep dancing with you and excuse your klutziness if you can learn to follow these dance steps.

S = STOP: *Stop Expecting and Pretending to Know*

Adopt a humble attitude and ask yourself, "What am I missing here?"

The cost of being taught indirectly (and sometimes directly) by a monocultural social structure as a white person that you are superior is that you don't know what you don't know. It is hard for any of us to be humble and to accept that our unearned privileges (receiving the benefits of being considered "better than" others by virtue of a social group identity) have put us at a disadvantage because we know so little about those in the groups that have been designated as "less than." On the other hand, those in the so-called "less than" group know lots about the "better than" group. They have to, in order to survive. A white friend of mine told me recently, "I was not at all in touch with my superiority complex. In fact, until I started digging really deeply into understanding race, I would have outright denied it. It wasn't that I thought I was superior, but I definitely felt others were inferior." The "digging" she referred to was a twelve-week racial identity course for teachers. She had been motivated to take the course after seeing the racial divide play out in the performance gap between the white and black students in her school system year after year. She explained further:

> Before that course, I knew people of color were disadvantaged; but by the end of the course, I learned that I had been advantaged as a white person by the very same systems that had caused that disadvantage. I didn't know that the black soldiers from World War II were denied benefits from the GI bill. I didn't even know that race wasn't actually a biological fact. I wasn't making the connections between my beloved New England family and our success and the lives of the black children who weren't faring so well in our school system—I thought my family did better because we were better. But when, in the course of reading, I read a quote by sociologist Allan Johnson along the lines of, "You can't have a short end of the stick without the long end of the stick,"[1] I got it.

During the exchange I had with Earl, my blind colleague, that I previously recounted, I found not only my ignorance exposed but also my sense of superiority. I felt like an idiot because I thought I should have known what to say in the situation, especially as a "diversity expert." But where did that thinking come from? Honestly? It emerged from an unacknowledged, but deeply rooted, sense that I was better than Earl; that, in our relationship, he was the one to be pitied and helped. I was the "knower" in our association. I was not prepared to learn from him. I am willing to admit this so as not to get stuck in some self-flagellating guilt. I was reminded once again that there is no way to be an expert in every area of difference, especially in an area where I have little actual experience. I see genuinely good white people relate to black people in the same way I was relating to Earl. They somehow expect that they should know what to say or how to treat black people even if they have had very little interaction with them. Or they have a patronizing approach that they are completely unaware of; they think they are helping, but, to the black person, it feels like they are demonstrating their self-importance.

Some white people assume that the Golden Rule will take care of everything. They reason that they know how they want to be treated, so they know what they need to know to interact with others respectfully. The Golden Rule is helpful sometimes, but it does not recognize that people from different cultural backgrounds and experiences may have different expectations, needs, and interpretations about what respect and love look like. Accepting that you don't know is an actual step in the direction of greater racial harmony. *Once you admit ignorance, you begin asking rather than telling, listening rather than proclaiming, and learning rather than teaching.* Besides, I find it less stressful not to have to pretend that I'm cool and I know everything, don't you?

A = APOLOGIZE: Don't Hide behind Your Intent

Your intent is not the same as your impact. If, because of my mistake, I felt so upset with myself that I grew reserved with Earl, I wouldn't have enjoyed the exchange we had after my blunder. I learned so much about him as an individual and increased my awareness about the issues with which he regularly contends. For example, he told me that when he boards a subway train, people talk to his dog but never talk to him. Shocking, isn't it? They don't know how to talk comfortably with a blind man, but maybe they know how to talk to dogs? I believe they are intending to connect with Earl, but the impact is to make him feel invisible and "less than" his dog.

Even though what you intended to say or ask may be valid and important, it isn't the whole equation. When we are confronted with the possibility that something about our behavior has upset someone, we naturally defend ourselves by sharing our intent. So often I have heard some white people protest, "That's not what I meant" or "My intent wasn't to insult you." I think most black people could accept this explanation if the white person would first acknowledge how the comment or action may have been offensive. I believe conversations, learning, and relationships between white and black people could expand if a white person when he is told about or realizes his misstep, would say something similar to one of the following:

- ⇨ "I'm sorry; I see that I offended you. What did I say to upset you?"
- ⇨ "I wish I knew, but I don't and I want to know."
- ⇨ "What should I have said?"
- ⇨ "Did I just call you the name of the other black woman? Sorry. Bear with me; I'm working on it."
- ⇨ "That was wrong, wasn't it?"
- ⇨ "Oh, shoot, that was racist, wasn't it?"

Some of my white male friends tell me that men will never utter an apology like the statements above because they have been taught "apologize for nothing," especially in the workplace. It is an admission of weakness. However, I think I have heard the guy version of these statements; it goes something like this:

> "Just ignore (kill, shoot, etc.) me. I'm an idiot (jerk, fool, Neanderthal, insensitive clod)."

These statements will work, too. Also, if you are a man who has been schooled against apologizing like my white male friends, all I can say is that apologizing in cross-racial interactions takes real guts. So, really, doing so is a sign of bravery not frailty.

A white friend I know who is hard at work on racial issues recently took a very courageous step in this regard. She told me that she was standing on the soccer field with a black parent and asked her about her daughter. But when she asked about the daughter, she called the daughter by the name of the one other black girl on the team. She noticed that for a brief moment the black mother looked confused, but then continued on with the conversation. After the incident, my friend realized what she had done wrong. She fretted about it all day. I can imagine how she felt. I remember when I was walking with Earl that sunny day, wishing that I had never opened my mouth or hoping that maybe he hadn't heard me. My friend told her husband about what she had done on the soccer field. He consoled her and told her it wasn't a big deal, and, besides, what could she do anyway? She sat with it for a few more hours and then she picked up the phone. She called the mother and apologized for calling her daughter by the other black child's name. The mother listened, thanked her for calling, and assured her that everything was fine. They talked a little about how their girls were enjoying soccer and life in general.

I love this story, because maybe the mistake wasn't a big deal, but the call and the apology certainly were. It so rarely happens that someone is willing to admit to a mistake when they are not called on it, especially across race. I can only imagine the possibilities for a real relationship between these two women, because my friend was courageous enough to say, "I made a mistake that may have offended you, and I want to account for it."

M = MISTAKES: It's Okay to Make Mistakes

You get to make mistakes as you engage in the process of ending racial exclusion. Don't be so overwhelmed with guilt and fear that you withdraw from the interaction and relationship.

My friend made a mistake, but she didn't let that prevent her from reconnecting with the black mother. However, some white individuals, especially in the work setting, live in fear of saying or doing the wrong thing with people of color. Lawyers seem especially afraid of making a misstep with people of color. I was in one workshop, and a partner remarked, "Well, you know when I work with a protected class person . . . ." I cringed when I heard that. I knew he had no idea what he was revealing. Can you imagine? Every time a woman, a person of color, or a person with a disability came innocently into his office for an assignment, he saw her or him as a potential lawsuit, "a protected class person." Just think about it. How does one talk, interrelate with, or mentor a "protected class person"? There has to be awkwardness, a distance, an arm's-length engagement that is perceptible on some level to this other individual even if the partner is unconscious of how this designation is influencing his behavior and the dynamic of the relationship.

When some white people make a mistake that involves a person of color, they feel so mortified, even if they are not afraid of being sued, they stop talking or trying to engage with the person they insulted. Here's what I mean: a young Asian man told me that he was in his law firm's cafeteria when a partner at the firm came up to him and quickly and emphatically instructed him to contact a client regarding an urgent matter. The Asian man, who wasn't an attorney, but a scientist in the firm's patent department, was so confused by the situation as it was unfolding that only after the partner had left did he realize what had happened. The partner had mistaken him for someone else. He hurried to his office and telephoned Jason, the one Asian male lawyer in the litigation department, since he thought the partner's instructions sounded like they had to do with a case.

He described the partner to Jason and tried his best to convey the partner's message. Jason recognized that it was a partner he was working with, but after the call, Jason still wasn't certain about what the partner wanted him to do. So Jason, in the most pleasant way possible, called the partner, explained that he knew some urgent matter needed his immediate attention, but that he was not the one in the cafeteria with whom the partner had communicated. The partner apologized; the associate assured him that it was no big deal and that he was only calling to find out what to do. After that day, Jason explained that the partner's behavior toward him changed: the partner seemed to avoid one-on-one meetings with him and when he saw the partner, the partner would never look him in the eye. He also never received any other work from that partner after the matter closed. The partner withdrew because he was embarrassed; he stepped off the dance floor with Jason because of shame, and by doing so, he added to his error by making Jason pay for it. I call this particular dance move "adding insult to injury."

Mistakes Have an Impact

Mistaken identity itself is not the end of the world, unless you deal with it in the same manner as the partner discussed above. I am not saying that you should just dismiss your mistake. I am suggesting that mistakes happen when engaging cross racially, and it is important to stop for a second and appreciate the possible impact on the person of color, so that you will commit to completing the E dance step—Engage—rather than running away. In the preceding case, the partner had been working with Jason, but obviously still didn't quite see Jason as an individual. Why? Why hadn't he stopped long enough to recognize who Jason really was? What is the impact on Jason? Remember, Jason is an associate who is trying to distinguish himself from others and impress his partners with the hope of being taken under someone's wing and nurtured into an excellent attorney.

At my consulting firm, VMCG, we refer to this phenomenon as "conspicuous but invisible." Jason is conspicuous with regard to his Asian group identity but invisible when it comes to his identity as an individual person. This type of mistake can wear people out and make them wonder, especially in the work context, if they are not only invoking group identity but also the stereotypes that accompany that group designa-

tion. Of course, mistaken identity is not only an issue that people of color and members of other traditionally underrepresented groups (women, for example) face in majority white male-dominated organizations. Certainly this happens to some white men, too. The problem for black people and other underrepresented group members is that they have to endure this same mistake frequently and from different majority group members. This is especially difficult to endure in the workplace, where they are trying to believe that success is possible, even though there may be very little proof of that in the upper echelons of the company.

If they look up the chain of command and see very few people who look like them, they begin to conclude that their prospects for success in the environment are doubtful. Unless they have solid work opportunities and relationships with majority people in the organization, they will often start to disengage from the organization and make plans to try their luck elsewhere; or they will stay put, but withdraw into a "do just enough to get by" strategy. I have seen among many black employees an attitude I refer to as "protective disengagement." They convince themselves that they don't want to succeed or may secretly believe they are not up to the task; in reality, it is just a way to protect themselves from what they see as the impossibility of success. This posture makes them appear as if they are uncommitted, uninterested, and unenthusiastic. Any potential dance partner will pass them by, assuming that he will be rebuffed if he were to get up enough nerve to ask them to step into the flow of things.

Micro-Inequities

I am sure that many of you have heard of the term "micro-inequities," also known as micro-insults or micro-aggressions. It is important as you learn the dance of inclusion to be aware of what micro-inequities are and how these tiny mistakes can have a much larger detrimental impact on your relationship with people of color and the environments in which we work and live. "In the world of business, the term 'micro-inequities' is used to describe the pattern of being overlooked, underrespected, and devalued because of one's race or gender."[2] Mistaken identity, forgetting to introduce a person of color to an important client, using the word "qualified" only to describe candidates of color, and assuring a black person that race had nothing to do with an interaction when the black person believes it does, are examples of micro-inequities. They are quick, small acts, slights, or indignities that black people endure in daily cross-racial interactions. They can be intentional, but many times they are not. Sometimes they happen verbally, or maybe even with a glance or the tone of voice. Even when they are unintentional, they reveal an offender's negative or erroneous assumption or stereotype.

One of my black friends told me that he was the guest of honor at a ceremony celebrating his excellent service as the president of a large professional association. He was all decked out in his tuxedo and feeling good as he walked into the hotel ballroom where the reception for the event had just started, when he saw a white woman in a lovely gown smiling and waving at him. He thought she must know him and wanted to be the first of many that night to congratulate him. He walked toward her, but when they met up, she said politely, "Can you get me a red wine?" He was crushed, but just for a moment, because it wasn't the first time he had experienced an incident like this. In his most recent book, *The Presumption of Guilt: The Arrest of Henry Louis Gates Jr. and Race, Class and Crime in America*, Professor Charles Ogletree includes a chapter entitled, "100 Ways to Look at a Black Man." In the chapter, he chronicles the stories of 100 prominent black men who have encountered the various incidents of race-based micro-aggressions, as well more serious racial profiling and unwarranted police aggravation.[3]

Micro-insults sting and shock. They happen before one knows it, and there is little one can do about them. They can create a profound frustration and often anger in those who are subjected to them because they are subtle, often unintentional, and hard to put one's finger on. They are not egregious comments or behaviors and therefore they are difficult to talk about and correct. Yet, when they happen over and over again, they accumulate and develop a weight of their own. They fester and become a wound that is reopened each time another slight occurs.

WARNING: *It is possible that in some situations you will encounter a black person, who may be carrying some emotional baggage based on their experiences with racism, or someone for whom your comment was the last straw. Sometimes, it may have nothing to do with race. You do need to take responsibility for your mistakes, but also realize that you cannot bear the entire burden in every incident. The problems of racism have a long and deep history. Everything you do to help dismantle racism and bridge the racial divide is part of reversing that history, but change will not happen overnight. Being able to listen to a black person who is upset at you for something you did that offended them or at a racial situation that doesn't involve you, may not be easy. However, it is part of learning to be an ally to black people. If you can make space for a black person to express herself honestly, it will be useful to her and to your growth and awareness and may deepen your relationship with that person. Difficult interactions with certain individuals cannot be your excuse for quitting or withdrawing. And remember to reserve judgment; who knows how you would react if you had walked in her shoes, or should I say, "in her skin."*

E = ENGAGE: Start the Dance of Engagement

Move toward the person you offended. Engagement helps you minimize and correct the mistake and enjoy the benefits of the relationship.

Engagement is maybe the most important step of this dance, but let's practice the first three steps again:

1. Stop pretending to know things that you don't, so that you can begin to learn more.
2. Apologize when you've made mistakes and acknowledge the impact of your actions.
3. Accept that mistakes are going to happen as part of the process of improving relationships across race.

Now, let's look at our last step: Engage. It is so important to move toward, rather than away from, relationships with black people. Remember how I told you earlier that sighted people sometimes talk to Earl's guide dog instead of to Earl? When he told me this, I realized that every time I rode the commuter rail in my neighborhood, there was a blind man on the platform. I had never spoken to him. I am a friendly person, and I usually greet my neighbors with some verbal or visual acknowledgment, even those I don't know. I became aware that because the blind commuter couldn't see me, I had rendered him invisible. After talking to Earl, I started saying, "Good morning" as I walked by my blind neighbor, and he would respond with a similar greeting and a smile. On that beautifully clear day with Earl, he made other blind people visible to me and gave me courage to do something different. I learned to engage.

What if the partner who mistook the Asian associate, Jason, decided as result of the little mix-up to make sure that he actually visited Jason's office, invited him to lunch, and worked with him on another project? He would have gotten to know Jason better, thereby minimizing the chance of confusing Jason with other Asian men in the firm. Jason would have felt more included rather than outnumbered and excluded, and he would have increased opportunities to develop. The feeling of connection that Jason experienced with the partner might have positively impacted Jason's performance on behalf of the partner and the firm's client. Jason's positive work experiences would increase his willingness to commit to and stay with the firm.

So, if you are a peer or supervisor of a person of color, like Jason, at work, the most important thing you can do is not to be careful and distant but be connected and collaborative—to purposefully look to engage with and support this person. If he does seem somewhat withdrawn or unengaged with others and his work, remember that it might be because he has been enduring microinsults and macroinsults that are affecting his opportunities, confidence, and sense of possibilities for his success in your organization. He may not even know that his actions and attitudes are communicating that he doesn't want to be there. If he knows you are on his side, he may be able to confide in you regarding his concerns, frustrations, and exhaustion. If you are able to listen to him, understand his situation, and help him find a solution, you will also help him be conscious and constructive about his behavior so he can gain control over his future.

> So, if you are a peer or supervisor of a person of color, like Jason, at work, the most important thing you can do is not to be careful and distant but be connected and collaborative—to purposefully look to engage with and support this person.

The actions above are some ideas for what you can do when you've made a mistake with a black employee, neighbor, friend, or stranger or when you are supporting someone who has had to deal with the mistakes of others. However, as may be obvious, this is a list for people who want to connect not just with black people but with people of all backgrounds whom they have offended or who have been insulted by others. Try them out.

Remember, *the S-A-M-E dance is not magical.* Be prepared for awkward moments. The actions listed above are not easy. They require self-examination, some courage, and lots of practice. Some days, in some situations, you might still let an incident go because you might have too many other problems to deal with at the time. There is no perfection here. The more you practice, the more confidence you gain in admitting to your imperfection! No matter what happens with one individual black person, just be prepared to persist with others, many of whom have been working hard and anxiously waiting for a dance partner.

Endnotes

1. A. G. Johnson, PRIVILEGE, POWER, AND DIFFERENCE (Mayfield 2001), 131.

2. D. W. Sue, C. M. Capodilupo, et al. *Microaggressions in Everyday Life: Implications for Clinical Practice*, 62 AMERICAN PSYCHOLOGIST 273 (2007). The term "microinequity" was created by Mary P. Rowe, Ph.D, of Massachusetts Institute of Technology Sloan School of Management as she was researching what made students feel excluded. She later published her observations in *Barriers to Equality: The Power of Subtle Discrimination to Maintain Unequal Opportunity*, 3 Employee Responsibilities and Rights Journal 153–163 (1990). Stephen Young, former Senior Vice President and Chief Diversity Officer at JPMorgan Chase and a management consultant, has written and spoken extensively on the subject of micro-inequities in corporations and the power of these small insults to negatively affect the work environment and individual and team performance. His recently published book, Micromessaging: Why Great Leadership Is Beyond Words (McGraw-Hill 2007), asks leaders to be aware that their expressions of indifference (and other micro-inequities) to their staff reports, etc., can have an impact. They can accumulate and negatively impact performance and morale. Employees who receive negative micro-messages tend to just complete assignments. A leader who deploys positive micro-messages can create an environment of inclusion.

3. Charles Ogletree, THE PRESUMPTION OF GUILT: THE ARREST OF HENRY LOUIS GATES JR. AND RACE, CLASS AND CRIME IN AMERICA (Palgrave Macmillan 2010). The list includes such prominent individuals as Attorney General Eric Holder, Johnny Cochran, Jr., and Justice Thurgood Marshall.

6

What's Everybody Staring At? Nobody's Perfect When They First Learn to Dance: The BASICS of Cultural Competence

Dance Lessons for this Chapter:

☑ Learning the BASICS of cultural competence

☑ How to interact without leading with your assumptions

☑ The type of questions that work best when interviewing black candidates

☑ What questions and statements white people should avoid

☑ Considering what "whiteness" means

☑ My favorite places to learn more about the varied culture, history, and experiences of African Americans

I went to China for the first time in 2006 to conduct diversity workshops with a U.S. client that had expanded to Europe and Asia. I was so excited about being in China. I had worked in several other countries in Asia, but not China. When I first arrived, I was certain that I was going to die either trying to cross a Beijing street or traveling by rickshaw one rainy night. But the biggest shock was not the traffic; it was the staring. At first I thought I was imagining it; then I thought maybe I was doing something horribly wrong and that is why everyone was peering. But a day into my trip, I just couldn't deny that 14 million people seemed to be not only staring, but pointing their fingers at me. They were grabbing their children by the nape of the neck and swinging them around to face me. People would almost crash their bikes craning their necks to look at me. Yes, I was definitely on display. It did not help that I, a tall, medium brown African American woman with blondish super short hair, was accompanied by a darker skinned African American with her hair in braids and a tall, mixed-race (Asian and white) American woman. We were the freaks of the week.

I wish I could tell you that my first response was "Wow, a new cultural experience!" Of course, I was interested in taking in a new culture, but I was not prepared

for the way in which the new culture was taking in me. My initial reaction to what I was experiencing was negative, but something unexpected happened. I leaned on the skills that I have learned to use whenever I am feeling uneasy in a different culture or cultural dynamic where I have little information. In my field, we talk about the concept of being culturally competent—having the appropriate attitudes, awareness, knowledge and skills to successfully interact across cultures.

Follow the BASICS

Well, when I arrived in China, I became aware of my own journey toward cultural competence. I have categorized the stages of my journey into something I call the BASICS. I want to offer them to you as a way to move more gracefully in your relationships with black people and others who may be racially or culturally different from you, even when you don't know as much as you would like about you own worldview or about their history and culture. Having culturally competent attitudes and skills will give you the confidence and ability to move toward a sticky or difficult cultural dynamic with a black person, rather than avoiding him or her or misinterpreting his or her reluctance to connect with you.

> **B** = Breathe: Suspend all judgments
> **A** = Assumptions: Question your assumptions
> **S** = Self-Awareness: Stay self-aware about what you are bringing to the dynamic
> **I** = Information: Get the information before making conclusions or deciding next steps
> **C** = Culture: Accept that all cultures are equally valid
> **S** = Steps: Take steps toward the person or interaction rather than away from the situation (sound familiar?)

B = Breathe: Suspend All Judgments

As I mentioned, my initial reaction to my "freak of the week" status was not positive. I was upset, and I felt unwelcomed. The first step, "Breathe," reminds us to take a deep breath and slow down, so you don't jump to conclusions and do something you might later regret. It is one thing to say, "Suspend judgment," but it is a difficult thing to do. However, if you don't find a way to calm down, you will never take the next five steps, and you will miss the opportunity to learn new things and to improve the interaction. This step reminds me of what my good friend, Dan, told me about the Mambo. Do you remember the dance routine they performed in *West Side Story* that took place on the roof, "In America?" That's the Mambo. Dan, who takes ballroom dancing lessons, tells me that you dance the Mambo on the second beat; you hold on the one. He says that it's not easy for some people to dance the Mambo, because it's hard to hold on the one and dance on the two. I know what he means! However, that's what I did in China. I rested on the one, took a deep breath, gained some composure, and spoke to myself, "You don't know what's going on, don't go making stuff up." Then I moved on the second beat; I questioned the "stuff" I was making up.

A = Assumptions: Question Your Assumptions

As I was standing in Tiananmen Square in the summer of 2006, I was thinking, "Everyone knows it's improper to stare, what's wrong with these people? They are so rude. Don't they know any better?" When faced with a troubling cultural dynamic, you have to expect that your interpretation of what's going on will be influenced by your bias (usually, but not always, negative) regarding the difference you are experiencing and/or some stereotype that you've picked up from somewhere. Initially, that's all you've got.

One of the hardest skills that I am learning when it comes to relating respectfully across difference is to ask open-ended questions rather than starting with questions or statements in which my assumptions are already embedded in them. It is a tough task for several reasons. Sometimes, I don't know that what I am saying is an assumption; I genuinely believe it is the truth. Also, I don't notice that my statements or questions are often prompted by my discomfort with difference and my need to prove that I am "cool," "hip," "with it," or "good."

The interview context is one area in which I have seen some white people make the mistake of leading with their assumptions. I have heard compassionate, but uninformed white interviewers make assumptions about black candidates and proceed to

Compassionate White Interviewer: "You have done so well in school; it must have been hard learning to adjust to your environment (referring to the predominately white school the candidate is attending).

Instead the interviewer might say: "You've done a great job at school. Your academic credentials are impressive. What were the most difficult obstacles you had to overcome to become successful?"

conduct the interview based on those assumptions. In some cases, the interviewer's intent is to give credit or take into consideration the distance some black candidates have traveled to reach their accomplishments. He assumes that all blacks come from underprivileged backgrounds, single-parent households, and predominately black, poor, and violent neighborhoods. Other women and people of color experience these assumptions, too. Many U.S.–born Asians tell me how frequently interviewers lead with what they think is a compliment: "Your English is so good; when did you come to the country?" One South Asian woman told me that an interviewer said to her, "You are Indian and I know that Indian parents are strict. Are you sure your parents are going to let you come to work in New York by yourself?" The woman was 25 years old and had completed graduate school. I call this "a little bit of knowledge is a dangerous thing."

The interviewer's first question in the circle above makes an assumption. If the interviewer's assumption is wrong, he runs the risk of insulting the candidate, knocking him off his center and possibly making it difficult for him to perform well. Even if the interviewer's assumption is correct, the candidate may not understand the question, or it may come off as condescending or patronizing. Acting too surprised that a black person has performed well sends the message that you are operating from the assumption that blacks are not as qualified. In both cases, the interviewee wonders whom the interviewer is seeing in front of him and how much race is "coloring" the dynamic and the interviewer's ultimate assessment. The alternative question suggested in the circle allows the candidate to reveal who he really is and include, if he deems appropriate and useful, how his racial identity and background might have been challenging or helpful.

Learning to ask open-ended questions like this is good even if you share the same racial background of the candidate. The second question would provide important information about any job candidate. We have assumptions about all sorts of people that cause us to miss seeing them as individuals. If the interviewer asks the same question of everyone, he will learn more about all the candidates and have the same type of information by which to compare them. I know some interviewers hate asking the same question of every candidate, because it doesn't seem to acknowledge the differences between interviewees, and it makes the interview feel too wooden. I am suggesting that you have a couple of open-ended questions like those suggested here for every candidate and then follow them up with a more individualized inquiry based on the candidate's responses and experience. If that still feels too stilted to you, instead of changing how you interview now, you might commit to observing the type of questions you do ask and to whom. You can use the exercise, "How Not to Lead with Your Assumptions," on the next page to start your examination.

An open-ended question is one that cannot be answered by a "yes" or "no." Some questions may seem like they are open-ended, but they are not. It's kind of funny, but I try to imagine opposing counsel in the courtroom, raising objections every time I lead with my assumptions: "I object your honor; leading the witness."

DON'T Ask "Yes" or "No" Questions	DO Ask Open-Ended Questions
"Did you grow up in the South?"	"Where did you grow up?"
"Was it difficult for you to feel comfortable and included in your last job?	"What was the work environment in your last job like?" or "Can you describe how you felt working at your last job? What type of environment was it?"

Here's is a simple exercise that you might try in order to improve your skill with asking open-ended questions and refraining from using statements that include your assumptions.

Exercise: How Not to Lead with Your Assumptions

1. For several days, pay attention to any conversations that you have with people who you don't know well or at all. (They can be exchanges at work, an interview, a meeting at your child's school or on an airplane.)
2. Keep a mental record of what you notice, including your observations based on the action items below.
3. If you catch yourself asking "yes" or "no" questions or making conjectures, stop and reassert the open-ended or open-minded version of the subject.
4. See if you notice any difference among those of whom you ask more closed questions and open-ended questions? (Sometimes, when I ask closed questions it's because I want the person to agree with me or confirm how I see the world. I've noticed that it happens more often when in I am in the dominant group interacting with someone from a marginalized group.)
5. Compare what you learn from people when you use "yes" or "no" questions or make a leading statement versus when you communicate more openly and without assumption. Which approach yields more information and connection?
6. The following week, see if your ability to converse without assumption improves, especially when talking with black people or others who are different from you.

S = Self-Awareness: Stay Self-Aware about What Are You Bringing to the Interpretation of the Dynamic

The next step in developing the attitudes and skills of cultural competence is self-awareness. If we go back to the streets of Beijing where I stood bewildered, trying to interpret the gaping of millions, I realized that once I had Breathed, and questioned my Assumptions, I needed to change my focal point. In other words, instead of looking and pointing at them and trying to figure out what was in the minds of the Chinese, I had to begin looking within myself.

When you are in a culturally uncomfortable situation, you are just as important a factor in the equation as the other person or persons. This important realization not too long ago caused consultants to change the cultural training curricula designed to teach executives in global organizations how to be successful doing business in other counties. Classes used to focus on teaching businesspeople the cultural customs, languages, expressions, and values of the other countries. After a while, people realized that knowing this information is only one component of doing well in other cultures. At least as important is the executive's recognition that she is also a cultural being with values, norms and customs, and her cultural programming will shape her response to and interpretation of the other culture, and the other culture's reaction to her.

So in China, I began asking myself, "Why are you feeling so upset?" "Where did you get the idea that staring was rude?" One reason of course, is that I had been taught as early as I could remember that staring was wrong. I was corrected and even reprimanded when I disobeyed this strict edict as a child. Adults around me were so serious about this standard of behavior; I assumed it was universal.

However, it wasn't just what I had been taught about staring as impolite that was the problem. I began to realize that some of my upset had to do with my African American identity. The glaring really riled and unsettled me and brought up all sorts of feelings of fear and anger. In the United States, the history of black people and my own experience suggest when someone who isn't black stares at you as a black person, it usually isn't good. The stare is a glower that communicates, "Your kind of people isn't welcomed here." Then I began to notice these Chinese were staring at all sorts of foreigners, not just me. I wondered if the circumstances had this particular impact on me because I was black. When I was able to understand what I was bringing to the dynamic, I was able to be more objective. I had to allow for the fact that some of my upset was due to a history that wasn't China's issue. That allowed me to challenge my own interpretation of the story unfolding and to stay open to seeking out more understanding.

Staying Self-Aware: "Whiteness"

Most white people recognize that people of color have a race, a distinct culture and history, but white-skin privilege makes it hard for many white people to see their race and its significance in the interactions they have with others—especially black people. Over the years, I have heard many white people say, "I don't think of myself as white." It takes more effort for some white people to see their race. They have to consciously work on identifying what "whiteness" means. However, if you are a white person who has found yourself in situations for any period of time where you are the racial minority (school, another country, neighborhoods, certain events, etc.), then you have already had the experience of noticing your race and its meaning. There has been a great deal of focus on the subject of whiteness in the last few decades; many books, conferences, and even courses in major universities across the country are exploring the historical, social, cultural, and psychological implications of being white in the United States.

I asked some of my white friends and colleagues what whiteness meant for them. Here is what they said:

"You never have to think about it. You just are."

"In some ways, I guess it means not black—being automatically a step up in the social hierarchy in the U.S. Out of that comes an individualism—I get to attribute my wins to me. I get to not describe myself by my skin color."

"I think of white people as those with ancestors from Europe during the time period when Europe was actively engaged in imperialism. Personally, it is complicated by the fact that I am Jewish and my ancestors were also oppressed in Europe. But I am clear that in the U.S., European Jews are treated as white people, and they treat people of color based on being considered white people."

"To me, whiteness is the mythology that white-skinned people are superior. It encompasses the idea of superior looks, but more importantly: superior beliefs, values, and priorities."

You will have a hard time going beyond superficial relationships with black people or understanding the obstacles they face if you insist that you are a raceless, well-intentioned individual. To be self-aware means that you are on the lookout for what you are bringing as a white person to any cross-racial interaction instead of focusing on the black person. If you've been working at this for a while, you may have noticed that some black people might not initially believe that you are committed to inclusion; they may question your motives, and it may seem that you have to work harder to gain their trust. Do not be surprised or offended by this skepticism on the part of black people. As a white person, you have a racial identity that carries with it an entire history and a way of doing things that have been shaped by a belief that to be white is to be superior to black people. With this recognition, you are better able to understand the reluctance of some black people to trust you and still determine to be patient and stay committed to reaching out to breaking down racial barriers.

Here are some ways that you can learn more about white racial identity.

Ways to Learn More about Whiteness

⇨ If you want to start with something light and humorous, check out Website, "Stuff White People Like," at www.stuffwhitepeoplelike.com. Christian Lander, the author of a book with the same name, writes this satirical blog that pokes fun at liberal, left-wing, well-educated, affluent, socially conscious North Americans, one of whom Lander admits to being. There is something so undeniable about how it captures, in a funny way, the things that make up a cultural group.

⇨ Read Shelly Stochluk's book, *Witnessing Whiteness, The Need to Talk about Race and How To Do It* and/or visit her Website www.witnessingwhiteness.com, which has many resources for schools, business, and churches, and information about upcoming workshops and conferences.

⇨ Watch one of Tim Wise's videos regarding whiteness and racism on his website or YouTube. He is also a prolific writer on the topic. Read his book, *White Like Me,* and check out his many essays catalogued on his Website www.TimWise.org.

⇨ View a short film by Aimee Sands called *What Makes Me White?* on YouTube.

⇨ Invite speakers and white anti-racism groups to your school, community, organization, place of workshop, etc., to lead presentations and discussions about white identity.

⇨ As I mentioned in Chapter Three, join an anti-racism group for whites or attend discussions that they sponsor.

⇨ Attend the White People's Conference (WPC) in Minnesota started by Eddie More eleven years ago. The Website www.whiteprivilegeconference.com describes the conference as one "that examines the challenging concepts of privilege and oppression and offers solutions and team building strategies to work toward a more equitable world." One of my white friends who attended the conference for the first time last year called it a love fest for white people working on racial justice.

Staying Self-Aware: What Statements and Questions Not to Use with Your Black Dance Partner

One benefit of being more aware of your whiteness is that it can help you avoid saying things that come across to many black people as overly familiar, intrusive, biased, and/or offensive. Earlier in this chapter, I gave you some suggestions about how not to lead with your assumptions and how to ask open-ended and open-minded questions instead. However, there are some questions and statements that as a white person, you should avoid when relating to a black person, unless you have a well-established, open, and honest relationship with him or her—no matter how you say them, closed or open. I have seen white people, so curious or troubled after attending one of my workshops or maybe viewing a movie about a black historical event that they charge full speed into a black person, asking questions and making statements that can cause major damage and abruptly halt any dance move right in its tracks.

Many black people have found ways to just ignore these questions or come up with snappy retorts. Others carry around a lot of silent frustration that occasionally spills out in the most inopportune times, earning them the label of "overly sensitive," or worse, "threatening." By the way, including a disclaimer in front of these types of questions and statements like, "No offense, but . . ." or "I know this is none of my business, but . . ." does not help the situation. If you have to put the "but" before the question, then it is probably a question you should reconsider asking.

I know it sounds like I am going against the advice I have offered thus far about being inquisitive about difference and not withdrawing, and on the whole, it's okay to make mistakes. Let me be clear: if you keep engaging and building relationships in a humble learning posture, you will be fine. You will be getting the information that will eventually answer the questions you have or gaining the trust you need to establish a more authentic friendship in which potentially sensitive questions can be asked. Remember, however, just because you can talk a certain way with a particular black person with whom you have a relationship, doesn't mean you can talk to black people you don't know that way.

Here are examples of the type of statements and questions you want to avoid.

The Situation	Don't Ask/Say	If You Must Say Something
A black woman in your department comes in after the weekend with a braided hairstyle that you have never seen before; on the Friday before, her hair was in curls and much shorter.	"Is that your real hair?" "Can you wash it?" "Can I touch it?" "Did you grow hair over the weekend?"	"Your hair is so fabulous and intricate. Will you indulge my curiosity a bit? And if you are tired of answering questions like these from uninformed people like me; please feel free to ignore me. I would understand completely." "Your hair is so beautiful."

The Situation	Don't Ask/Say	If You Must Say Something
You meet a person of color at work whose name is quite interesting and unusual to you; you wonder what ethnic group or culture it comes from and how he got this name; also, you worry that you are mispronouncing his name.	"_____, wow! That's a weird name? Where did you get that name?" "What kind of name is that?" "Is that Swahili for George?" (ha, ha!) (probably said by a "Cool Moves but Still in Need of School" dance partner.)	"I want to make sure that I say your name correctly. Can you please say it for me one more time?" (and then write down the pronunciation to practice later without the person's further assistance; call voice mail when he is not around and listen to how he pronounces it; or ask someone who knows how to pronounce his name) Or later, ONLY IF YOU HAVE BUILT A RELATIONSHIP: "Would it be okay to ask you the origin of your name? Does it have a special meaning?" "That's a great name."
A recent college grad just started working at your company. You are on the same team. She has a very fair complexion, and her hair is wavy. You noticed that she joined the black employee resource group (ERG). You see her in the pantry on your floor getting coffee and you strike up a conversation. Or, after a few months of knowing her, you see her coming back from an event sponsored by the black ERG.	"I can't quite tell what your background is. What's your racial category?" "Where are you from?" "I don't know why you are in that group, you're whiter than me." "You don't strike me as someone who would need a group like that"	After you've introduced yourself and have had a few opportunities to chat: "Can you tell me a bit about your background?" "Your group seems like they are doing interesting things, how are you enjoying it?" or "One day when you have time and are willing, I would love to know more about your group and what kind of things you are doing."

The Situation	Don't Ask/Say	If You Must Say Something
Your have been assigned a new mentee, a black male who joined the company a few days ago. You stop by his office and he stands up to greet you. He looks to be 6'5." You are 5'9."	"Wow! How tall are you? Do you play basketball?" "You must play basketball." "Did you go to school on a basketball scholarship?" "So glad you joined our firm; our basketball team could really use some help." "Can I call you 'Shaq'?" (ha, ha!) (probably said by a "Cool Moves But Still in Need of School" dance partner)	"It's a pleasure to meet you. Should we plan a time to do lunch soon?" Or later, ONLY IF YOU HAVE BUILT A RELATIONSHIP: "How is it going for you here so far? What more can I do to make you feel included? I was wondering, but didn't want to assume, what it's like for you as one of the few black males here. How many annoying things have you had to hear about your height?"

The last thing I will mention here is that it is important to question your motivations for wanting to ask particular questions of a black person. If you find yourself in a situation with a black person you don't know well and you are just dying to ask a question, please first stop to ask yourself a few questions. For example: Are you asking because you want to get to know the person better? Are you looking to try to support the person? Are you trying to prove to the black person and/or others that you are a "good white person"? If, after pondering these and other questions regarding your motivation, you still feel that you have to put a possibly offensive question or statement out there, remember to lead with a positive assumption or compliment. For example, one day I walked into a restaurant and the host was one the most gorgeous young men I had ever seen in my life. I could tell that he was multi-racial, and I was so intrigued. So I said, "You've have got to tell me what combination makes a person as beautiful as you." He blushed and said, "My mom is Puerto Rican and my dad is Middle Eastern." I said, "Wow, well they did a really great job." He smiled broadly, thanked me and showed me to my table.

I = Information: Get Information before You Decide What's Going On

My question to the handsome host was admittedly a risky way to get information. I wouldn't advise you proceed in similar fashion. Again, being aware of who you are and how you might be perceived is always useful to consider first. No doubt, it helped that I was black, I was a woman, and I was smiling as I asked the question. Knowing how to seek out information about what you don't know, haven't been taught, or have not yet experienced is an important skill for operating fluently across race and cultures different from your own. You will want to make sure the information you get is reliable, and that you are learning from a source that is familiar with and respectful of the culture. The resources can be individuals from that culture, someone who has spent time getting to know and respect the culture or events, books, magazines, documentaries, and films.

As you can imagine, during my first trip to China, I was anxious to get an answer to the staring problem and I hadn't been able to find anything helpful in my glossy guidebooks. So that first night in Beijing, we were at dinner with a Chinese-born man from one of the company's U.S. offices. I figured he would have a balanced and informed perspective, having worked in both countries over the years and would be willing to act as my cultural informant. I mentioned the gawking, and I asked him to help me understand. He explained, "They've never seen anybody who looks like you before. Also, it's the summer, and many people from the countryside come to Beijing because it is the cultural center. If you live in a big city, you may have seen a black person, but the folks from the countryside definitely haven't seen anyone like you." He added, "Also, we are not taught that staring is bad or impolite." This all seemed reasonable to me. What I was witnessing was genuine curiosity. I knew that if it hadn't been drilled into my head for years by my parents that staring was wrong, I would definitely gape at a human being that came in packaging that I'd never seen before. Okay, I thought, I have some context.

I know that some of you might be thinking, "Well, of course it takes skills to function comfortably in a foreign country, but black and white people live in the same country, speak the same language, work and live in the same places." Really? Think about it. Blacks and whites living in the United States share much in common, but there are some distinct cultural leanings, languages, and experiences, even when they share the same educational, social, and economic background. It's different being black than being white in the United States. For the most part, we don't live together. There are only a few truly integrated neighborhoods in the United States.[2] Even in our workplaces, we tend to segregate, especially socially. So, remembering to get information before you decide what is going on in a particular situation involving a black person is still an important step.

Remember Not All Black People Are the Same

As a white person trying to understand what's going on in a dynamic between you and another black person, the very first thing you want to remember is that not all black people are alike. Some difficult scenarios develop between black and white people, when white people assume the black person grew up in an underserved community within a large city, when in fact the person is from a military family and lived all over the world or grew up in a predominately white community in the Midwest or the suburbs outside some major city. West Indian blacks and U.S. blacks may have common ancestry, but they have different histories and experiences, and thus attitudes toward race. If you delve even more deeply, you will discover differences among Caribbean Americans. So the best thing to do is to be open to learning more about those differences, rather than assuming you know who the black person is. That way you can have a more accurate picture of what might be influencing a particular situation.

Learn about the Experiences and Triumphs of Black People

Some of the most important information that you will need to increase your cultural competence has to do with learning not only where black people come from, but what they have gone through—their life experiences, attitudes, and feelings. Just as valuable is learning more about what black people celebrate as their cultural heritage. You can do some of this work by purposefully participating in facilitated conversations with people of color, black people, and other individuals from traditionally marginalized groups.

One of the most amazing workshops that I have ever attended was sponsored by the National Coalition Building Institute (NCBI).[3] The participants were a mixed group of men and women, gay and straight, of color and white. We each worked with a partner who was of a different social identity group. I was paired with a white man, and we were exploring our attitudes about gender. He had to share what he liked and didn't like about being a man. I had to express the same with regard to being a woman. When I listened to him speak about what he liked about being a man, I was reminded, "Oh yeah, you men do great things. You aren't only the group that oppresses; you are the group that builds and protects, explores, and parks the car." I had seriously forgotten these positive things about men. Another revelation: as a man, he disliked many of the same things about the male group that I did: its suppression of women and men who don't cooperate with male norms and expectations. I spoke about the virtues of women and I divulged some of the issues that I see within my own gender group. It was a fascinating experience for me as a woman.

Later that afternoon, I participated in an exercise at this workshop that made me cry for days. One by one, individuals volunteered to stand in front of the group and describe a time they were mistreated because of a difference. The stories that people told were so moving—both crushing and inspiring at the same time. I remember one person who spoke about how she stopped talking for years when she was a little kid because of how she was teased about her accent. Others shared indignities suffered in the workplace that were ignored and, as a result, caused them to abandon their dreams. On the other hand, some incidents ended in victories won through determination and stamina, despite opportunities unfairly denied.

After they shared their stories, the volunteers were encouraged to speak out about what they wished someone would have done differently to prevent or interrupt the bigotry they suffered. Then we, as the listeners, were asked to put up our hands and promise to remember the story, and then to make an increased commitment to stand up against the particular "ism" (racism, sexism, elitism, ageism, etc.) they had endured.

These kinds of group experiences will help you to see the direct impact of stereotypes and bias, even unintentional ones, on black people and others (including a group to which you may belong) who have suffered oppression. They also allow you to appreciate how much black people and others from traditionally excluded groups have overcome, despite the odds. These encounters enable you to be a witness and invite you to be part of the solution. Without these personal stories being told, you may never have access to such information, especially delivered with so much passion and freedom. It was not for the faint of heart, but then again, justice is not for the squeamish. Sessions like that stick with you.

C = Culture: All Cultures are Equally Valid

Let's review where we are in the BASICS of cultural competency. We have reminded ourselves to Breathe and suspend all judgment about a situation, to question our Assumptions, to Stay Self-Aware about what we are bringing to the dynamic, and to get more Information about the other person, his or her culture, and other factors shaping the dynamic. The next step in the BASICS dance is C = Culture, believing that other cultures are valid.

Culture is a big word and has been explained in a million different ways. One way to think about culture is to view it as a large and complex system of meanings that helps a group of people organize and interpret their environment, their experience and also understand and make judgments about the behaviors of others.[4] What is intriguing is that culture operates on both a conscious and less conscious level, organizing our perceptions and understanding of the world in very subtle ways. People's cultures therefore make sense to them. Many of us are interested in the cultures of others, but we don't necessarily see them as legitimate or as sensible as our own.[5] Often that is because we do not know enough to understand and appreciate the historical circumstances, experience, and context in which the culture developed. This can be even truer for groups that have among its tenets the belief that their culture is superior.[6]

There is so much still untold and misunderstood about black culture and the history that has created it, as well as the events that continue to shape and expand it. Often the culture of the marginalized group in a society is ignored, disparaged, appropriated without credit, or hidden. This has certainly been true for black people. Whereas I think much has changed in America to acknowledge and celebrate black culture, history, and achievements, there is so much that white people don't know because it is not part of their everyday education, life or experience. There is a great deal of information out there, but the best of it is often not available in the mainstream media. One has to know where to find it. So I thought I would share just a few places I go to find out and keep up with what is happening in black America; I also discuss below some of the books, videos, movies, and events that have had a profound effect on me as a black person and some of the things that make me feel great about being black. Hopefully you will explore and enjoy my list, but I would encourage you to make your own list of resources and experiences that give you insight into and appreciation for what's going on with black people and culture. Ask your white and black friends for their ideas as well. In addition, I have included A Resource Guide for Dance Partners you can consult in the Appendix to this book.

Pop Culture

Read black magazines. The first place I start to catch up with what's happening with black folks is my sister's house. I resist clutter, so I don't subscribe to magazines, but thankfully she does. I love reading the magazines *Ebony*, *Essence*, and *Jet*. These publications have been around for a long time, and they are chock-full of information about people that I could never find in *People*, *Time*, or *Shape*—the lives and accomplishments of beautiful black movie stars, politicians, scientists, businesspeople educators, musicians, and everyday black people who rarely get ink in the popular press. These publications and Websites such as The Root, www.theroot.com, also specialize in issues directly related to black life (black love, the black community, educational opportunity, criminal justice, jobs, racial discrimination, etc.)

If you want to know what many black people in the United States are tuning into in the morning, listen to the *Tom Joyner Morning Show*, a nationally syndicated radio program hosted by Tom Joyner, the first African American to be elected to the Radio Hall of Fame. Okay, some of us are listening to NPR too in the morning; and yes, I love that Cornel West and Tavis Smiley now have a show on the weekend! However, if you want to get some insight into what's on the minds of everyday black people, try to catch the Joyner show—an entertaining combination of music, news talk, comedy, gossip and cool guests like: Bill Clinton, Oprah, Spike Lee, you name them.

TV and Movies

Watch the HBO series *The Wire*, which was one the most compelling and insightful series on TV (now on Netflix). The five-season drama centered around the gritty drug wars on the streets of Baltimore and offered a chilling social and political critique of America—how our educational, law enforcement, political, and media systems have failed many Americans and caused great distress in the underserved black community. It is a drama that illustrates the interplay between the individual and the system and makes clear that intelligence, hustle, resilience, and morality come in all colors, ages, genders, classes and positions. Both Harvard College and Harvard Law School have recently created courses dedicated to *The Wire*.

There have been so many great movies and documentaries depicting black history, culture and experience, but here is a small sample of the many that have moved me: *Roots*, *Eyes on the Prize I & II*, *A Soldier's Story*, *Hollywood Shuffle*, *Glory*, *Do the Right Thing*, *Love Jones*, *The Color Purple*, and *Imitation of Life*.

History, Literature, Art, and Music

Indulge in the Harlem Renaissance. I was in college before I realized that black people wrote drama, poetry, and plays. Now, most people can name several black authors off the tops of their heads, including Toni Morrison, Maya Angelou, and Ralph Ellison, all of whom have written amazing books. However, the Harlem Renaissance of the 1920s and 1930s produced hundreds of talented artists of all types in many genres, along with brilliant thinkers. If you haven't already treated yourself to the writings of Langston Hughes, Jean Toomer, Zora Neal Hurston, or Countee Cullen, you will be amazed. Can you imagine W.E.B. Dubois, James Weldon Johnson, Paul Roberson, Billie Holliday, Ella Baker, Louis Armstrong, and Duke Ellington walking along the streets of Harlem, dancing at the Cotton Club, and performing at the Apollo Theatre?

How could I possibly talk about music, and how could I not? Luckily, many white people have a great appreciation for the contributions that blacks have made to the world of music, and I mean literally the world. I went to a dance club in Hong Kong not too long ago. When I looked around, I was dancing to Jay-Z and everyone on the dance floor with me was Asian! It was definitely a new cultural experience. I grew up listening to rhythm and blues and funk and people in my generation complain about rap and hip hop and how music is just not as good as it was in our day. Are you kidding? Check out the brilliant lyrics, music and truth-telling of people like Mos Def, Talib Kweli, India. Arie, Lupe Fiasco, the Roots, John Legend, Liz Wright, and José James. They are taking the old and making it better.

Education

Become acquainted with the rich legacy and accomplishments of historically black colleges and universities (HBCUs) located throughout the South. A pernicious stereotype has been perpetuated over the years, not just about the intellectual capacity of blacks, but also their commitment to education. If you spend any time learning about the 105 HBCUs, you will find out that many black people and some generous and caring white people over a long period of time have dedicated themselves to making sure that there were secondary educational opportunities available for black people who were often excluded from white institutions.[7] These schools are also famous for their black fraternities and sororities that perform hours of community service. In addition, their marching bands are out of this world. Check out the many YouTube clips of HBCU Band Battle—it is the most exhilarating, colorful, choreographed combination of dance, rhythmic syncopation, crazy athleticism, and bravado you'll ever see.

Religion

Visit a black church. The black church is not a monolith. There are different denominations, practices, and worship services, but most embody the tradition of gospel music and powerful preaching. The church has also played a prominent role as an institution in the African American community. I love the singing, the preaching, and the community outreach that is part of so many black churches. I visited a black church in Chicago during black history month recently. A huge multi-generational choir dressed in gorgeous African outfits sang "Lift Every Voice and Sing" (the black national anthem by James Weldon Johnson) and "Nkosi Sikelel" (the South African National Anthem). It was magic! The sermon was delivered by a guest preacher educated at Morehouse College (a HBCU) and trained in the undeniable oratory style of the black southern preacher. This church had seventy ministries designed to meet the needs of its parishioners and the communities of color surrounding it.

Read books on black theology and liberation. I wandered into a classroom on black theology and politics at Union Theological Seminary (UTS) where I discovered Professor Cornel West and a deep tradition of the black struggle in the African American community through the Christian faith. We read books by Martin Luther King, *Strength to Love* and *Where Do We Go from Here: Chaos to Community*; Paulo Friere, *The Pedagogy of the Oppressed*; and writings by James Cone and many others. I heard for the first time about the famous theologian Howard Thurman and met Dr. James Melvin Washington who was teaching at UTS. Dr. West taught us with so much erudition and energy, it changed my life.[8]

S = Step Forward

Step Forward is the last of the BASICS, and it is extremely important. Developing all the attitudes and skills that I have suggested in this chapter are useless unless you add this last piece—the forward motion. You might be worrying, "Do I have to wait to move forward until I have thoroughly examined my white identity, gathered all the information I can, and done all my cultural homework before I can ever speak to a black person?" Some of you may even be still back in the earlier part of this chapter trying to memorize the "Don't Say" chart. I didn't give you the BASICS to stifle you, but rather to give you a guide for your approach to relationships across race and culture. Again, this is not about being perfect. Missteps are inevitable but hopefully with this guide, there are some mistakes you can avoid. The main thing is to keep finding ways to improve your understanding and your personal and professional relationships with black people. With new culturally competent attitudes and skills, you can venture into more authentic and meaningful associations and be more aligned with the people you want to help. The great Dutch social psychologist Geert Hofstede said this about culture and why it is important for all of us to have the skills to step forward,

> Our shared human nature is intensely social: we are group animals.
> We use language and empathy, and practice collaboration and

intergroup competition. But the unwritten rules of how we do these things differ from one human group to another. 'Culture' is what we call these unwritten rules ... We tend to classify groups other than our own as inferior or (rarely) superior. But to get things done, we still need to cooperate with members of other groups carrying other cultures. Skills in cooperation across cultures are vital for our common survival.[9]

You may be wondering what finally happened in China once I had good information and accepted that the Chinese had their own culture and way of doing things that was different than mine. Well, the very next day after the dinner with my Chinese cultural informant, I went outside my westernized hotel and when people stared, I smiled and waved, not wildly, just a small wave. To my surprise, they smiled too and waved back! I found out happily from my little experiment that my initial fears about the ogling were wrong. It wasn't that these Chinese people were saying, "We don't like you; take your kind and get out of here." They were pointing at me and my colleagues—like people do when rock stars are walking down the street—with awe and excitement! Needless to say, by the time I left Beijing I had met and taken pictures with many friendly Chinese people. I often chuckle when I think about the idea that maybe somewhere in the countryside there is a picture of me in a photo album—my tall brown self towering over and surrounded by the smiles of a lovely Chinese family with the caption: "Our Trip to Beijing—Summer 2006."

Endnotes

1. Mercedes Martin & Billy Vaughn, *Cultural Competence: The Nuts and Bolts of Diversity and Inclusion*, Diversity Officer Magazine available at http://diversityofficermagazine.com/cultural-competence/cultural-competence-the-nuts-bolts-of-diversity-inclusion/; DTUI.com, What Is Cultural Competence and How Is It Measured?" Diversity Officer Magazine available at http://diversityofficermagazine.com/cultural-competence/what-is-cultural-competence-and-how-is-it-measured/.

2. W. H. Frey & D. Myers, Neighborhood Segregation in Single-Race and Multirace America: A Census 2000 Study of Cities and Metropolitan Areas (Fannie Mae Foundation 2002). *See also* W. H. Frey, *New Racial Segregation Measures for Large Metropolitan Areas: Analysis of the 1990–2010 Decennial Censuses: Racial Segregation For Largest Metro Areas*, Population Studies Center, Institute for Social Research, accessed Apr. 10, 2011 http://www.psc.isr.umich.edu/dis/census/segregation2010.html.

3. The National Coalition Building Institute (NCBI) is an international, non-profit, leadership training organization based in Washington, D.C. Since 1984, NCBI has worked to eliminate racism and all other forms of prejudice and discrimination throughout the world.

4. *See* Clifford Geertz, The Interpretation of Cultures (Basic Books 1973).

5. This set of meanings categorizes people and things (including people outside the members of the cultural group), orders them into systems of rank and power, and provides rules that often work to legitimize an existing structure of power. For instance, the notion of whiteness as superior, the fact that whites seem to be unconscious of their privilege illustrates the ways in which culture works within the U.S. For this perspective on culture, cf. Pierre Bourdieu in David Swartz, Culture and Power: The Sociology of Pierre Bourdieu (University of Chicago Press 1997).

6. While it is important that people's cultures make sense to them, that framework of "common sense" can become an obstacle when they encounter a culture that is different. In a country as large as the United States that has a history of welcoming immigrants from other

cultures around the world, this assumption of superiority can cause problems. This is especially true when we Americans implicitly assume that being American and American culture is equated with whiteness, as a key research project uncovered. T. Devos & M. R. Banaji, *American = White?* 88 J. PERSONALITY SOCIAL PSYCH., 447–66 (2005).

7. Most HCBUs were established after the Civil War, many in response to the fact that many southern land grant colleges specifically excluded blacks. Of the 105 HBCU institutions in America today, 27 offer doctoral programs and 52 provide graduate degree programs at the master's level. At the undergraduate level, 83 of the HBCUs offer a Bachelor's degree program and 38 of these schools offer associate degrees. Nobel Laureate Toni Morrison, writer Alice Walker, Marian Wright Edelman, Dr. Martin Luther King, filmmaker and actor Spike Lee and former Bank of America Chairman Walter E, Massey are just a few of the famous alums from these colleges.

8. Martin Luther King, STRENGTH TO LOVE (Collins + World 1977); Martin Luther King, WHERE DO WE GO FROM HERE: CHAOS OR COMMUNITY? (Beacon Press 1968); Paulo Friere, PEDAGOGY OF THE OPPRESSED 30TH ANNIVERSARY EDITION (originally published in 1968).

9. G. Hofstede & G. J. Hofstede, *Why Is Culture So Important*, accessed Feb. 8, 2011, http://www.geerthofstede.nl/.

7

Are You Sure He's Our Waiter? I Think He's the Band Leader: How Is Your Lens Shaping What You See?

Dance Lessons for this Chapter:

☑ Examining your diversity lens: seeing the world through your particular identities and life experiences

☑ Considering what you might be missing in a racial dynamic

☑ Learning ways to stay open to other viewpoints

☑ Discovering the differences between how some white and black people experience the world around them

☑ Appreciating the different ways people from different cultures work and play

everal years ago, my good friend Nan and I got out of a taxi late at night in the Wall Street area of New York City. Nan is Asian American. Like me, she is a diversity consultant and former attorney. We are about the same age; okay, she's younger. She is cool and fun, and we love talking about and working on diversity issues together. We had come from LaGuardia Airport and were on our way to a hotel room for a good night's sleep before a full day of workshops with a client in the area. As we neared our destination, our cab driver announced that there was too much construction on the street for him to take us to the front door of the hotel and it would actually be faster if we got out and walked up a little back street that would lead us right to our hotel. He pointed, and for some reason, we complied. If you know anything about Wall Street, it's a ghost town at night. So we stood there, bags in tow, on a dark and deserted street not knowing exactly where to go. Then I saw this person across the street and I was immediately relieved. My friend Nan was stunned by my reaction.

The person I saw was a black man. I thought, "Yeah! It's a black guy; we're saved!" I mean, in my worldview, black men always know where they are going. Black men are chivalrous too; it comes from our deep southern roots, I think. Black men will say hello and good morning to a woman, almost like they are tipping their top hats as you go by.

They are always willing to assist. At least that is my experience. In my mind, a black guy is exactly who I want to see when I'm lost. But when I mentioned this to Nan, she confided in me, "You were saying, 'Yeah! It's a black guy!' I was saying, 'Oh no, it's a black guy!'" and she gestured like she was running away in the other direction. She and I looked at each other, both our eyes wide with surprise. Then she began apologizing profusely, "I'm a woman of color and a diversity consultant and I did that whole black guy thing; I can't believe I did that. I should know better."

I felt bad for her, "Look," I said, "Don't do the blame, shame thing. Think about it . . . I go way back with black guys: my dad is a black guy! My grandfathers were black guys. I was married to a black guy. My 6'4" son is a black guy. My world is so wide and so deep with black guys; I was pretty confident about that black guy across the street." I wasn't upset with Nan because I realized that Nan had much less exposure to and experience with black men. She had, as we all have, been bombarded with the negative images of black men as threatening.[1] It was clear to me that Nan and I had looked at the person across the street and did the same thing. We looked at the world through our lenses, the breadth and depth of our experience, and made an assessment. It was just that our lenses and our experiences were different.

After the encounter, she and I talked a great deal about the concept of one's "diversity lens," which I want to share in this chapter. It's the idea that all of us are sorting the world and giving meaning to what we see based on our own identities, experiences, and cultural teachings, those chosen and those that were not ours to choose. That night we were looking at the exact same person, at a given time of night, both needing to get off the deserted street and into the hotel; yet we had completely different reactions. I went toward him, and we danced. If I hadn't been beside Nan and this particular party, she would have turned on her heels and run off the gym floor to the girl's bathroom. He was, by the way, my black guy. When I asked him if he knew where the hotel was, he replied, "Sure, I know where you ladies are going. I'll show you there." Nan was amazed!

Start to Explore Your Diversity Lens

Take a look at the diagram on the opposite page created some years ago to help people see and explore their diversity lenses.[2] I really appreciate this graphic representation because it is so simple, and yet it helps us to look at the complexity of who we are and to consider how each of us is a composite of different identities and experiences. It reinforces that we are all diverse; no one person is only one identity. We sometimes forget that about diversity and people get pigeonholed and defined by one of their group characteristics. I specifically resist using the term "diverse people" to refer to people of color because I believe such a term would include everyone. We are also reminded by this figure that each of us has a race, a sexual orientation, a political view, and a family

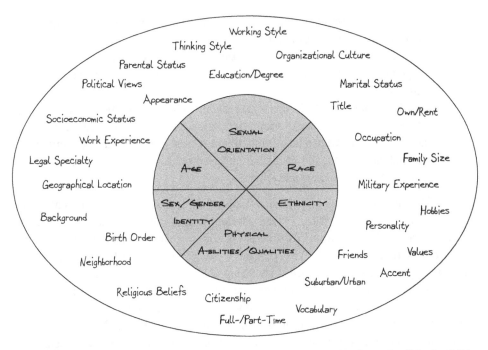

structure that we can explore. Diversity awareness is not only about the "blacks," "the gays," "the conservatives," and "the single mother." If you look at the inside circle, you will see what might be thought of as primary identities: salient descriptors for many people that create significant experiences and worldviews. They are also some of the first categories that come to mind when we think of diversity. You will also notice that most of them are legally protected because there is a history of legal discrimination against groups of people who were considered different or outside the "norm" in these categories.[3] The types of groupings on the outside circle give us an opportunity to consider more secondary dimensions of experience and identity, which can be very important in shaping and filtering our world as well. I used to comment that some of the secondary dimensions are chosen and can be changed over time, but I have become aware that this is also true for those in the inner circle; sex, gender and gender identity, sexual orientation, physical ability, and age can all change.

In our workshops, we ask participants to look closely at these dimensions of classifications of identity and experience and tell us what they see as it pertains to them. I invite you to participate in the exercise below. Take a look at the six dimensions in the inner circle: age, race, ethnicity, sexual orientation, sex/gender identity, and physical abilities/qualities. Write down the answers to the following questions for each of them. The first question you might remember from the "Exploring Our Cultural Diversity" exercise in Chapter Three.

⇨ What is/are your age, ethnicity, physical abilities/qualities, race sex/gender identity, sexual orientation?

⇨ How relevant is/are age, ethnicity, physical abilities/qualities, race, sex/gender identity, sexual orientation in your life?

⇨ How many people from your age, ethnicity, physical abilities/qualities, race, sex/gender identity, sexual orientation group are in your workplace, neighborhood, and social circle?

⇨ How do people from your age, ethnicity, physical abilities/qualities, race, sex/ gender identity, sexual orientation group fare at work?

⇨ Has your membership in this age, ethnicity, physical abilities/qualities, race, sex/gender identity, sexual orientation group influenced how you see yourself? If so, how?

⇨ How does your identity in this age, ethnicity, physical abilities/qualities, race, sex/gender identity, sexual orientation group shape how you regard, interact, and judge others whose identity is different from yours in this category? Have your judgments changed over time or based on the environment in which you are operating? If so, how and why?

We also ask these types of questions with regard to the categories of identity and experience on the outside circle. In one session, a man quickly raised his hand and said enthusiastically, "I'm farm." At first, I was silent because I thought I hadn't heard him correctly; then I repeated, "You're farm?" "Yes," he said, as a few folks chuckled. "Can you explain?" I replied. "Sure. I spent my whole life on a farm, and everything I do has been influenced by that. I can see it all the time in the way I do things and act and expect others to do things. It doesn't always go over so well at work." There was no need to say anything more after he spoke, except "Class dismissed."

In the following box are some of the many discoveries that I have made using this diversity lens concept and the above exercise, especially as it relates to race.

Diversity Lens Discoveries

⇨ We all have so many identities and experiences; so while we have some visible identities, no one can really tell who we are by just looking at us. We get tricked by the apparent, particularly when it comes to race. My experience is that the more I get to know a white person or others from a race or ethnicity different from my own, the more I realize how much I made up about them before I knew much about them at all.

⇨ Even if I know of some less-visible aspects about a person's identity (e.g., his parents were divorced when he was young, or he is Roman Catholic), I still can't predict how he will react to any particular situation. I know that an individual's identities and experiences will influence his reactions, but I don't know how. As a person who grew up in a working-class family, I favor working-class people. However, I know people who grew up as I did, including some black people, who are now well-off and want nothing to do with anyone from their working-class identity. In fact, they are of the opinion that no one helped them, so why should they favor or help anyone else?

⇨ There are so many commonalities in places you didn't expect because you didn't notice that while someone is of a different race, he shares your love for knitting or he grew up in a small town, just like you. If you can remember as a white person that even though race is a significant factor to many people of color, there are also other identities and experiences to connect to and in which to engage, it will help you to cultivate meaningful relationships across race.

⇨ There is also a dynamic happening between and among the identities in each circle that creates a layering effect. That's why I asked you in the exercise to look

> ## Diversity Lens Discoveries *(continued)*
>
> at more than just your racial identity. When it comes to race, your experience and interpretation may have been shaped differently based on many things, such as your political affiliation, job status, military experience, hobbies, or religion. Most people would agree that men and women often see the world differently, but they assume that women mostly see the world the same. Gender is just one layer of a person's identity. If you add other dimensions of race, geography, socioeconomic status, and age to the gender lens, you may be talking about totally different worldviews. For example, the life perspective of an older white woman born in the South to a poor family is quite different from that of a younger woman of color born in New England to a middle-class family. The woman of color may have more in common with her male colleague or neighbor from a similar class and geographical background than she does with her southern sister.

I hope that by looking at the questions above, you will make your own discoveries like our "I'm farm" participant and like Nan and I did that night on Wall Street. After you have completed the exercise above, start observing yourself and others through the concept of "lens." See if you can notice your filters sorting in a particular situation, particularly in situations where you are not connecting well with a person of color for some reason. Look for what story you might be telling yourself about him without knowing much about his other identities and filters. Ask yourself if it is his race or your race that is making a difference in your interaction and causing you or him to withdraw.

Before you decide to avoid making contact, also consider if maybe there are other dimensions that might be affecting your interaction: personality, language differences, appearance. Maybe you are reacting the way you are because you come from a big family and you were the oldest; therefore, you learned to take charge, and you expect cooperation. Perhaps he is looking at the situation through the lens of work style, and he sees you as a micromanager who is bossy and risk-averse. It might have nothing to do with race, or perhaps race is having a secondary or layering effect but isn't the main issue. The possibilities are endless, so the best thing to do is

⇨ dig in and do not move away,
⇨ get to know the person better,
⇨ share more about yourself,
⇨ explain your specific expectations and ways of working and ask for feedback,
⇨ ask what will make the relationship work better, and
⇨ look for the commonalities you share in order to build upon them.

With all of the many identities we have, such aspects of ourselves are bound to be there, waiting to be discovered.

Go Looking for the Gorilla

Sometimes our brains make it hard for us to notice our commonalities with another person or to even see that individual at all. A couple of years ago, we started using a fascinating video clip by Professor Daniel J. Simons; it is a selective attention exercise.[4] The video is of two teams of people, one in white shirts and one in black shirts passing a basketball to others on their respective teams. The audience is asked to count the number of passes among those in the white shirts only. In the workshop, after the very short clip is over, we ask the group how many passes they counted; there are different answers, but most people are within two or three passes of each other. Then we ask if anyone saw anything else while they were counting. Some people report seeing a gorilla, while a good number of the people in the room look incredulous. We replay the clip and ask the group not to count; lo and behold, everyone sees the gorilla (a man in a gorilla suit, actually), who not only walks among those passing the basketballs but stops in the middle of the circle, pounds his chest, then slowly walks off. Those who didn't initially see the gorilla begin to chuckle.

When we are focused on a particular task and are not expecting to see something, we may actually miss a major event. Or, as the scientists who study these mind glitches point out, we may even add items to make the world make more sense to us. We will swear that we saw something in a picture that actually isn't there simply because our brain thinks it should be. Malcolm Gladwell made some of these concepts popular in his book *Blink*.[5] He presents a number of studies that suggest that people are pretty good at assessing dynamics quickly without a lot of information, but there are situations where we as humans get it wrong. Gladwell used a term that may be helpful here: "thin-slicing." Thin-slicing refers to the ability of our unconscious to find patterns in situations and behavior based on very narrow slices of data. Gladwell's research shows that our minds are quite accurate at assessing any given situation quickly without lots of information; but when we make snap judgments, sometimes we make mistakes.

At one diversity conference I attended, a black senior-level executive graciously stood up and recounted a compelling and disturbing story about a time he walked out of an elevator and up to the receptionist on the main floor of a prestigious company. Before he had a chance to open his mouth, the receptionist was directing him to a part of the office where he could find and fix the copier. The company had just extended him an offer to join their senior executive team. The receptionist was seeing a copy repairman when there was a senior manager in front of her. Her brain missed all the indicia that would normally register "executive" because her brain could not get the image of a black man to match with her picture of a high-powered executive.

Before you oversee that multimillion dollar acquisition, will you take a look at our copier?

I know this sounds really bad. It can be kind of heartbreaking, but I also know that how we learn to put images and concepts together can change. I remember that shortly after the lens experience that Nan and I had on Wall Street, we were working together in Los Angeles in a tall, glassy sky-scraper in the business district downtown where many black men were working at the front desk on security. Every time we entered the building in the morning and at lunchtime, they would say with broad smiles, "Hello, ladies, how are you all doing today?" My friend Nan looked at me one day and asked, "Where did these black guys come from?" I said, "They were always here; you just couldn't see them."

One Person's Mugger Is Someone Else's Brother

Nan and I discovered that while we had different lens and life experiences, we were both better off because we had each other to expand the way we see the world—her potential mugger was someone I saw as a brother. There are opportunities to expand our lenses everywhere, at all times, if you are interested in finding them. In the box below are some tips for seeing someone else's point of view.

Tips for Seeing Another Person's Point of View

⇨ *Don't be afraid to mix it up and try on different perspectives.* Worldviews and habits of thinking are hard to break. Don't worry; if you want to return to the way you used to see and think, it will happen easily enough.

⇨ *Be patient.* Again, worldviews are stubborn; it takes time for entire shifts to happen, and sometimes revelations are fleeting.

⇨ *Listen very closely to what the other person is saying.* See if there is anything that you can agree with about his or her perspective. Start off your response by acknowledging what you can see: "I see your point about ..." or "What resonates with me is ..." Then you can add, "Where I see things differently is ..."

⇨ *Don't be dismissive of others' experiences. Ask others what they see and why they see it the way they do,* especially those who often see things differently from you.

⇨ *Look for the gorilla.* Did something happen that you missed because you were focusing on something else or not expecting it?

⇨ *Ask yourself: "How would I feel if I were a black person in this position?"* This is tricky because, of course, you don't know from firsthand experience how it would feel, and, as a white person, you may not account for how much of your reality has been "colored" by whiteness, or the privilege that your race has afforded to you. But the exercise can work if you follow the next tip.

⇨ *Think of an identity where you were the outsider, the one who was marginalized or looked down upon* (e.g., poor or working-class, lesbian, Jewish, visibly disabled, female, non-U.S.-born). How would you feel if the same or analogous thing happened to someone else based on those outsider identities? Being able to access these feelings allows you to understand some of what the black person might be feeling. **Empathy is a powerful inclusion tool.**

⇨ *Be kind to yourself when you discover blind spots or the ways that you have been shaped by racism.* You didn't create this system that excludes others, and you don't believe in it—you are working to change it. **It's about low guilt and high responsibility.**

⇨ *Check your cultural leanings.* If, for example, you are attempting to understand through the lens of an individual, shift to see if thinking more through your cultural group identity (e.g., white, straight, Christian, senior, able-bodied) helps you to see things differently.

Get on the Bus: Look for Opportunities to Expand Your Lens about Black People, Their Experiences and Culture

The last suggestion above, looking at your cultural leanings and paying attention to the way your group identity (not only your identity as an individual) is shaping your experience, will help you understand why many black people often see and experience the world very differently than many white people. I know my statement sounds a bit too general to be right, but I am trying to make a point about black and white people as groups, not individuals. Dr. Milton J. Bennett, who is well known for his work on intercultural communications and teaches corporate executives all over the world about intercultural competence, says,

> Useful cultural generalizations . . . refer to predominant tendencies among groups of people, so they are not labels for individuals. Any given individual may exhibit the predominant group tendency a lot, a little, or not at all . . . So cultural generalizations must be applied to individuals as tentative hypotheses, open to verification.[6]

Dr. Bennett also warns that these generalizations should be used cautiously because of their similarities to stereotypes. So, as I tread carefully, I would like to share with you what I have observed about different worldviews and experiences of blacks and whites.

Although it may be difficult and go against all you have learned as a white person, if you want to support more racial inclusion, you will want to examine all you have come to know about race. You have to be willing to ask yourself, as a member of the white group, what you have been missing or filtering out about the black experience. I thought comedian Eddie Murphy did this brilliantly in an NBC *Saturday Night Live* skit years ago. In the skit, he decides to go underground to explore the assertion by some that there are two Americas, a white and a black one. With the help of a makeup artist, he disguises himself as a white person and visits different places to experience the world as a Caucasian man. He boards a regular New York City bus and when the only visibly black person on the bus gets off on 45th Street, a party breaks out on the bus. The bus driver turns on the music "Cabaret," riders start dancing with each other and a cocktail waitress emerges with a tray of drinks and begins serving the passengers.

After visiting a bank in his white man disguise, where he is given a cash loan by a white banker without credit or even identification and being told by the shopkeeper that he doesn't have to pay for his newspaper at the store, he concludes that America has a long way to go before everyone is equal, but until then, he's got plenty of makeup. The skit is really quite hilarious. Eddie Murphy even developed a new "white man walk" that he uses to travel in this role. The piece is exaggerated, but memorable, because it is easy for many people to imagine that changing one's race would change one's perspective and everyday experiences.

Of course, there have been more serious treatments of the differences in life experiences and outcomes of whites and blacks, including the book, *Black Like Me*, written by John Howard Griffin, a white journalist who artificially darkened his skin and proceeded to travel through the south as a black man in 1959, experiencing what it felt like to be black. The book was later made into a film, and additional books have been written about Griffin's eye-opening journey into the world as a black man.[7] I am not asking anyone to go to the lengths that Griffin did, but there are ways to get a better understanding of the experiences of black people in the United States. For example, some white people have told me about their experiences of being in an African country or having to speak in front of a black organization or getting lost on a subway and ending up in the black section of town. These opportunities have given them a small window into what it feels like to be in the minority.

Watch Out for How Your Lens Interprets Expressions of Black Culture

If you have been raised in the United States or another Western country, you have been taught to think a certain way and to value certain things and ways of being. As a person from this country, so have I, but as an African American with parents from the South, I have also been surrounded and influenced by more traditional African or collectivist culture and values. Most of us in the United States have been taught or have imbibed that Western cultural values are superior to others. However, I, like many Black Americans, struggle with various aspects of Western culture, because I personally see and experience the downsides of a culture that regards itself as better than others.

For example, in the workplace, I have heard white people comment that something a black person did was not proper and professional because of the person's informal mannerisms or ways of relating, or because they demonstrated emotion in a particular situation. As an African American, I watched the tightrope that candidate Barack Obama walked throughout his campaign, especially in the debates. I know I wasn't the only black person who marveled at his refusal to show anger or any intense emotion, no matter what the situation or the bait was. Of course, it may be that President Obama isn't an emotional person and his behavior reflected his personality, rather than it being influenced by racial or cultural concerns. However, I believe we were witnessing an individual deftly navigate through treacherous waters of Western cultural norms about what constitutes appropriate expression and racial stereotyping that view black men as loud, angry, and volatile. So many people, black and white, felt certain that if candidate Obama showed the slightest negative emotion, it would translate as a lack of "professionalism," or he would trigger white America's negative assumptions about black men. Either way, his candidacy would be doomed. There were also blacks, however, who wanted Senator Obama to get angry when the circumstance called for it. It is also interesting that as President, one of the criticisms leveled against him by many, including Democrats of every racial and ethnic background, is that he is too cerebral and rational, and he doesn't display enough emotion, especially anger. I wonder what they would say if he actually did demonstrate the emotion or frustration he (and every President) must experience. I truly wonder if he has that luxury as a black man, especially as the first black man in that role.

In professional sports, too, there is the question of what constitutes professional demeanor and proper decorum. When a black football player celebrates his touchdown with a dance, I love it. It seems right. Dance is great way to celebrate. But for others, it is seen as shameful, unseemly, and improper sportsmanship. In 2006, the NFL passed a rule (the so-called "excessive celebration" rule) that football players could not demonstrate in the end zone, and if they did so, they would be fined.[8] Many people of color and some white people, as well, saw the NFL rule as racist. Herbert D. Simons, a University of California Berkeley professor, in his article entitled, "Race and Penalized Sports Behaviors," explains,

> Celebrating, dancing, high stepping, spiking, dunking, [and] taking off one's helmet are reflections of the expressiveness and performance aspect of African American culture . . . They are designed to encourage spectators and teammates to validate one's performance by responding to it. The desire for audience involvement may be related to the call and response features of African American churches.

He goes on to say,

> The invisibility of one's own culture makes it difficult to recognize behavior that conflicts with one's own cultural expressions as an expression of a different cultural pattern. Behaviors that differ are seen as abnormal and deviant . . . In other words, when whites decide that their cultural expression is the correct expression and make rules that require others to follow that norm, that's racism, whether it is intentional or not.[9]

Whereas not all black people would agree with Simons, I definitely think he is pointing out on the field what I see in many predominately white organizations, especially the corporate workplace. The right and proper way to be in the workplace seems to be defined by the dominant culture. How we celebrate, how we mourn, what we value, how we express emotion, and what we think is right and proper is culturally shaped. If what is considered right and proper comports with your cultural programming, you don't notice it. However, when it doesn't, you see it all the time and have to work harder to align yourself with it. Workplaces have their own fines if you run afoul of these cultural norms (e.g., being frozen out of opportunities, excluded from informal networks, passed over for promotions); they are just not as clearly pronounced as the NFL's.

I come from the black church culture that practices the "call and response" tradition that Simons mentions. In my world, when someone is in front of a group of people speaking, it is the audience's job to speak back to the speaker. The orator expects it; she "calls" for it. When I came to the corporate world, I noticed that when someone is presenting, the participants sit blank face with their arms crossed, not making a sound. This is a sign of respect for the speaker. But for me, it was difficult to learn to speak in that type of environment. It felt invalidating, confusing, and devoid of energy; and I couldn't figure out if I was reaching my audience. I am used to an "amen corner"—someone who testifies to the truth of what you are saying. Still, occasionally, I forget the acceptable way, and I slip and say, "Amen" when I hear a speaker make an undeniably excellent point. Classical music concerts are still hard for me, because I want to clap or yell "You go 'head, Mr. Solo Cellist; play those strings!" but I dare not.

Individualism and Collectivism

There is a real emphasis on rugged individualism as a cultural value in the United States and in the corporate arena; "survival of the fittest," "pulling oneself up by one's own bootstrap," and self-sufficiency are all ways this value gets expressed. Leaders of organizations I work with have no problem telling me, "We are a self-starter culture" or "This is a sink-or-swim culture." In these workplaces, they establish formal mentor programs, but they have limited success. This is because the underlying culture speaks more loudly than any program: the more you can do and achieve on your own, without help from others, the smarter and more valuable you are. Competition, rather than cooperation, between individuals is an extension of this ideal and is seen as the best way to determine who is most talented.

Professor Geert Hofstede, whom I mentioned in the last chapter, conducted a very well-known study of 116,000 IBM employees who were employed in 53 countries in the world, to explore cultural differences between countries. From his analysis of the survey, he ascertained that countries have four (later five) distinct cultural patterns. Individualism/Collectivism was one of these dimensions. Individualism is defined as the tendency to view ties between individuals as loose; everyone looks after him/herself (and immediate family). Collectivism is defined as the tendency to view oneself from birth onward as being integrated into a set of strong, cohesive in-groups, often extended families; the group protects its members in exchange for loyalty. In Hofstede's study, the United States scored as the most individualistic country—number one out of fifty-three.[10]

Black people come from a collectivist culture because of our African ancestry that was traditionally rooted in a more collectivist culture or what is sometimes referred to as a "relational" or "indigenous culture." Most people of color come from these type of cultures. This was never clearer to me than when I had a very difficult conversation with an attorney who had just become the first black partner in his large law firm. I had been working with the firm on improving its diversity. I was thrilled for him, because he was an amazing person and excellent lawyer. One day, soon after the announcement, I saw him and I excitedly congratulated him and commented about how proud he must be. I was not prepared for his response. He said, "What do I have to be happy about? How can I be proud when there is no one here with me?" He went on to explain, that he would only be satisfied when he saw many more people of color coming up behind him. As long as his group still seemed to be having problems being hired and retained (there were very few attorneys of color in the firm), there was nothing to celebrate.

His sense of achievement was tied to his group's success. This is something that I knew well but had forgotten. To be the sole person to have accomplished a certain feat is not quite the same when you are still the only one like you and may be for a long time. From my own experience and the black people with whom I have spoken, I know about the additional burden of carrying and caring about the group. If they have decided to leave their companies, they worry about what their departures will mean for other black people coming up in the organization. Some black people stay much longer at the organization for this reason. They have concerns about how their mistakes and failures might make white people doubt the capabilities of other blacks. These are part of being shaped according to the values of a collectivist or relational culture.

The chart below captures some tenets of two cultures that often can be at odds with each other and therefore cause conflict, misunderstanding, and distance between white and black people. It illustrates how our lenses are shaped by different cultural norms. Although divided into two columns, the chart is not meant to suggest that there are only two types of cultures or that you can only be influenced by one of them. I, for one, can see that both have influenced my worldview and ways of doing things.

Collectivist Culture	Individualist Culture
Collectivism: The focus is the group, the community, and relationships. The individual exists in relationship to the community. *"Ubuntu"*—We are, therefore I am (a South African concept)	Rugged Individualism: The focus is the individual as primary, the most important. "Survival of the fittest."
Bonds are long; responsibility is to the extended family and larger community.	Bonds and responsibilities are more limited to immediate family (nuclear family).
Emotion is expressed and valued.	Rationality is key, and emotion is opposed to reason. Emotion is not expressed or is expressed with little to no affect. "I think, therefore I am."

Look back at the lens diagram on page 77, and you will see that we have only begun to scratch the surface. There are so many experiences and identities that are filtering our realities, even more than are listed there. The whole point of the lens concept is that there are many ways to see things and that your way is not the only way. The skill that I am encouraging you to develop here is the ability to appreciate your own lens and to stay open to seeing the lenses of others, as my friend Nan did when she looked through my lens at black men that night on Wall Street.

As a white person who wants to connect in a genuine way to black people, you will need to do two things:

⇨ accept that the way you have seen the world has been influenced by your racial and cultural lens, and

⇨ become more curious about how a black person may see the world differently.

When you hear a black person explain how she experienced your or someone else's behavior, how she sees racism in a particular incident or policy, or what she finds enjoyable, you should lean into, rather than resist or immediately question, their perspectives. Don't say "I just don't (can't) believe that." When you do, it shuts the black person down and cuts off your access to new information. Be inquisitive like Eddie Murphy and get on the bus to find out what you are missing or how your culture and experience cause you to see a different world. You can't be John Howard Griffin and blacken your skin, but you could think about trying on the lens of a black person in your company or on your board of directors. How different would the dance floor of your committee or boardroom look to you if you were black? How comfortable would the rhythms be?

The more you are able to explore and challenge your lens and appreciate the worldviews of the black people around you, the more expansive your lens will be, making you a worthy dance partner. Your black acquaintances, friends, colleagues, and supervisees will want to cut the rug with you—to share their views, their experiences, and their joys. Together, you can build the racial amity and equity we so desperately want and need.

Endnotes

1. JASON MARSH, RODOLFO MENDOZA-DENTON, & JEREMY SMITH, ARE WE BORN RACIST? NEW INSIGHTS FROM NEUROSCIENCE AND POSITIVE PSYCHOLOGY 9 (Beacon Press 2010) ("When white men briefly saw pictures of unfamiliar black male faces, their brain activity spiked in a region known as the amygdala, which is involved in feelings of vigilance generally, and in the fear response specifically; the amygdala lights up when we encounter people or events we judge threatening."); *see also* A. J. Golby, J. D. Gabrieli, J. Y. Chiao, & J. L. Eberhardt, *Differential Responses in the Fusiform Region to Same-Race and Other-Race Faces,* 4 NATURE NEUROSCIENCE 845–50 (2001).

2. This diagram has been adapted from M. LODEN & J. ROSENER, WORKFORCE AMERICA! (Bus. One Irwin 1991).

3. No federal law bars employment discrimination on the basis of sexual orientation or gender identity. The Employment Non-discrimination Act (ENDA) S. 811/H.R. 1397 would extend federal employment discrimination protections now applied to discrimination based on race, religion, sex, national origin, age and disability to sexual orientation and gender identity. Since 1994, ENDA has been introduced in every Congress except the 104th but has never passed. The legislation has been sent to committees in both houses of Congress in 2011. In addition to Washington D.C. and the 13 states that provide full employment non-discrimination protection for transgender people, nine states have executive orders that mandate protection for state jobs. Efforts on the federal level to establish workplace protection rights have stalled since 2007. http://motherjones.com/mojo/2011/04/transgender-lgbt-employment-map; https://secure.aclu.org/site/Advocacy?cmd=display&page=UserAction&id=1601.

4. Simon & Chabris, *Selective Attention Test,* YOU TUBE (1999), http://www.youtube.com/watch?v=vJG698U2Mvo; *see also* www.invisiblegorilla.com/videos.html (accessed Jan. 19, 2010).

5. MALCOLM GLADWELL, BLINK: THE POWER OF THINKING WITHOUT THINKING 23, 53 (Little, Brown 2005).

6. DAN LANDIS, JANET BENNETT, & MILTON BENNETT, HANDBOOK OF INTERCULTURAL TRAINING (Sage, 3d ed. 2004), 151. Dr. Bennett is well known for his Developmental Model of Intercultural Sensitivity and the Intercultural Development Inventory, which are used internationally to guide intercultural training design and to assess intercultural competence. In 1986, Dr. Bennett cofounded the Intercultural Communication Institute (ICI), a private, nonprofit educational foundation designed to foster an awareness and appreciation of cultural difference in both the international and domestic arenas.

7. In the Deep South of the 1950s, journalist John Howard Griffin, a white male born in Mansfield, Texas, decided to cross the color line. Using medication that darkened his skin to deep brown, he traded his life of privilege as a Southern white male for the disenfranchised world of an unemployed black man. His eyewitness history is a work about race and humanity that in this new millennium still has something important to say to every American. JOHN HOWARD GRIFFIN, BLACK LIKE ME (Penguin 1960).

8. The limitation on end zone demonstrations includes push-ups, sit-ups, boat rowing, snow angels, and worm crawls, as well as the use of props by football players. D. Pierson, *NBC Sports,* NBC.com (Apr. 4, 2006), http://nbcsports.msnbc.com/id/12070684/ (accessed Jan. 21, 2011).

9. H. D. Simons, *Race and Penalized Sports Behaviors,* 38 INT'L REV. OF SPORTS SOC. 5–22 (2003).

10. Australia, Great Britain, Canada, and Netherlands followed the U.S. ranking (2, 3, 4, and 5, respectively). On the collectivist side of the spectrum were Latin American countries: Guatemala was number 53; Ecuador, Panama, Venezuela, and Colombia were not far behind as 52, 51, 50, and 49, respectively. Hofstede cautions that the cultural findings describe the country's score and not every individual in each country's view of the dimension. There are huge differences that individuals display within countries.

8

He's Black. What Do You Mean He Can't Dance? Check for Your Biases When Things Get Bumpy

Dance Lessons for this Chapter:

☑ Why our minds conjure up the image of someone white and male when we hear the words "pilot," "doctor," or "executive"

☑ Why stereotypes keep us from seeing the person in front of us

☑ What implicit bias is and how it may differ from our explicit beliefs

☑ How to find more about our own implicit biases

☑ How to correct for our implicit biases

As a consultant, I am always on a plane. I can take two bins from the stack, throw them on the conveyor belt, whip off all my outer layers, remove my shoes, dump them in the first bin with my Ziploc bag of essential liquids, snatch my computer from my tote, place it the second bin, and have them along with my suitcase rolling toward that TSA-manned X-ray box in thirty seconds. So, as a seasoned flyer, I was pleasantly shocked one day when just as the plane soared to 30,000 feet, the pilot began to speak over the public address system, and it was the voice of a woman. I was so excited. It's a female pilot! Pilots are so rarely women, and I was just thrilled to be riding with a woman who had not only broken through the glass ceiling but was reigning in the stratosphere. However, later into the flight, we encountered terrible turbulence, the ride got bumpy, and the plane started bouncing up and down. I thought, "Oh God, I hope she can drive!" I was so worried that it didn't even occur to me that my thinking was a problem. Not until I was on the return flight and the pilot was male and the plane began to experience turbulence did I notice my gender bias. The pilot is almost always a man, and it is often a bumpy ride. I couldn't ever remember thinking, "I hope he knows how to work this vehicle." Yes, I have been afraid for my ultimate safety. I've wished I had read the safety card in the back of the seat and watched the video more carefully, but I have never questioned the competence of the pilot through the lens of gender. I have never wondered if he was "qualified."

Where did this bias come from? After all, I am a woman and I can drive and I know many men who can't. However, somehow, when the ride gets rough, I feel safer with a man. At the beginning of the trip, when I heard there was a woman at the helm, I had been all "Rah-rah! Diversity!" But the minute there was a problem, I lost my enthusiasm.

Our Problem Is Implicit

My problem isn't that I believe that women are incapable of "manning" large, fast-moving engines. To the contrary, I actually assume any woman who has become a pilot must have overcome great odds and therefore be excellent at what she does. My problem is that my explicit belief is not the whole story.

As I am starting a workshop, many intelligent, kind, and caring people come up to me and say, "I believe in equal opportunity and fairness. I don't have a biased bone in my body." I don't know how to tell them that unless they are aliens, the bias is not only in their bones but also in their brains and probably in their behaviors. I understand what they are trying to tell me. They are trying to assure me. In other words, "Hey, Ms. Diversity Lady, I am not the problem; I am a good person, and I treat everyone the same. I have nothing against black people or any other group of people."

Bias is not about being good or bad; it's about being human.

Many of us believe that bias has to be intentional and conscious. We believe that if we had stereotypes for or against groups of people, we would certainly know it. Bias is not about being good or bad; it's about being human. The more I meet and work with white people who care but are still in the early stages of their journey, the more I realize that the biggest barrier to racial progress is not their *explicit* biases, but their *implicit* ones.

Get Familiar with Your Implicit Biases

When we are not conscious of the stereotypes and assumptions we are keeping, it is called implicit bias. Our implicit biases come up quickly and naturally, especially when we are in stressful situations. Every day is filled with turbulence, and, as humans, we are programmed to make quick decisions for our own survival. Most of us move toward the path of least resistance. However, countering unconscious bias requires us to see what we are doing before we get too far down the path, stop the movement, and back up from the bias. The first step on this road is to admit you have biases. The second is to get familiar with what they are. However, the initial admission can be a problem for many well-meaning people who pride themselves on being open-minded and supportive of the principle of equal rights. If you can't own up to having biases, you can't see them or catch yourself unconsciously acting upon them. Our second step, getting familiar with your biases, isn't easy at the outset either. They usually have to be pointed out to us until we get into the habit of looking for them.

Unintentional Biases: Katrina Survivors

During the Katrina disaster, there was a great deal of discussion about racial bias in the media accounts of the survivors and how reporters were characterizing black and white victims of Katrina differently. The two published pictures below and their interpretations were used to illustrate the point. In the top picture, there appears to be a young black person; the description reads, "A young man walks through chest deep flood water after *looting* a grocery store." In the picture below it, two white individuals are reportedly "*finding* bread and soda from a local grocery store." It is hard to explain why "looting" is used for one victim and "finding" for the others since there were no grocery stores open and conducting business. "Finding" is not "buying." So why is the black person described as a criminal and his fellow white victims as industrious? The reporters are reporting what they see, but perhaps the scene is being interpreted through stereotypes hidden in their unconscious minds.[1]

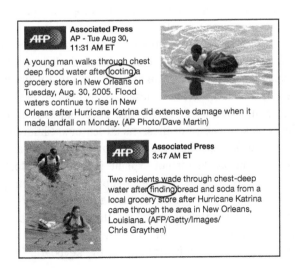

Remember when we talked about Malcolm Gladwell's research? He also discussed a concept referred to as priming. Priming is a concept that refers to subtle triggers influencing our behavior without our awareness of such influence.[2] We talked about this in the last chapter. The reporters, like all of us in the United States, have been "primed" to see the black men, especially young black men, as criminals. This was the same issue that my friend Nan and I ran into that night on Wall Street. There are many white criminals, but we have been primed to see white people as good law-abiding citizens. So when the reporters are primed by these stereotypes without knowing, it influences what they report.

Take the Implicit Association Test

Luckily, some very clever scientists have done us all a favor by developing the Implicit Association Test, or the IAT.[3] This test, which was launched online in 1998, is a great way to help us face the fact that we all harbor stereotypes, biases, and assumptions for and against groups of people. I am grateful for the IAT because it has provided us with information that pierces through our denial, but also takes away our guilt. Social scientists know that sometimes people have thoughts and feelings about themselves and others that they don't want to share publicly and that individuals possess attitudes they don't know they have. The web-based test measures the attitudes and beliefs that people have about other groups that they are unwilling or unable to report. In addition to the Race IAT, there are many other tests that you can take (e.g., Age IAT, Gender-Career IAT, Arab-Muslim IAT, Sexuality IAT). Each test takes about ten minutes. First, you are asked to share your explicit views with regard to the issue or group to be measured by the particular test. The next part of the test requests you to classify a set of words, images, or names.

The Race IAT measures your racial bias by timing how quickly you can associate a black face with a pleasant word as compared to the speed with which you can match a pleasant word with a white face and vice versa—how easy it is for you to associate unpleasant words with the image of a white person, as compared to a black person. At the end of the test, you will be told whether you have a slight, moderate, or strong automatic preference for European or black, or no preference at all.

I encourage you to go to the IAT website https://implicit.harvard.edu/implicit/ and take the Race IAT. If you are white and end up showing a preference for Europeans, don't worry. You are in good company. Of the millions of white and Asian Americans who have taken the test, 75 to 80% reveal an automatic preference for whites. Sadly, almost 50% of black people demonstrate a bias in favor of whites as well.[4] This should also not be a surprise. We have all been taught or intuited that white is good and black is bad, even if we don't believe it. Those lessons are hard to erase. We've all been breathing in the same air. Even as we attempt to teach our kids differently, the Race IAT testifies to the pervasive nature of these racial lessons. Children as young as five years old who have taken the test show the same pattern as white and black adults.[5]

I stated earlier that our problem is not explicit; it is implicit. Most of my white clients find themselves surprised when their tests show a bias for European Americans. They tell me that the test must be wrong. Or they argue that they are left-handed, or that they were distracted when they were taking the test and this accounts for their results. They wonder aloud how they would score if, for example, the order of the test changed, or the first task was on a different side of the keyboard. I tell them what the scientists have explained to me: none of it matters. The test is capturing a real and large effect. If you want, you can take the test several times to see what, if anything, changes about the outcome. Also, you will see that the site provides answers to a long list of frequently asked questions. Millions of people have tried their best to make their Race IAT test results match their explicit views but most have been unsuccessful.

I have to admit that I was relieved by the results of my Race IAT score, but I know what it feels like to show a bias on the test that is different than what you explicitly believe. I took the Career-Gender IAT, which measures the how quickly the test taker matches female names with careers and male names with family- or home-related words and vice versa. Even before the computer told me my preference, I knew I would show an automatic preference for men and careers. In my distress about the results, I reminded myself of how I attempt to console my clients. I say, "It's not your fault. This is to be expected. We have been bombarded with these messages forever." We have to be able to accept our biases. If we cannot accept them, we cannot see how they hamper the way we want to relate, operate, and support others who we see as different.

Use Your Explicit Beliefs and Values to Correct Your Implicit Biases

Those on the Project Implicit Team and other researchers have taken the results of the IAT a step further and determined that the IAT test score predicts how people behave in particular situations. When I interviewed Professor Mahzarin Banaji, one of the test creators, about what the Race IAT suggests about our behavior, she explained,

> One can no longer walk away from the data by saying "but these are artificial laboratory tests"—the test has been shown to predict people's behavior in over 50 studies done in real-world settings like business, politics, and medicine. It predicts who will be hired, who will be treated well, and how comfortable one is in the presence of another.[6]

Some people feel so discouraged when they learn about implicit bias and hear that it is predictive of behavior. They plead, "Don't my conscious beliefs and values mean anything? I just can't accept that I have these biases and I can't do anything about it." I am happy to respond, "Yes, the IAT shows your automatic response, not your ONLY response." It is your explicit beliefs that black and white people are equal and your value of fairness that will make you commit to keeping watch over your biases and learning to minimize them. Professor Banaji put it this way,

> The data from the IAT tells us what we are likely to do, who we might be under certain circumstances. But let us remember that knowing that we are likely to be the sort of people we have no wish to be, however disappointing, is powerful knowledge. It is our conscious thoughts and values that can get us out of the mess we create unknowingly. This is possible because the arguably greatest gift that evolution has bestowed on *Homo sapiens* is the ability to imagine a future unlike the present and to do something to get us there.[7]

Steps You Can Take to Check Your Automatic Responses

It is probably not possible for us to get rid of all our biases, nor is it desirable. Our brain's way of sorting through lots of stimuli quickly is what allows us to move through the world and survive. What we need to learn is how to slow down the biases that betray our values long enough for us to act in a way that is more aligned with what we believe.

To give you an idea of what you can do when you catch yourself acting according to your unconscious bias, below are some conscious steps you can take to create the future that we all want to be a reality.

How to Use Your Explicit Beliefs to Check Your Automatic Responses:

⇨ STEP ONE: Work on recognizing your biases—notice when and where they pop up.

⇨ STEP TWO: Stop the behaviors that naturally follow these biases.

⇨ STEP THREE: Remind yourself of what you really believe and value—pay attention to what is true instead of what you fear based on your stereotypes and biases.

⇨ STEP FOUR: Substitute new behaviors that are fair, and act to minimize the biases.

⇨ STEP FIVE: Expect to make new discoveries about yourself and others.

⇨ STEP SIX: Find ways to make up for the initial biased behavior.

Now, I want to tell you a story about how I learned these steps. Years ago, I had been up all night nursing my sick child. I was in a frenzy by the time we arrived at his doctor's office early the next morning. His regular physician wasn't there. A very young, petite South Asian woman wearing a white coat and a stethoscope around her neck walked into the exam room and introduced herself to me as the doctor. Without knowing what I was doing, from almost her first statement, I started questioning—or should I say interrogating?—her: "So, have you ever taken care of kids with these symptoms before? How many?" Also, she spoke with an Indian accent, so when she answered my questions I would add in a raised voice, "What? I don't know what you are saying." It was like I was a member of a medical licensing board and acted as if she were lying about being a doctor—I treated her like she was an imposter.

Then, somehow, I caught myself. Somewhere in the middle of the inquisition, I became aware of my posture. I was on my heels leaning back from her; my arms were crossed, and my tone was stern. I don't like to imagine what my face looked like. "What are you doing?" I asked myself. Then I realized what was happening and why—I was treating her this way because she was a young Asian woman. Her youth and diminutive stature brought up additional biases for me. I knew right then that if a white man had walked in that room, even without a stethoscope or introduction, I would have immediately felt at ease, in the right place with the right person—in good hands. If he had been young and short, I probably would have been a little uncomfortable, but I would have reasoned that he was some Doogie Howser type, brilliant and beyond his years. If it had been a black woman, I am sure I would have been at least friendlier and more trusting. Yet, my automatic response to this Indian woman was that she wasn't qualified to take care of my son.

Below are the steps I took to check my automatic responses.

Personal Experience: Using My Explicit Beliefs to Counter My Automatic Responses

⇨ STEP ONE: I became aware of what was happening.

⇨ STEP TWO: I stopped. I could have kept going on. I was the worried, frantic mother; she wasn't my son's real doctor; and my child was sick. I didn't know her. Why shouldn't I question her? There were many excuses available, but I knew I was wrong. So, I said to myself, "Cut it out."

⇨ STEP THREE: We must have been ten minutes into the interaction by then. I felt terrible, but I went into self-correction mode. I changed my posture and leaned into what she was saying. I relaxed my face. I softened my stare. I started listening instead of questioning. I stopped pretending that I couldn't understand what she was saying. Once I stopped resisting her, I realized she was speaking perfect English.

⇨ STEP FOUR: Changing my behavior made it easier for me to recover my conscious compass. I replaced my negative stereotypical thinking, my implicit response with my explicit beliefs. I talked to myself, "You believe that people of every background are smart and competent. She stated that she was a doctor. She has on a white coat. She is working at this reputable institution. There is no reason to doubt that she is a highly capable doctor." When she explained what she thought about my son's illness, I nodded my head up and down. When she asked me a question, I was forthcoming with the information and openly shared my concerns.

⇨ STEP FIVE: Once I settled down, I discovered that she was not only competent but calming. By the end of the interaction, I realized that I really loved her approach and style. I actually liked her better than my son's usual physician.

⇨ STEP SIX: My son was feeling better by the end of our appointment. As we were leaving, I made sure she knew how much I appreciated her. I smiled as much as I could, repeated many "thank-yous," and offered several compliments. I did not apologize. I was too embarrassed. However, whenever I saw her after that day, I made sure to greet her warmly, inquire about her health, and update her on my son's health.

I was shocked and ashamed by my initial reaction to this woman of color. However, it was the fact that I could see what I was doing that allowed me to correct my behavior. I comforted myself all that day by saying, "Well, at least you caught yourself." I tried to remember S-A-M-E from Chapter Five. I had Stopped pretending. I punted on the Apology, but I had tried to acknowledge how sorry I was by being solicitous afterward. I had made a Mistake; mistakes are part of the process, I told myself. Once I realized my mistake, I stayed Engaged.

I am not fooling myself. She was so pleasant throughout the whole exchange, but I am sure she knew exactly what was happening. People of color are used to being underestimated, although I think it is particularly disappointing when the prejudice comes from someone who is similar to you and whom you feel should know better. I'm certain that I was not the first person who had misjudged this wonderfully talented, small, short, young South Asian physician. Sadly, I thought about my then husband, a black doctor, who had been asked several times by new patients who came to his office, even with his white coat on, "Where's the doctor?" I hated that I had made her work so hard—that I had committed a microaggression against her, adding to the many slights she had already experienced. I found myself just grateful that she was willing to persevere through my ignorance and that her grace allowed me to find my explicit self.

When I am brave enough to share this story with people, they try to excuse my behavior by suggesting that I was not myself: my son was sick, and I had been up all night. All this is true, but it is still bias that informed my behavior. Having said that, I think my sympathetic audience has a point that we need to examine. Our automatic responses get the best of us when we are in difficult situations—such as when the turbulence comes—when we are afraid and are looking for someone whom we can trust or when there is a lot at stake and we are determining who should handle an important matter or relationship.

Change Your Brain's Diet

When I spoke with Professor Banaji, I asked her what else she thought we could do to change our behavior so it doesn't conform to our implicit biases. Her suggestion is one that we have already started working on as part of the BASICS in Chapter Six—expand your life to include information about the culture and experiences of those with whom you are not familiar. She explained,

> The brain needs a diet that is healthy in the same way the body does. Some of us are smug about this. We say that we live in a big city, a liberal environment, and that therefore we are protected from bias. But I would argue that if you live in a relatively more diverse city like L.A., you may be at greater risk for bias than somebody who doesn't hear and see the regular creation of stereotypes. But here's the critical thing—cities like L.A. afford us social experiences (a diet) that is more balanced and with more options. If you actually partake of it, really partake of it, through the people you count among your best friends, your intimate relations, the music you hear, the media you consume more generally, the roads you travel, there the daily diet can change the associations that the IAT detects. Every choice, every decision becomes relevant in the same way as the number of calories we consume. Think molecular when it comes to changing your mind. What are the daily, small units that are consumed?[8]

Somewhere near the end of my interview with Professor Banaji, I confessed to her my embarrassing Indian female doctor story. Mahzarin is Indian and petite just like the doctor in my story. Instead of shaming me, she proceeded to tell me two of her more recent biased moments. It was like we were comparing war wounds. "You did what? Please, girl, let me tell you what I said the other day." We were following one of the guidelines we evoke in all our trainings: "No shame, blame, or attack—yourself or others." This guideline and another, "Keep a self-focus," is what we need to work against our biases and the behaviors that follow.

In this chapter, I have tried to be open and honest about my struggles as a way of keeping a self-focus; and my hope, of course, is that these admissions will not invite blame or shame from others. I am hoping you will say, "Well, if Vernā has these biases, I can accept that maybe I do, too," and then you will be inspired to go looking for your own. I truly believe that if we can accept our implicit biases, start recognizing how they impact our behavior, and begin using our explicit good selves to examine our choices on the cellular level, as Professor Banaji suggests, we will change our behaviors. Our new and healthy ways of acting will, in turn, change our relationships, our communities, and our organizations. Eventually, with all these changes, our implicit mind will have to reshape itself, and our automatic responses will better reflect what we hold true: All of us are equal, and no one group is automatically better or worse than another.

Endnotes

1. D. A. MARTIN, MEDIA AWARENESS NETWORK (Aug. 30, 2005), http://www.media-awareness.ca/english/resources/educational/teachable_moments/katrina_2_photo.cfm (accessed Jan. 21, 2011).

2. MALCOLM GLADWELL, BLINK (Little Brown 2005).

3. B. NOSEK, M. BANAJI & T. GREENWALD, PROJECT IMPLICIT, https://implicit.harvard.edu/implicit (accessed Jan. 21, 2011).

4. B. Nosek, M. Banaji & A. Greenwald, *Harvesting Implicit Group Attitudes and Beliefs from a Demonstration Web Site*, GROUP DYNAMICS: THEORY, RES. & PRAC. 6, 101–15 (2002).

5. Interview with Professor Mahzarin Banaji, in Cambridge, Massachusetts (Dec. 22, 2010).

6. *Id.*

7. *Id.*

Dancing with Peggy McIntosh: Breaking the Thirteen Deadly Habits of Workplace Oppression

Dance Lessons for this Chapter:

☑ The Thirteen Deadly Habits that make it hard for us to create inclusive work environments

☑ The Instead behaviors that we can use to build more inclusion

hab·it -noun \'ha-bət\

7a: a behavior pattern acquired by frequent repetition or physiologic exposure that shows itself in regularity or increased facility of performance **b:** an acquired mode of behavior that has become nearly or completely involuntary.[1]

In the last chapter, we discussed the implicit biases that shape our behaviors and how important it is for us to acknowledge these biases so that we can begin to counter them. In this chapter, you will discover that some of these unconsciously biased behaviors have become habits, a pattern of behavior. The habits reinforce exclusion and dominance of one group over another in the workplace.

I learned about these habits from Professor Peggy McIntosh, who is well known and respected for her illuminating work regarding white privilege. Her article, "White Privilege: Unpacking the Invisible Knapsack," has shaped the awareness and the conversation about privilege for many people of every background for more than twenty years now. In her original 1988 article, Peggy created a list of forty-six small and yet very substantial ways that she experiences "unearned overadvantage" in her everyday life as a white woman by comparison with her African American colleagues at Wellesley Centers for Women.[2] We will talk more about that list and the concept of white privilege in our next chapter.

When working with Peggy recently, I was thrilled to discover that she had developed another very valuable list—"Thirteen Deadly Habits of Oppression in the Workplace"—and I wanted to share it with you.[3] The chart below contains a list of the thirteen Deadly Habits in the left hand column and, what we called for the purposes of our conversation, the "Instead Behaviors" in the right-hand column.

Thirteen Deadly Habits of Oppression in the Workplace	
Always Being:	**"Instead Behaviors" to Practice:**
The Knower	Listen
The Manager	Learn
The Authority	Observe
The Authorizer	Relate
The Judge	Relax
The Jury	Reflect
The Gatekeeper	Consult
The Challenger	Connect
The Competition	Settle down
The Speaker	
The Synthesizer	
The Generalizer	
The Clown	

I had a chance to talk with Peggy about the Deadly Habits and how they hinder some people from becoming real actors in promoting equity and inclusion. We also discussed how the "Instead Behaviors" need to be cultivated by people in a dominant group in order to round out and expand their humanity toward others, especially those who have been marginalized and oppressed by the Deadly Habits.

Our conversation really made me think about the ideas of sameness and difference that I discussed in Chapter Three—how black and white people can be the same in some fundamental ways, but history, worldview, experience, and culture can cause them to value and approach the same things differently. For example, both Peggy and I were taught that excellence was a virtue, but we were taught very different things about how to behave excellently.

What I also found intriguing about our conversation was Peggy's understanding that the Deadly Habits are linked to white men's history of mastering people and things, women and black people among them. The connection can be painful for white and black people to consider. However, throughout our conversation, she reminded me that overreliance on the Deadly Habits by white people like herself is not their fault; these are behaviors taught by culture. People learn them and are rewarded in a system of hierarchy for using them. In addition, our conversation helped me realize another way I have learned to be cross-cultural. As a black woman who has been able to progress in mostly white male domains, I have had to learn to use both sides of this chart to survive and thrive. I have also encouraged the decision makers in these domains to value the "Instead Behaviors" in order to increase the inclusion of others who have been historically excluded. At the end of our conversation, Peggy suggested the Deadly Habits are not bad in themselves, as they are part of a larger range of human traits. However, people who want to break down racial barriers and build more inclusion need to hone the "Instead Behaviors" to mitigate the oppressive ways that the Deadly Habits have been used over time to maintain exclusion and dominance.

I found our conversation so enlightening and encouraging, that I thought you might want to eavesdrop. So below, I have included a portion of our interview. We have edited it for length and flow, and added some of our follow-up conversations as well. However, one thing I hope you will see is just how wonderfully instructive and enriching a genuine conversation about race between a black and white person can be. There is so much that black and white people can learn from each other and do together to eliminate racism, if we commit to self-awareness, connection, and action.

Vernā: Peggy, can you tell us about the genesis of the Thirteen Deadly Habits?

Peggy: As a white person I was taught that these are traits of excellence in public life. I was taught that a leader is the one who *knows* the most; can *manage* or get people to do his bidding; is the *authority* on a subject; is the *gatekeeper* who keeps the undesirables out and maintains the enclave. I generated the list on the left based on my own experience of feeling oppressed by bullies and excluded by know-it-alls. I saw how hard it was to make any kind of community if a few people are behaving in bossy and argumentative ways. But when I began to hold jobs, of course, I wanted to play these dominating roles because I saw they led to what the world calls "excellence" and "success." And I was shot down for trying, because I was seen as not behaving as a woman should.

Vernā: And the "Instead Behaviors," where did they come from?

Peggy: As a white woman in my social context, I was taught that the list on the right contained what I was expected to specialize in. Well, maybe not *relax;* but we were expected to hold it all together no matter what was going on, and smile while doing so. And because women were considered weaker than men and inferior to them, these relational behaviors in the right-hand column were regarded as weak and unimportant. These behaviors were not about maintaining control. And as a white woman, I also learned not to respect these specialties that I had learned so well. They are more apt to lead to a sharing of power, which, when I was growing up, was seen as a loss of leadership capability. I now know that, sadly, for men, development of the behaviors in the left-hand column has required the subordination of many aspects of themselves. There are important human traits on the right side of this chart that men were discouraged from developing and/or demonstrating because when they did, they were considered weak or submissive. I now see that "Instead Behaviors" have a vast importance for improving workplaces, though they are not one-on-one antidotes for dominant behaviors. Spending your work time only in listening and connecting can allow the dominants to run rampant. But all oppressive colleagues are improved by practicing some "Instead Behaviors."

Vernā: What makes you call the habits on the left deadly and oppressive? Many of my white clients have asked me to remove the word "oppression" from my presentation materials. A director in a quasi-government service organization informed me that "no one is oppressed here; we don't ask people to go around wearing armbands." A corporate client exclaimed, "The people here make too much money to be oppressed!"

Peggy: They are deadly habits because they have to do with keeping control, and they are really based on fear. They have become habits for many of us as white people in the workplace and in life generally. We are not taught to think of them as habits that oppress other people. For me, the sad thing is I was taught that these habits showed excellence. I thought excellence in economic and public life was about mastery—mastering a skill, a subject, a situation, one's environment . . . for some, even the universe. But the roles in the left-hand column translate to mastering or subordinating—taking control of not just things and situations but also people. For white people, especially, these habits have a racial, gender, and class history. For example, slave owners learned certain behaviors in order to master their slaves. Men learned certain behaviors in order to master women. Classwise, owners of land and human labor were masters of the economic system.

Vernā: Some of the behaviors on the left-hand list are self-explanatory, I think, but what about being The Clown or The Generalizer or The Synthesizer? Why are these behaviors deadly? How do they keep white people from creating an environment where black and white folks can relate and work well together in the workplace?

Peggy: If you are The Clown, for example, you use humor to interrupt or derail a presentation or conversation; you make light of everything so that the person who is speaking doesn't know where they are psychologically with you. The speaker is thrown off course. The Clown usually does this just as something is about to happen; something is about to be exposed or confronted.

Vernā: Yes, it's like The Clown causes us to miss out on what the black person has to offer that might be different and prevents us from going deeper in the discourse.

Peggy: Yes, and The Generalizer loves to speak for everyone about everything. He or she may throw out adages: "It's a dog-eat-dog world" or "It takes all kinds to make a world" or "White people have problems, too." These can be conversation stoppers. These ideas are introduced and may be seen as irrefutable, ending the discussion. The Synthesizer is the person who can "pull it all together." If you can take all the various thoughts and find a way in the moment to pull it all together, you are considered "excellent," as in, "What I hear us saying is . . ." But this is also a way of hijacking all that has been said and putting your interpretation onto it.

Vernā: Yes, and taking credit for others' ideas. Also, some ideas shouldn't be synthesized. If I am trying to contribute a perspective that is pointed and different from others' perspectives and someone comes along and synthesizes it, my opinion usually gets blended in with what has already been said and loses its sharpness and emotion. It has the effect of quieting me down and confusing me because now my point is all wrapped up in someone else's nice, neat package with a bow. It happens before you can even get a word out; everyone is packing up their files and walking out of the room by the time you realize what has happened. Can you explain The Challenger?

Peggy: I was taught that being The Challenger was an excellent role to play. You were separating the sheep from the goats. When you challenge what people say or do, you imply that you can ferret out the people who don't know what they are talking about.

Vernā: Yeah, it's also like the "devil's advocate" thing. People say, "Let me just play the devil's advocate." I am always thinking, "Let's not!" It's like they get permission to kill your idea. It's especially difficult for a black person who is concerned about the perceptions regarding the negative stereotype out there about her ability to think, speak, and articulate her ideas well.

Peggy: The Challenger thinks he or she is doing the whole world a favor by cutting out the deadwood, winnowing the chaff. But it is deadly and oppressive because The Challenger puts people on the defensive and tries to humiliate the speaker. It's top-dog alpha behavior. Challengers reinforce pecking orders. Often, a male Challenger will say things to a woman or person of color that he wouldn't say to a man or to other whites.

Vernā: When I look at the Instead Behaviors, I see them as important social skills and the behaviors that lead to self-awareness and awareness of others. They are the very traits that help you show respect for others. But you are right; one would not operate in this "instead" way if one wanted to get or remain in power, especially in a corporate environment.

Peggy: Yes, they are relational skills, often associated with women in general and men in subordinated groups. The political history is that these differing characteristics were projected onto people of color and whites, men and women, and at the same time ranked as superior and inferior.

Vernā: Yes, but I see white women, people of other races, and even myself adopting the traits on the left side, almost as second nature.

Peggy: Well, I still often avoid them even when I need them. But there has been a generational shift toward them in public life for women across class and race and ethnicity.

Vernā: You know, you are right. As a woman of color I have definitely been schooled on the "Instead Behaviors"—they were the ways I learned to survive working with those practicing the Deadly Habits. My mom taught me to act this way as a sign of respect; however, I have sometimes rejected, and I have seen many other people of color reject, these "Instead Behaviors" as soft—and therefore weak and ineffective—especially in a workplace that is predominately white.

Peggy: I used to see them that way, too.

Vernā: Do you think young people are still getting these messages about what behaviors are appropriate for them as women and men?

Peggy: Things have changed somewhat for men and women in this regard; the projections of opposite traits onto "opposite sexes" have lessened. There is more understanding that everybody needs to develop their own capacities on both sides of this polarity, which is a social construction anyway. Awareness of what you are doing is important to keep your competence from becoming oppressive. Another way of saying it is that what works best in a particular situation may be oppressive if practiced all the time, as an unexamined habit. The definitions of leadership and competence in business and management have changed somewhat over the last twenty years in the United States, toward the "Instead" column. But often, it is the financial bottom line that determines the shift away from the behaviors in the left-hand column rather than any aspiration to have a better quality of human life in general, or to have business care about the public interest.

Vernā: Yes, I see that financial motivation among some of my clients as well. I am hoping that adopting these new competencies will help them to see the bigger human picture as well.

So just to be clear about the habits on the left side: you are not saying there is something wrong with being smart, knowledgeable, and competitive, are you? After all, isn't this the way that we know who is capable of leading our organizations and teams?

Peggy: The problem is that the list on the left stems from a sense of superiority and is not balanced with the "Instead Behaviors." The characteristics on both lists are in all humans, and they need to be balanced with each other. The deadly habits can be egotistical behaviors. Being "The such and such" means you are The One who *knows* or who can *speak*, or who has the *authority*. It has to do with being in charge, superior, and not in equitable relation with others.

Vernā: Yes, I see. *Knowing, competing, clowning,* and *synthesizing:* these aren't bad. It's the "The" and the "-er" that silences or presses down the skills on the right side of the chart.

Peggy: Exactly.

Vernā: Being The Knower is a problem if it keeps you from *learning.* Being The Speaker often prevents us from *listening.* The Judge and Jury rarely *consults.* It's hard to *reflect* when you are The Challenger or The Competitor. If white people want to be able to converse with black people openly and genuinely, they will have to modify these behaviors. The Instead Behaviors allow black people, who are often in the minority, to be heard and appreciated.

Peggy: You are pointing out wonderful connections between the two sides of the list. I feel that white people must become aware—and this has to do with our class backgrounds and every aspect of economics—that we were taught to take control. The skills in the left column are useful in many ways, but we need to go easy on all those habits. We need to work on completing our personality by strengthening the characteristics that we were taught to consider inferior if we hope to develop as full human beings and break down systems of white power and privilege. For example, the *consult*ing behavior begins to build community. It also allows you to *reflect;* reflecting on new information shows you your edges, your bounded assumptions.

Vernā: One's assumptions can be so revealing and so embarrassing. One thing I see a lot with nice white people is that they feel so guilty when they make mistakes, and they have a hard time acknowledging that systems have designated them as superior and powerful.

Peggy: Yes. I feel this should not be about guilt. It is not our fault that we were taught these things. Guilt is one way that whites draw attention to themselves. It is arrogant for us to think that we made this history; it is very self-centered. We have inherited a history, and the question is how we develop as full human beings despite such history.

Vernā: All of this makes so much sense to me, and yet I know that when I get into an uncomfortable position because of a difference, my instinct is to go "deadly." What can I do? What can white people do to get to a place where the Instead Behaviors come more easily and naturally, especially when they are interacting with black people and they are worried about making mistakes?

Peggy: It is a hard row to hoe. It takes intervention and intention to get to the right-hand side. It takes practice. Unless I practice the right side in my job, I will enact those behaviors on the left side of the chart. My race and my class have allowed and encouraged me to do this, though not as much as the men of my class and race have been encouraged to do it. But it is hard to move from these deadly habits. They are about keeping "weakness" and relationality at bay, especially in the professional fields, and are about remaining in control. Yes, I was taught that if you Consult with other people, you lose status. White people worry about losing status.

Vernā: Yes, I see that as one of the costs of being white. The more status you have, in a society that values status, the more you worry about it. It is definitely a different mindset, one that equates sharing with weakness. Black people and other people of color are considered to be from more communal or relational cultures. Our cultural leaning is toward sharing as a strength; really sharing is just expected, because another's well-being in the community is related to your own.

Having said that, why would a white person do something that might endanger his or her status?

Peggy: There has to be an incentive to let go of what you were trained to believe. Someone has to say to you that you will lose out if you don't change; or that the behaviors on the left-hand column are not working for you anymore. Or maybe you can see that you could fail in a relationship if you continue to be The Challenger. For organizations like law firms, the impetus might be what they are hearing from their clients about needing more diversity on their staff; or maybe that they are going to lose out on talent; perhaps there is new product or market in a different part of the world that requires a firm to learn a new approach. Often the motivation comes because there is threat to the bottom line. Or people come to realize in their personal lives that they need more than the attributes and behaviors of the left hand to make up a full life.

Vernā: So once there is an impetus, then what does one do?

Peggy: Well that's where you come in. You do the workshops, the dialogues, the exercises. It is like an intervention. You are reteaching people to consider how they respond in different situations.

Vernā: But what if you aren't in a workshop? What would you advise my white readers then?

Peggy: For them to think twice about what they are doing or saying:

- **Notice your power moves—when you start being The Knower, The Challenger, The Judge and so on.**
- **Notice how meetings work, how the left-side traits take over a meeting. Listen to the people who have the right-side traits, if you want to learn and you think you are democratic.**
- **If you are chairing a meeting, apportion time so that everyone will be heard, in a group of twenty or fewer, time everyone at one minute, and then take a minute for yourself. No more.**

- Determine to learn and use those behaviors on the right-hand side better than you ever have.
- Agree to be on a different footing with colleagues—when the dynamic with a black person becomes uncomfortable, decide not to be The Knower, but rather someone who wants to Learn and Listen.
- Relax and reflect—and you can say, "I'm sorry, I don't want to come on wrong here; I'm confused, I'm working on trying not to take over everything."
- And settle down—don't try to be in every discussion, fix everything, or make everything right. See yourself as a continuing learner.

Vernā: Wouldn't it be great if we could get to a place where we saw discomfort and mistakes as a chance to practice new behaviors? When you got that feeling in your stomach, or your heart started racing because you put your foot in your mouth with a black person— that would be the signal to switch sides, abandon your Deadly Habits and transition to the "Instead Behaviors"? There would be less of that paralyzing guilt that draws all the attention to you. You would see the situation as a triggering moment that allows you to practice. In that case, you would avail yourself of places and experiences where you could fail rather than trying to avoid them all.

Peggy: Yes, that would be great. In addition, we as white people need to actually use our privilege to change things. I feel much more empowered than I ever did when I was oblivious to being white in a society that favored whites.

Vernā: I am so glad you are willing to use your privilege that way. It is inspiring to me and to so many others. Thank you.

Endnotes

1. http://www.merriam-webster.com/dictionary/habit (last accessed June 5, 2011).

2. P. McIntosh, White Privilege: Unpacking the Invisible Knapsack (Wellesley Center for Research on Women 1988); P. MacIntosh, White Privilege and Male Privilege: A Personal Account of Coming to See Correspondences Through Work in Women's Studies (Wellesley Centers for Women 1988).

3. Peggy McIntosh, *Thirteen Deadly Habits of Workplace Oppression*, in K. Dace (Ed.),"Why Can't We Just be Friends": Women of Color and White Women in the Academy (forthcoming).

(10)

White People Have Always Been Center Stage: Understanding White Privilege and Other Forms of Unearned Privilege

Dance Lessons for this Chapter:

☑ Understanding what white privilege is and is not
☑ Doing the line dance of opportunity
☑ Understanding other forms of unearned advantage and disadvantage, target and non-target groups
☑ Considering the complex interplay between our target and non-target identities

One of the most thought-provoking and enlightening conversations happening these days among those who are interested in improving race relations and racial equity centers around the concept of "white privilege," which Peggy McIntosh mentioned in the previous chapter. I would like us to spend more time understanding what white privilege is, and exploring other types of unearned privilege as well. White privilege is the name given to the implicit advantages that occur to white people in U.S. society, because they belong to a group that was long ago deemed "better than" or superior. The idea has been discussed in anti-racism circles for years, because without understanding white privilege, it is hard to grasp racial inequality and its causes. More recently, it has been making inroads into mainstream discussions.

White privilege exists without people with white skin asking for it or even wanting it. It exists whether white people believe in their own superiority or not. In fact, most of the white people I know don't believe they are better than any other group of people, and yet, they haven't quite reckoned with the fact that they still experience the benefits pertaining to these old beliefs. It is also true that many of my white friends and colleagues recognize and are upset by the disadvantages that blacks encounter daily, but they are less aware of the day-to-day over-advantages they experience. Intellectually, of course, it makes sense: if one group is being unfairly disadvantaged, the other is being unfairly over-advantaged. It is just the other side of the coin, but it is so much harder to notice.

For example, in many department stores in America, a well-dressed black man can enter the establishment to shop and almost immediately notice that someone from its security team is following him. Or, many professional black men joke about the several sets of car keys they have been handed by some unknown white couple who has mistaken them for the hotel valet, even though they have just attended the same high-class event. How many of these micro-inequity stories do I have, you might ask? Too many! When many white people hear these stories, they are outraged by the fact that black men are assumed to be in service positions no matter what they are wearing or have accomplished. However, the new work for many white people is to fully appreciate what it means to be part of a group that walks with ease through any department store where they are assumed, by virtue of their skin color, to be trustworthy or that attends lovely formal affairs where they are assumed to be the patrons rather than the staff.

Get a Working Understanding of White Privilege

The first thing to know about white privilege is that it has nothing to do with intentional acts of discrimination. In fact, it is a system that is on "automatic" all of the time. Most white people are completely unaware that they experience an unfair advantage because they grew up being in the racial norm in our society, having the experiences that they had, and having those experiences interpreted in a way that reinforces their sense of the norm. Many white people assume that the treatment they receive is the normal treatment, or just "the way life is."

The second thing to know is that white privilege doesn't deny that white individuals have worked hard to get what they have in society. What it points to is the positioning that white people receive at birth because of skin color, which gives them more of an opportunity to realize the benefits of their hard work. Some of you have heard that expression, "People are born on third base and go through life thinking they hit a triple."[1] This idea is similar to that of white privilege. It suggests that a great deal of what white people experience and possess that was not earned. Unearned advantage is a destabilizing concept because it flies in the face of all that we have been taught in the United States about meritocracy. If people are not successful in our country, we are taught that this is due to their lack of individual effort and/or smarts.

Of course, we recognize that some people start behind the eight ball, but we don't consider that maybe others start off in front of it. For example, before 1920, it didn't matter how keen your political skills were or how hard you were willing to work, if you were a woman, you weren't going to get elected to Congress. How could you, when your group wasn't even allowed to vote? If you think about it, when you have a society that has sanctioned discrimination for centuries where only certain groups could vote, hold land, and go to certain schools, those groups are able to excel and solidify their dominance over time. So even when the laws are changed, these groups still maintain their power and control over opportunities in that area. The institutions they have built and the resources they have accumulated and passed down help them remain in power to the exclusion of others, even if they don't have the legal right to bar others as they had in the past.

So it is now 2011. Women have made progress on the political landscape, but we have never had a female president of the country; there are only 17 women U.S. senators out of 100, and only 75 of the 435 representatives in Congress are women.[2] As we dig more deeply, we begin to see that even though we dismantled the discriminatory laws in our country, we did not disable the systems or attitudes that allow the dominance of the privilege group to prevail. When we think of politicians, we think of men, not because they are the best at it but because they have dominated this area for so long. The same is true for race and ethnicity. White people are seen as better, smarter, more industrious, and more responsible, not because people of other races are not, but because this one group of people has dominated our society and thinking for so long. This view of whites as superior affects how resources and opportunities are distributed in our institutions, and this in turn reinforces the group's power.

Make Your Own List of How You Experience White Privilege

As I mentioned earlier, I was first introduced to the concept of white privilege when I read Professor Peggy McIntosh's articles wherein she explains her personal journey discovering and enumerating the ways she experiences white privilege in her daily life.[3] Her piece is so powerful because it is personal and autobiographical. There is something about her list that makes the invisible, visible and allows other whites to consider ways in which their skin color may have given them the benefit of the doubt and contributed to their success. Four items from Peggy's inventory of daily effects of white privilege in her life include the following:

> "I can if I wish arrange to be in the company of people of my race most of the time";
> "I can take a job with an affirmative action employer without having coworkers on the job suspect that I got it because of my race";
> "I can be late to a meeting without having the lateness reflect on my race"; and
> "I can swear, or dress in secondhand clothes, or not answer letters without having people attribute these choices to the bad morals, the poverty, or the illiteracy of my race."[4]

Many white people have read the list and found themselves challenged to reconsider their strongly held beliefs about meritocracy and how they operate in the world. I realized once I read her article that I had been aware of white privilege for some time, but I couldn't name it. McIntosh says,

> I did not ask for the unearned advantages that I put on my list. They came to me because of my placement within systems of privilege and disadvantage that do not have to do with merit. I have come to see white privilege as an invisible package of unearned assets that I could count on cashing in each day but about which I was meant to remain oblivious. White privilege is like an invisible, weightless knapsack of special provisions, maps, passports, codebooks, visas, clothes, tools and blank checks. Seeing this, which I was taught not to see, made

me revise my view of myself, and also of the United States' claim to be a democracy in which merit is rewarded and life outcomes are directly related to deservedness.[5]

Peggy's list is not intended to be a universal list of white privilege. I would like to suggest, as Peggy does in her article, that you make your own list. Just take a pad of paper and a pen and write down what you notice as you go through your day, as you consider your interactions and perceptions. This is one way to make the invisible more apparent.

Do the Line Dance of Opportunity

Occasionally, when I talk about unearned privilege in a workshop, some white men protest on the grounds that they worked hard for what they have. As I mentioned, what the white privilege concept asks you to do is to acknowledge that there is a larger societal context in which you were able to make your diligence and smarts work for you. It is asking people to be courageous enough to consider where they think they would have landed in life if they had identities from the groups that were historically labeled and treated as inferior. What can you count as merit only and what is a function of the circumstances in which you were born that you had little control over?

Sometimes, it is hard to intellectualize these difficult questions, so when we have the right space and group composition, I ask people to take the Opportunity Walk with their colleagues. Sometimes it's called the Privilege Walk. It is quite a compelling exercise. Every time I include it in a workshop, participants tell me that the exercise opened their eyes. People who were in workshops that I conducted fifteen years ago see me at conferences and tell me that the exercise changed their lives. I want to describe the Walk and share some of the questions. However, I always tell my clients not to attempt this exercise without a trained facilitator. Many emotions come up during the exercise; and unless it is debriefed correctly, people may go away without being able to process their feelings constructively.

To start the exercise, I ask everyone in the group to create a line, shoulder to shoulder, going horizontally across the room. It is important that people create an even line and everyone is starting at the same place. I tell them that I will be asking them to take steps forward and backward according to various questions, so we practice taking steps. Then I begin asking a series of questions. I also make it optional to not move. So, if for any reason someone feels uncomfortable answering a question, he can remain still. One other direction is that I will be using the term "major identity marker" (MIM), which refers to the perceptions other people have of your race, ethnicity, gender, religion, sexual orientation, and visible abilities. Here are some of the questions so that you can imagine how you might be moving if you were participating in this exercise:

⇨   If your ancestors were forced against their will to come to the United States, step *back*.

⇨   If most of your family members worked in careers requiring college education, step *forward*.

⇨   If you were ever called hurtful names because of your MIMs, step *back*.

⇨   If there were more than fifty books in your house when you grew up, step *forward*.

➡ If you were often embarrassed or ashamed of your material possessions, step *back.*

➡ If you attended a private school or summer camp, step *forward.*

➡ If you ever tried to change your appearance, behavior, or speech to avoid being judged on the basis of your MIMs, step *back.*

➡ If your parents told you that you were beautiful, smart, and capable, step *forward.*

➡ If your family owned its own house, step *forward.*

➡ If you ever were offered a good job because of your association with a friend, mentor, or family member, step *forward.*

➡ If you believe that an employer turned you down because of your MIMs, step *back.*

➡ If your parents did not grow up in the United States, step *back.*

➡ If your primary ethnic identity is American, step *forward.*

➡ If your racial or ethnic group constitutes a majority of your organization's leaders, step *forward.*

➡ If the head of your organization is of your same race/ethnicity, step *forward.*

➡ If you've been mentored at work by someone of your own race/ethnicity, step *forward.*

➡ If most of your clients (customers) are of your same race/ethnicity, step *forward.*

➡ If you frequently are the only person of your race/ethnicity at work meetings, step *back.*

At the end of the exercise, I stand in front of the group and hold up a fresh $20 bill. I tell them that it represents a valuable opportunity and that anyone in the room can have it if they are the first to get to me after I count to three. I count to three and yell, "Go!" Sometimes people run forward, but most often people stay where they are. Despite the fact that we all started off the exercise in the same place, at this point there are some people right in front of my face because of the steps that they have taken forward, and some are way in the back. No matter how fast or capable those in the back rows are, they will not be able to get to the $20 bill before those in the front. The message is clear: The

I don't care how fast Doris is, she's NEVER going to get that $20 before me!

life circumstances in which we find ourselves, the ones we did not choose or make happen, position some of us better than others to take advantage of opportunity.

As you can imagine, people have many reactions to the Walk. Obviously, you can quibble with the questions or whether a particular question should entitle a person to move backward or forward. However, the visual of the group starting all together in the same place and then breaking apart as the questions sort them is profound. The whole group is moving constantly, but each person is taking his own journey through time as he considers the questions, what they mean for him in his own life, and how he compares to others.

People are more than they appear, as we learned in Chapter Seven when we were trying on the concept of a diversity lens. Of course, you cannot predict ahead of time where any one individual may end up in the exercise. However, of the many times that I have done this exercise, without fail a person of color has been the farthest in the back; and it is always a white person, most often a male (especially given the questions that are targeted at the workplace), who is the closest to the front. People in back rows tell me they feel validated or recognized for the struggles they have endured and overcome to be there in the same place in reality with others who have had greater opportunities and fewer obstacles. Some participants, especially those in front of the line, talk about feeling shame and guilt as they move forward. They sometimes admit they began to shorten their steps as they got too far in front.

I have to remind them that all these questions are about things that they had no control over. They are not responsible for where they end up in the line. Others share that they felt solidarity with certain people who were stepping back with them, but then they would lose that sense when suddenly they found themselves moving up or falling farther behind the pack. Also, when I have done the exercise among people who know each other, sometimes people are surprised to learn that they have very different life experiences than their peers. They remark that everyone may be working in the same workplace, but the exercise made them realize that people have taken very different paths to get there. Where do you think you would be in the line compared to people in your organization?

Privilege Isn't Just a White Thing

Earlier in this chapter, I explained that I found the subject of unearned privilege thought-provoking and enlightening. You may have assumed that I was talking about it from the point of view of a black person examining the racial hierarchy in our society. However, the most fascinating discovery I have made by exploring white privilege is my own unearned privileges, not with regard to race, of course, but in connection with several of my other identities.

I was a participant in a four-day workshop with Visions, Inc., when we were asked to find ourselves on the chart on the next page.[7] As you can see, the chart itself is not rocket science. It is a table that captures the historical classifications of groups—the "in" and "out," "more privileged" and "less privileged," and the "one-up" and "one-down" groups in our society. Most people from the United States who are my age or older could piece together the right-hand column if you asked them to list the groups that were designated as inferior and were discriminated against in the history of our country. In many cases, they are "protected groups" under our federal and state laws.[8] The third column, labeled "Historically Advantaged (Nontarget Groups)," is just the corollary to the column

Types of Oppression	Variable	Historically Advantaged (Nontarget Groups)	Historically Disadvantaged (Target groups)
Racism	Race/ethnicity/ color	White	People of color (African, Asian, Native, Latino/a Americans)
Sexism	Gender	Men	Women Transgendered
Classism	Socioeconomic class	Middle, upper class	Poor, working class
Elitism	Education level Place in hierarchy	Formally educated Managers, exempt, faculty	Informally educated Clerical, nonexempt, students
Religious oppression Anti-Semitism	Religion	Christians, Protestants	Muslims/Catholics and others Jews
Militarism	Military status	WWI, WWII, Korean, Gulf War veterans	Vietnam veterans
Ageism Adultism	Age	Young adults Adults	Elders (40+ by law) Children, youth
Heterosexism	Sexual orientation	Heterosexuals	Gay, lesbian, bisexual, transgender
Ableism	Physical or mental ability	Temporarily able-bodied	Physically or mentally challenged
Xenophobia	Immigrant status	U.S. born	Immigrant
Linguistic Oppression	Language	English	English as a second language Non-English

on the right. The "Variable" column makes clear the factor on which the distinction of the nontarget and target groups has been made.

The column on the far left side is hugely important because it adds the concept of power to the idea of prejudice. Prejudice isn't necessarily about power. A person in the target group can be prejudiced or biased against someone on the nontarget side of the chart just as easily as the converse. However, a prejudice becomes an "ism" because the nontarget group occupies a place in social structure that gives group members the power to reinforce or ignore prejudice against the target group, or the condition of inequality that persists for the target group. This is the distinction that I make between racism and racial prejudice or bias.

Just to be clear and recap: No one is accusing anyone of oppression here. Of course individual personal racism exists, but this idea of unearned privilege suggests—the chart represents—a system that was created long ago and is undetectable as an actual structure because it has existed for centuries and is so pervasive. It needs no action to sustain itself on the part of those who are now in the nontarget group. We will talk more about this in the last chapter, but as a white individual, you don't have to commit any act of racial bias in order for racism to persist and for you to continue to enjoy the unearned benefits that come along with your nontarget status.

So why was this chart so revelatory to me as a black woman who has known about and experienced racism, sexism, and elitism since I was a young girl? Up until the time I saw this chart, I could wax eloquent about the trials, tribulations, and oppression of blacks, women, and those who are poor and working-class (three of my target group identities) in the United States. However, what I realized when I was instructed to do so is that I had several group identities on the nontarget (historically advantaged) side as well. That would mean that I was experiencing unearned advantages just like my white, male, and wealthy brethren. Who knew? My advantages as a heterosexual, Protestant, able-bodied, well-educated, U.S.-born adult were just as invisible to me as whiteness was to my white colleagues, clients, and friends. It was a humbling epiphany, and it also gave me great insight and empathy for people in the three nontarget groups that were situated directly across from my target identities.

In fact, every time I think, "Why don't white people know more or see this or that when it comes to people of color?," I try to remember to ask myself, "Why don't you, as a Protestant, know more about other people's religions?" Or when I find myself judging the comments from a white man that reveal his unconscious, but nevertheless offensive, assumptions about the capabilities of a black woman, I recall insensitivities I have shown as an able-bodied person toward someone with a disability. When I wonder why some white people of means can't see how much respect they receive simply because of their group status, I recall how I first became aware of how much deference and freedom I received from people simply because I belonged to the heterosexual group—not because they knew me, but because I am in the accepted norm.

Now that I know I have privileges, I am trying to work on my privilege identities, searching for what I don't know about groups and using many of the tips and steps that I have suggested in previous chapters. I am learning to own and acknowledge my privilege identity as I have suggested white people do with regard to whiteness. I have begun to say, "as a heterosexual" or "as a U.S.-born citizen" so that I am not proceeding as the unspoken norm and I am acknowledging that my views are shaped by the lens of my dominant group identity. I am examining my own biases and seeking more contact with those "across the aisle." I am learning more about what their experiences have been and trying to keep my eyes open to how my identities afforded me certain opportunities. I have started to ask myself, "What can you do about the fact that you landed in this group? How do you change this chart?"

In fact, I started noticing all sorts of things once my eyes had been opened. Sometimes I would be at a party with friends, at a cocktail reception in a professional setting, at the grocery store, or on an airplane. During a conversation in one of these places with a white person that I didn't know, the subject of what I do for a living would come up. Somewhere in the explanation, I would reveal that I used to practice law; then the white person would ask where I went to school. When I would say "Harvard," in almost every situation, I could feel a shift in the interaction; a warming; a smile; and then an effusive acceptance, embrace, energy, and increased chatter:

"Oh wow, really, Harvard? That's great."

"I went to Harvard," or "My son [my father, my niece, my neighbor's son] went to Harvard."

"Did you like it?"

"What year did you go?"

"Do you know ___?"

I was amazed when it happened so often. It was like I became one of them. Before, something created a distance—maybe it was my race—but my Harvard identity made me okay: acceptable, knowable, and special. When I was trying to find work outside the law field and people heard that I went to Barnard and/or Harvard, they seemed ready to give me whatever I wanted without knowing much about me at all. I have often joked with my friends, noting that once people know I attended Harvard, their attitudes change so much that it is like they are saying, "Oh, you went to Harvard—do you want to hold my baby?" I had become immediately trustworthy in ways that had nothing to with intellect. For many well-educated white people, my elite school identity trumps my black and working-class origin identities.[9]

Several years ago, I was in the market for a house, and I had arranged to meet a seller agent at a property that I was interested in seeing. It was a Saturday and so I was dressed nicely, but casually. I don't know if I noticed this before or after my exchange with the realtor, but at some point when I was getting dressed for my appointment, I dug in my closet and found the one baseball hat that I have (I usually don't wear hats) and put it on my head; it was my Harvard Law School (HLS) hat. I realized that somewhere in my unconscious mind, I was aware of the advantage I enjoyed as an HLS grad and the disadvantage I might encounter as a black person trying to buy a house in an affluent white community. I was hoping my hat would hide the color of my face—cancel out the part of my identity that makes some white people worry that my living in their neighborhood will bring down their property values or be disruptive in some way. With my hat, I was subtly saying, "Don't assume what I can afford and what I can't." I guess I was implying, "I'm not one of those blacks you have to worry about." Eeek!

I guess that I have admitted here what is true for many of us wrestling with the issue of privilege; it's hard not to use it to your own advantage even when you know it is unfair and contrived.

I imagine that the more unearned privileges one has, the harder it is to see them. I realized that the reason I can see what I am doing with my Harvard hat and why it bothers me is because I grew up on the other side of the chart as a working-class person. I know what it feels like to be thought of as "less than" by people who don't know you, just because you don't have the best car, live in a middle-class neighborhood, have parents who finished college or went to select schools, backpacked in Europe, or wear expensive clothes and jewelry. Now I have moved across the chart into the group that the system favors. I am experiencing the flip side of elitism. If I thought the underserved treatment that I experienced when I was on the target group side was wrong, don't I have to reject the unmerited favor that I now receive on the nontarget side?

> I imagine that the more unearned privileges one has, the harder it is to see them.

To be clear, I am not saying that having money and a good education is bad. Something is very right in this country when a skinny, pigeon-toed, little black girl from Poplar Grove Street in West Baltimore can make it to Harvard and create a good living for herself. What I am refusing is the system of thinking that deems me "better than" and superior to other human beings and treats me with more respect because of it. In Chapter Thirteen, the last chapter, we will talk about how we can use the privileges we do have to help break down this system and create fairness for black people and, by extension, other groups that have landed on the target side of the chart. For me, it means finding ways to remove the obstacles that prevent so many poor and working-class black girls who were like me from reaching their true potential.

Realize How Group Identities Interrelate and Compound Each Other

Most people have multiple identities, as I do, that have them crisscrossing the chart from advantaged to disadvantaged. The categories all seem separate when placed in a two-dimensional layout, but, in real life with actual people, they link up to compound both privileged and disadvantaged. There is no hierarchy of oppression; all forms of oppression are unacceptable. It is, nevertheless, worth looking at how multiple identities compound and offset others so that you can examine how you experience advantages and disadvantages and be open to learning the experience of others. Being a black woman lawyer is a different life experience than being a white woman lawyer; women may share the experience of gender bias, but the issues black women encounter because of their race may be invisible to their white female colleagues. A Jewish man may suffer a lack of privilege based on his religious identity but experience great opportunity due to the fact that he is also white and male. Many lesbians talk about the issue of male superiority in the gay community, and certainly women of color have had to suffer through the sexism that has existed in many male-dominated black organizations.

Sometimes, white men will say, "Well, I am white and male, but I had a hard life, too, and I don't feel privileged at all." First, I remind them that the chart is a "group" analysis. The chart speaks to the statistical odds for success by groups (success as defined by standard indicators: employment, health, housing, etc.) over time. So, for members of historically advantaged groups, the odds for success are greater by virtue of being born into and/or entering such a group; and for members of historically disadvantaged groups, the odds for success are less. However, this does not mean that all individuals in a particular group will have better or worse life outcomes based on their group designation.

Usually after I learn more from many of the white men who have this reaction, I discover that they grew up poor, their parents were immigrants, they had a learning disability, or they grew up with some group identity that doesn't appear on this chart; and they were treated as "less than" by the mainstream of our society (e.g., identities around size, appearance, or certain types of Christian religions). They are not really arguing with the categories or the concept of oppression or mistreatment because of group status; they are just not seeing how their multiple identities interrelate and influence life outcomes. They have advantages as white men, but they also may have disadvantages due to some other identity, such as socioeconomic class.

In this country, we don't give much attention to socioeconomic class because we are a country in which the circumstance of our birth is not supposed to be determinative of our life outcomes. This is the land of opportunity, and for many people that has been true; but depending on your other identities, the climb out of poverty can be easier or harder. All white people are not the same. Being a poor white man is very different from being a wealthy white man. However, when you add the overlay of race to socioeconomic class, you will be surprised how race continues to define one's opportunities. Studies suggest that the statistical odds for life success are less for a poor black man than for a poor white man.[10] Chip Smith argues in his book *The Cost of Privilege: Taking on the System of White Supremacy and Racism* that white privilege still exists even when you compare black and white working-class people. In the appendix of this book, I have included Mr. Smith's eye-opening table, entitled "Lifetime Benefits of being a working-class white person in the Early 21st Century," which includes data comparing the life experiences of working-class white people with those of black and Latino people, and, in some instances, Asian/Pacific Islander and native people.[11]

Many of my white clients and friends are very aware of and detest the active forms of racism that Peggy McIntosh describes as "the individual acts of meanness" in her article "White Privilege: Unpacking the Invisible Knapsack."[12] The chart on page 115 makes sense to them as a historical picture of discrimination in our country and the bigoted behavior of some people in the country still. However, they have a harder time grasping the column on the left that names the oppression. In other words, they see the prejudice, but they don't see the "isms." To see the "isms" is to understand that entrenched in the diagram is a dynamic system that operates to reinforce the power and hierarchy of the traditionally advantaged groups. This is the idea of systemic or structural racism. Meanness is not needed to perpetuate the system, only inaction.

Seeing racism as a system and noticing your unearned advantage as a white person in that system are huge steps. It is not necessarily a pleasant discovery, but, like implicit bias, knowing means you are now in the position to do something about it. For one, you will be able to notice and better appreciate the unearned disadvantages that many black people are facing in our workplaces and society. However, the biggest benefit of being able to see unearned advantage is that you can use it on behalf of those in the target group to improve the society as a whole.

Endnotes

1. B. Switzer, The Quotations Page, http://www.quotationspage.com/quote/23536.html (accessed Feb. 8, 2011).

2. List of Women in the 112th Congress 2011–2013, http://womenincongress.house.gov/historical-data/representatives-senators-by-congress.html?congress=112 (accessed Apr. 18, 2011).

3. Peggy McIntosh, White Privilege and Male Privilege: A Personal Account of Coming to See Correspondences Through Work in Women's Studies (Wellesley Ctr. for Research on Women 1988).

4. *Id.* at 10–11.

5. *Id.* at 10.

6. Fig. 1. This chart is included in four-day multiculturalism workshop, "Changing Racism and Other 'Isms.'" Reprinted with permission from Visions, Inc., Boston, MA, Oakland/Pasadena, CA. (2000).

7. The following characteristics are "protected classes" that have developed through the Civil Rights Act of 1964, the Age Discrimination in Employment Act of 1967, the Equal Pay Act of 1963, the Americans with Disabilities Act of 1974, the Vietnam Era Veterans Readjustment Assistance Act of 1974, and the Genetic Information Nondiscrimination Act; race, color, religion, national origin, age (40 and over), sex, familial status, sexual orientation, gender identity, disability status, veteran status, and genetic information.

8. Despite my experience, many blacks and other people of color with educational backgrounds similar to mine have told me that white people ask them about their GPA and/or LSAT scores. In fact, recently, a young woman of color told me that one of her white peers at work asked her about her law school grades and LSAT scores. She was convinced that he was upset that he had not attended a first-tier law school as she had and that behind his question was the presumption that she didn't deserve to be there.

9. In 2008, 37.5% of all black households (total of 14,595) made $25,000 a year or less compared with 22.9% of white households (total of 95,297) which made $25,000 a year or less. U.S. Census Bureau, *Money Income of Households—Percent Distribution by Income Level, Race, and Hispanic Origin, in Constant (2008) Dollars, 1980–2008*, STATISTICAL ABSTRACT OF THE UNITED STATES: 2011, accessed January 28, 2011, http://www.census.gov/compendia/statab/2011/tables/11s0689.pdf.

10. C. Smith & M. Goff, THE COST OF PRIVILEGE: TAKING ON THE SYSTEM OF WHITE SUPREMACY AND RACISM (Camino Press 2007), 236.

11. *Supra*, note 3.

12. P. McIntosh, WHITE PRIVILEGE: UNPACKING THE INVISIBLE KNAPSACK (Wellesley Center for Research on Women 1988).

Five Old Dance Moves That White People Do: Updating Your Dance Moves to Support the Success of Black People at Work

Dance Lessons for this Chapter:

☑ Small ways that implicit biases can create a sense of exclusion for black people in their daily lives at work

☑ Five implicitly biased behaviors and how they impede black people's success at work

☑ New dance steps that can contribute to the success of black people and the power of inclusion in your organization

Now that we know what privilege is, how do we stay aware of it and detect when we are receiving benefits that we didn't necessarily earn, while others are not being given the consideration and opportunities they deserve? In particular, how can we be effective dance partners at work where people's careers are at stake? In the next two chapters, we are going to examine closely how bias and privilege and the behaviors that stem from them can harm not only those in the target groups but also the entire work team or organization.

A lack of awareness or denial about bias and privilege, for example, will set up a white manager to make inaccurate assessments and poor predictions about the interests, concerns, abilities, and performance of a black supervisee. Remember my experiences with the female pilot as the flight got turbulent and with the Indian doctor when my child was sick? As humans, we are programmed to make quick decisions, especially when things get stressful, for our own survival. Therefore, it is in the most important circumstances that we are likely to lean into our biases. For this reason, we really have to watch out for our biases at work, where most of us are under great pressure to perform every day. In this context, quick and unfair judgments are made about all individuals—not only black people—all the time. If we know this, we can be on the lookout for our automatic response mode that seems to be programmed for stereotyping and prejudice.

In institutions where most of the decision makers and supervisors are white, if those in charge don't pay attention to and check their implicit biases, they will miss the chance to retain and advance talented people of color and the opportunity to enhance the productivity of their multiracial teams and organizations. They also run the risk of depriving themselves of the prospect of developing authentic personal relationships and powerful alliances across race and the skills to operate cross-culturally.

It is also important to remember that biases run in favor of as well as against people. Sometimes the problem is not that some white people have biases against black people; it is that they unknowingly favor white people. They don't notice that they have a positive bias toward whites with whom they agree about so many principles and rules regarding appropriate performance, behavior, and ways of being. So when judging who the best person is for the opportunity, they unconsciously prefer candidates with whom they feel a greater level of comfort, a sense of familiarity. They excuse mistakes, inappropriate behavior, or inconsistent performance in the favored person that they would not in a person outside their favored group. They may see promise and potential in the person they favor, but they will demand evidence of demonstrated competence in another person. Favoritism, as we discuss later in this chapter, is often harder to detect in ourselves than bias against groups and individuals.

This issue of implicit bias, whether it be preference for white people or against black people, has major consequences. As you will see below, the professional livelihoods, reputations, financial and psychological well-being, and futures of individuals and institutions are at stake. In the workplace, white folks who seem to be operating on autopilot often negatively affect black people and other people of color.

Stories that People of Color Tell

I have done many interviews and focus groups with people of color in predominately white organizations, and the stories they tell range from disappointing to devastating. There are the situations, for example, where a black lawyer has been working with a client for six months; and when the client meets the attorney in person for the first time, the client's jaw drops open. She shakes the black attorney's hand, looking a little confused, and mutters something like, "You don't look anything like I imagined." When some white people hear a story like this, they hasten to tell me that this kind of thing has happened to them with another white person: when they finally met the other white person, the person didn't look anything like they had imagined. Of course they are right; we all make up ideas about what folks look like before we meet them. However, I encourage them to go a step further in the analysis and ask themselves whether their jaws flopped open when they saw this white person.

I also suggest they consider the impact of the same kind of exaggerated surprise from the white client when it is experienced by a black attorney as compared to a white attorney. The white attorney doesn't have to worry about whether the client is surprised because she expected the attorney with whom she had been conversing for months to be a white person or whether her surprise reflects some kind of implicit bias against black people. Maybe there is no bias at all, and the client is reacting to the fact that the black attorney is taller or better-looking than she imagined. Even then, there is this extra mental calculus that the black person has to go through to sort out the meaning of and appropriate reaction to the situation—a computation that a white attorney in the exact same scenario does not have to do. **This is the difficult work of inclusion—not being afraid of seeing bias as a possibility and remembering to**

weigh the differential impact on various groups even when the situation is the same. We have to be willing to pose these questions and go deeper into the analysis if we are going to unearth and counter our implicit bias.

When the black person asks the gawking client what she expected, usually the client can't explain. She might say something like, "Just different," or the more revealing and honest, "You look different than you sound on the phone." The black person would love to say, "How did I sound?" but they don't go there, to save the white person the embarrassment and the possible negative repercussions if the client can't get beyond the confrontation. What black people have learned from repeated experiences is that people think they can detect the voice pattern of a black person on the telephone, and some white people are not expecting black people to be as articulate as the white people with whom they have worked. Their lens is limited because they usually have not had much exposure to professional black people.

I learned about this expectation as a little girl when I would overhear my mom place an order from the Sears & Roebuck (as it was called then) catalogue by telephone. I called it her Sears voice. She would ask for the linen department in a tone of voice that was so light and proper it was almost British. It was as if she were playing a role. She knew, and I learned, that if she "sounded white" she would get better service. As soon as she hung up, she would go back to her regular voice that had a heavier, more southern flavor to it. There was nothing wrong with her normal voice or diction, but she had learned to adapt who she was to counteract the negative biases of others. The stories I hear in focus groups suggest that blacks still have to deal with these biases, no matter who they are or how they try to adapt.

The more distressing stories have to do with situations where black people at work are excluded or ignored by peers, underestimated, and overlooked for opportunities by managers, and subjected to shocking comments when they least expect them. One black attorney told me that he was part of a team arguing a case in a predominately black city. All his peers were white, and they had spent weeks together in this city working day and night. One night, after a tough day in court where the defense had gained the upper hand, all the associates from his firm were hanging around discussing the case. One of the white associates said about the black lead attorney for the defense, "You know they only got him because the jury is black; think of all the excellent attorneys they could have gotten to argue this case." The black associate recounted how stunned he was by the comment. He thought the black defense attorney

I told him to forget our strategy and
just play up the *black thing!*

had been brilliant; not to mention, the attorney was well-educated and had an amazing win record. Apparently, all this white attorney could see was the opposing counsel's race; and for this white associate, "black" did not translate into "excellent." "Excellent" was white. The black associate explained to me how he felt betrayed, excluded, alone, and suddenly uncertain of his standing on the team. His colleague's comment made him wonder, "What must they think of me? Why do they think I'm on this case?" You can imagine the impact of the situation on the attorney's work: he either feels less motivated to work, or more motivated to prove he belongs on the team, or some debilitating combination of the two.

Someone might argue that this type of statement is not unconscious, that it is blatant racism. What is blatant to some is unconscious to others. If you told this person that her statement was racist, I am sure she would resist that label and attempt to explain what she meant. I feel fairly certain as well that she would have no idea of the impact of her statement on the black person or the team. When she spoke, she was not trying to sever the sense of cohesion on the team or the lone black associate's feeling of connectedness and sameness with his teammates. She thought she was stating an obvious truth. It is just that embedded in her truth is unacknowledged racism—a belief that white people are superior to black people. If anyone on the team noticed the racism, they didn't mention it. The black associate told me that no one spoke up, so it appeared that others also agreed. In Chapter Thirteen, we will review the techniques that you can use to speak up and interrupt bias if you should find yourself in a similar situation.

While comments are hurtful and cause black people to feel less connected and respected, they are not the biggest issue. The problem that concerns many black people the most in the professional setting is the unconscious, unintentional, and implicit biases that hinder their opportunities for meaningful, challenging assignments and retard their advancement in their organizations and careers. Some years ago, Professor David Thomas of Harvard Business School conducted a longitudinal study tracking the careers of highly successful black executives.[1] One of his findings was that these black executives, who were ultimately successful, had a very different career trajectory than their white counterparts. Their white peers moved up in the institution at a steady pace, while the black executives would advance and plateau for several years and then advance and taper off again until they eventually reached the top levels. The research showed that it took blacks longer to achieve the same levels because they had to prove themselves over and over again to their white managers. They had to find managers who were comfortable enough with them and thought they were capable of taking on more difficult substantive and supervisory managerial responsibilities, so they would be promoted.

I talked to Dr. Thomas about his research and all the work he has done to educate business students and leaders about the barriers to and solutions for enhancing the inclusion of people of color in corporations. When I asked him what, based on his experience, white managers need to do to create real advancement opportunities for black people in their organizations, he responded,

> The first thing is to acknowledge that without monitoring and focus, people of color will often be overlooked or undervalued with regard to their talent. If they don't accept that as a fact, they will actually not be able move the needle because they won't intervene. For example, I know of a CEO who decided that he was going to put a black woman on his executive team. He took the view that, "If I don't focus on this and recognize that there are some biases with the way we look for people, we just won't get it done."[2]

Five Old Dance Moves that You Don't Want to Do

According to Dr. Thomas, accepting bias as a fact is key to making progress on race in our work environments. Therefore, I want to share with you five behavioral patterns that are shaped by unconscious racial bias. These behaviors make it difficult for organizations to recruit and retain the best and brightest African American candidates. They also prevent some well-intentioned white people from being able to create the fairness and inclusion they want in their workplace. Some of these patterns are experienced by other racial minorities and traditionally excluded groups as well.

Take a look at these dance moves. The goal of defining this set of old dance moves is simple. It clarifies, or makes more visible, the unconscious ways of acting that limit the ability to recruit and retain blacks and other people of color. Of course, not every black person has the experiences listed below, but I have seen these behaviors frequently enough and in so many different institutions, that I want to bring them to your attention. These may be difficult to hear about or to see in yourself. Or they may not be your patterns, but you have probably seen them in others. This is not about blame. I am trying to make these unconscious ways of acting more visible, in the way that the IAT does. I have also included steps that you can take to avoid, minimize, and/or correct for these patterns. With increased awareness and new ways of working with black people and others, we can have the organizations and the relationships we want and can benefit us all.

The goal of defining this set of old dance moves is simple. It clarifies, or makes more visible, the unconscious ways of acting that limit the ability to recruit and retain blacks and other people of color.

Old Dance Move No. 1: The One-Mistake Rule

Many blacks working in majority white organizations have the experience of seeing their mistakes magnified and their accomplishments minimized.

Black people seem to come into a job, a department, or a project having to prove that they belong there, while most white people are presumed to be intelligent and capable from the beginning—they would have to prove they don't belong there.

The most difficult stereotype that black people have to try to overcome, especially at work, is that they are not smart or not as bright as everyone else. This is a significant hurdle for black people that some other historically excluded groups do not have to face. Black people seem to come into a job, a department, or a project having to prove that they belong there, in contrast most white people are presumed to be intelligent and capable from the beginning—they would have to prove they don't belong there.

So when a black person misspells one word, misses a single deadline, or analyzes a solitary issue incorrectly, the presumption is that he can't write or isn't intelligent enough. If he upsets an individual manager, the black person is not responsible or has bad judgment. The one mistake is not just one incident; it becomes proof of the assumption of inferiority that some white people are holding quite unconsciously. By contrast, often the same type of error made by a white person is considered one mistake, or even an aberration. Sometimes when a black person does well, some white people regard the accomplishment as an anomaly, or, as I mentioned earlier, the success is minimized instead of using it to counter the negative stereotype. The unrealized negative bias about black people's capabilities means that other white people seem to react with surprise when a black person is bright, speaks well, or writes persuasively. Once these stereotypical judgments are made about black individuals (sometimes without being spoken), it is almost impossible for them to be successful. Their work dries up, they get staffed on less significant projects, their reputations are diminished, they feel demoralized—and it is a downward spiral from there.

The negative stereotype about the intellectual capacity of blacks has persisted despite the many examples to the contrary. Worst of all, now diversity efforts have been equated with affirmative action, which many people have defined as hiring and promoting unqualified people.[3] This confusion makes all black people suspect, no matter where they have been educated and how they have performed in the past. Thus, diversity—the focus on hiring black people into an organization for the sake of numbers—brings us up short. Diversity produces a revolving door of black people coming and going because the environments and the individuals in the environments have not changed enough to counter this stereotypical thinking and treatment. *Inclusion is cultivating the type of climate where the success of the talented black people who are hired is expected and supported at all levels of the organization.*

On the opposite page you will see steps you can take to avoid the One-Mistake Rule.

Old Dance Move No. 2: Sloppy Sentimentalism[4]

This old way of working with black people is the opposite of the One-Mistake Rule, but it is just as troubling. Sloppy Sentimentalism happens when a white person finds it hard to give negative feedback to a black supervisee or to hold him accountable for his behavior. It is also demonstrated when the supervisor gives the black person less challenging work assignments or responsibilities even when there is no evidence that the person isn't capable of doing higher-level work.

New Dance Moves to Avoid the One-Mistake Rule

⇨ Ask yourself, "If this person were white, how would I assess this situation? Have I had a similar circumstance with a white person? How did I evaluate him or her?

⇨ Look at the entirety of the person's performance, considering the person's experience level—do you have enough information about his or her work? Are you being too hasty?

⇨ Consider your work experience; what mistakes did you make? How were your mistakes regarded? Were those assessments fair?

⇨ Evaluate how you and others might have affected the person's performance. Were you clear with your direction and expectations? Did you make assumptions about what the supervisee knew? Were you direct? You may be attributing the problem solely to that person when there are other contributing factors, including the work and responsibility of other individuals. This is also known as attribution bias.

⇨ Encourage questions. Black people know the stereotype that haunts them. Remember "stereotype threat," which we talked about in Chapter Four? They often do not ask questions about assignments because they don't want to run the risk of saying something that may confirm the negative perception in their supervisor's mind. Of course, in many instances, this concern prevents them from getting the information they need to perform successfully. Make sure you encourage questions and offer information and other resources that will support the black person's success.

The white person may believe he is reserving judgment, in a way similar to the concept of color blindness we referenced earlier. He is committed to diversity and wants to see more black people succeeding in the institution. His approach to the black supervisee may maintain diversity for a short while, but this is not inclusion, so it is just a matter of time before that same door of diversity starts revolving. The impact, however, is to set up the black person to fail. Being patient with and supporting an individual's development is a good practice and should happen with everyone. However, when critical feedback and growth opportunities are withheld, a supervisee is put at a disadvantage. She will not develop sufficiently and will have no idea, until it is too late, that she is underperforming.

Dr. Valerie Batts of Visions, Inc., has labeled this behavior, "dysfunctional rescuing"—the help that doesn't help.[4] How does this behavior reveal a negative bias? If a white supervisor is holding the black supervisee to a lesser standard of performance than her white peers, he is treating her as less capable. Perhaps somewhere, deep down in his implicit mind, the white supervisor thinks that if he held her to the same standard, she would not be able to meet his requirements. So sloppy sentimentalism, or "dysfunctional rescuing," is not only helping the black person based on an assumption he or she cannot help themselves, but also behaving in a way that limits the black person's ability to help themselves.

It is also true that some white supervisors are afraid that if they are critical, the black supervisee will assume they are racist. The white supervisor may be telling himself that he is helping the supervisee, but actually he is protecting himself. The other troubling impact of this situation is that when that black person crashes and burns,

some in the company will think (if not say so publicly) that this individual's failure is proof that diversity compromises the enterprise's core value of excellence.

You might be reading this with a person in mind and thinking it is not negative bias and fear that cause you to be less critical of her. Quite the contrary, you see her raw talent and great potential. You believe she could be terrific for your company, and you want to encourage her. She is a little behind her peers with regard to certain skills and there are other aspects of her performance that require some refinement, but you don't want to dampen her energy and enthusiasm or make her self-conscious. If you feel this way, then you must be willing to have a very clear and honest conversation with her and explain the potential you see, as well as the areas that must be strengthened, if she is going to advance in the organization. You must be prepared to support her development and offer constructive advice when needed. If you see commitment on her part to improvement and positive results, you should also be prepared to defend her and intervene on her behalf, if and when necessary, and to create opportunities for others to see her worth. This is what you do when you really believe in a person. This is what several of my white teachers and bosses have done for me. This is how all people succeed. We rarely come in a perfect package. If you are not willing to do these things, the person whom you think has so much to offer will probably never reach her potential. This means both you and she lose, and so does your organization.

On the next page are New Dance Moves to Avoid Sloppy Sentimentalism.

Old Dance Move No. 3: Guilt by Association

This bias is really quite difficult for most people to detect in themselves. It occurs when some white people in majority white institutions have had only a few work experiences with black people, or when they have had no work experiences at all with a black person, but they have noticed several black individuals who have not fared well in their department or organization. As I mentioned at the beginning of the book, sometime when I interview leaders, they will mention their "spectacular failures" with black people in the organization. They have not done an analysis of why this is so; the assumption is that the individuals, not the organization, were at fault. I will talk

---

New Dance Moves to Avoid Sloppy Sentimentalism

⇨ Make your standards and expectations clear; don't expect that these are obvious to everyone.

⇨ Communicate that you have high expectations and you expect them to be met—most people perform up to expectations.

⇨ Do not ignore problems early on; it is harder to correct issues later, and if the person gets too far behind, it will be harder to catch up.

⇨ Give good accounts and challenging assignments first; then if the person doesn't do well, consider less demanding or more developmental work—make sure you are not testing the black person but are assuming success and supporting that success from the beginning.

⇨ Have a regular practice of giving constructive feedback to everyone you supervise—this way if someone accuses you of racism, you can point to your practice of giving feedback to everyone.

⇨ Offer support and encourage questions—as mentioned, sometimes black supervisees worry that they will be perceived as stupid if they ask questions.

⇨ Show interest and concern in the individual's career development—this puts your critical feedback in context: you care and want them to succeed. (Consider what we learned in Chapter Four about how to offset "stereotype threat.")

⇨ If there are competencies that are underdeveloped, offer options for improving performance or other opportunities that would be more suitable within and outside the organization.

---

more in detail about this assumption in Chapter Twelve, where I offer a framework for bias proofing organizations systems. Many of these leaders also don't seem to notice, acknowledge, or count the "spectacular failures" that they have had with white people in the organization. When people get focused on black people in this way—noticing and clumping each individual black person who doesn't make it into the "black people group," quite unconsciously, they begin to avoid hiring, working with, or promoting black people in general. This, of course, creates an obstacle for every black person who steps through the organization's doors, no matter how talented they are.

Why does this behavior indicate implicit or unconscious bias? When a person cannot be judged on her individual merit because of the presumptions against her racial group, this is the essence of racial bias. If you think about it, we are not concerned about hiring or working with a white individual because another white person or many white individuals have not performed as well as expected. In many professional organizations, when it comes to blacks, we suffer from a small sample size problem. We know from research that we make wrong judgments when there are too few in the sample. When there are only a few of any type of person, each person's action from that group is magnified and extrapolated to the group, especially those actions that reinforce our implicit biases—the one person becomes guilty because of his association as a group member.

This is why many black people cringe every time someone black is interviewed on the news or is responsible for some terrible crime that makes the front page. We worry that the transgressions, behaviors, attitudes, and inarticulate speech of one black per-

---

New Dance Moves to Avoid Guilt by Association

⇨ Consider each person on his or her own merits.

⇨ Avoid comparing the person with another black person whom you knew or with whom you worked. Remind yourself that they are two separate individuals.

⇨ Make sure you have enough information about the individual so you can make a proper assessment, and don't rely on information gleaned from your prior experience with others or your sense of the person, which may be biased.

⇨ Check to see if you are giving the black people you work with less autonomy or leeway and less demanding assignments than you do white team members— your behavior could be based on an experience with someone else.

⇨ If you must compare, recall a positive experience or accomplishment of a black person in your organization or elsewhere, and assume this is possible for all black people in your work environment.

---

son will taint the whole group and that white people, many of whom have very little personal contact with black people, will assume we are all (or mostly) like the individual being interviewed or arrested. I have noticed that I don't recoil as much as I used to when I watch television. I am sure it has to do with the advent of Colin Powell, Condoleezza Rice, and, of course, President and Michelle Obama, the numerous black officials that President Obama has appointed since he took office, and the numerous well-spoken black professional athletes and entertainers. I am hoping that these more visible black images of excellence are beginning to cancel out the negative assumptions about blacks that the IAT suggests most Americans still carry in their heads.[5]

When the presumptions in the work environment are that black people are going to fail, because one or some have not succeeded in the department or organization, black people are fighting an uphill battle to prove that they are not the individuals who came before them. It is a heavy burden, because they also worry that if they make any mistakes or leave the company, they are making it harder for the black person coming behind them. This is an additional weight that they face in work environments that are already stressful and demanding, no matter who you are. It contributes to their fatigue, diminishes their motivation and loyalty, undermines their performance, and hastens their exit.

Instead of leading with a presumption of failure, we have to frame the possibility for the success of black people positively, looking for data that might support the person's value rather than the negative implicit biases swirling around the environment. Above are other dance moves to avoid Guilt by Association.

Old Dance Move No. 4: The Prince Syndrome

This old dance move is characterized by the phrase, "If they could all be like X, we wouldn't have a problem." X is the one black person who has reached the highest levels of the institution. X is a superstar: I mean a Maya Angelou, Oprah Winfrey, Michael Jordan, Denzel Washington, First Lady Michelle Obama, President Barack Obama-type of superstar—the kind of people who broke the mold. A black law partner I know calls this the "Super Negro Syndrome." I refer to it as the Prince Syndrome because a white managing partner was expressing to my colleague and me his frustration with

---

New Dance Moves to Avoid the Prince Syndrome

⇨ If you have a black superstar in your organization, appreciate just how amazing he or she is.

⇨ Ask yourself if you are requiring more from a black person than you are of other white individuals whom you have hired or promoted. Compare with the average person who is successful in your organization, not the one or two superstars, black or white.

⇨ Have an articulated set of competencies for hiring and promotion, including for promotion to the highest position in the organization; be rigorous and consistent with the application of this criteria; be willing to examine and revise competencies.

⇨ Apply these criteria fairly: if a black person meets the criteria, don't ask for more.

⇨ When thinking about promotions, consider the potential and promise of black individuals in the same way you would with white candidates, especially if they have a great performance record in the positions in which they have been.

---

the firm's failure to make more black partners. He said earnestly, "We have X (black partner); if everyone could be like X, we wouldn't have this problem. X is a prince." My colleague, without skipping a beat, responded, "Are all your white partners princes?"

Why is this unintentional bias? What the managing partner could not see was that there were white partners in his firm who had been able to progress by being capable and good, but who were not necessarily superstars. For those who are stars now, they were not always stars. Someone saw their potential and invested in them. Why is the standard higher for black people? As long as he keeps looking for the superstar black partner X, it will take him a long time to make a difference in the complexion of his partnership. That is the nature of superstars. There are only a few of them.

Believe me, I understand the attraction. The black superstars are usually quite intelligent. More than smart, they are charismatic, able to get along with everyone, industrious, even-tempered, and able to put white people at ease. In my work, this double standard also affects women, especially when it comes to advancement. There are always one or two women who get pointed out as the ideal, and decision makers get stuck looking for that same woman over and over again. Their group of male executives consists of a wide variety of men, but the band of women who are successful in the institutions is quite narrow. As you can imagine, to succeed as a black woman in these corporate environments is twice as difficult.

I also see the Prince Syndrome in hiring, where the credentials of many of the people of color (multiple degrees from Ivy League schools) accepted into the organization are higher than many of their white peers. It is the negative stereotyping of blacks that causes some people to worry that they are taking a risk when hiring or promoting a black person. Without knowing, they are looking for the black person who will alleviate all their concerns, which are actually based on stereotypes. Even the greatest supporters of diversity, including people of color, fall into this trap of requiring candidates to be more exceptional than their white colleagues. They know they face ignorance, resistance, and doubt from some people in their institutions. They fear if they bring in a new black person or advocate for a black person's advancement and that person is not successful ultimately or leaves, it will negatively impact the chances for success of other people of color in the organization and the diversity effort generally. (They are aware of the Guilt by Association bias.) Instead of operating in this biased way, they might consider growing more diversity in their organization by hiring and promoting capable individuals, not stars, and finding ways to develop and support the success of these individuals. See the new dance moves I recommend for overcoming the Prince Syndrome on the previous page.

Old Dance Move No. 5: In-Group Favoritism

I want to point out one other significant type of unconscious bias about which many of us have to be vigilant. It is called "In-Group Favoritism." As explained in a wonderfully helpful Harvard Business School article entitled, "How (Un)ethical Are You?" it is the bias that favors your group.[6] As I mentioned at the beginning of this chapter, it is not a prejudice *against* any group; it is about favoring and giving opportunity to others who you know, those who are part of your group. Let's face it; we like ourselves and therefore we like people who share our same background, social status, language, culture, personality, religion, club membership, you name it. Furthermore, we trust people who are like us; we think we know them and we want to help them out with opportunities. We don't see anything wrong with that; it's not that we are recommending that someone hire or give a break to a person who's bad or incapable.

While this behavior may seem blameless, in predominately white organizations, it can have a disproportionately negative impact on those who are in the minority group. The authors of the Harvard Business School article mentioned above state,

> When those in the majority or those in power allocate scarce resources (such as jobs, promotions, and mortgages) to people just like them, they effectively discriminate against those who are different from them. Such "in-group favoritism" amounts to giving credit for group membership. Yet while discrimination against those who are different is considered unethical, helping people close to us is often viewed favorably.[8]

So the intent is positive toward the person you like, but the implicit bias can been seen in the impact on those who are not like you.

I will give you an example from my own life that demonstrates the impact of in-group favoritism. I used to think that I was a great interviewer: ethical, fair, and open—until one day, while working as a young lawyer, I was asked to interview a young, black law student from a top-ranked law school for a new associate position. She had received her undergraduate degree from a Seven Sister college and had competed in intercollegiate sports during her time there. I liked her immediately. I found her easy to talk to, interesting, and personable. I glanced at her resume quickly, asked her some rather perfunctory questions, and then I was practically ready to invite her out for a drink! We continued to have a wonderful conversation, and when she left, I quickly and enthusiastically completed her evaluation.

Intellectual ability:	✔ Excellent
Oral communication skills:	✔ Excellent
Interest in the Firm:	✔ Excellent
Leadership skills:	✔ Excellent

Additional comments:
She's terrific! Poised, creative, great sense of humor.
Would be a great addition to the firm.

I had no idea that I was acting in a biased way in favor of her, until after she exited and the next candidate, a young white man, entered my office. His resume indicated he was from an elite law school, had served in the military, and was the captain of the golf team in college. As soon as the interview began, I discovered that the excitement I had just experienced with the black woman was absent. There was no joking. I didn't explore to see if we had common experiences to compare. With the black woman, there were several exchanges along these lines: "Do you know so and so?" and "Oh, I worked there. How did you like ___?" I don't think I asked the second candidate anything about his military service. There may have been a great deal to learn about his motivation, ability to deal with difficult situations, and his leadership skills, but because wasn't really familiar with the military, I didn't ask him about his experience. I tried to focus on other things on the résumé and ask relevant questions, but it was a lackluster interview, to say the least. When it was over, I am sure we were both relieved. I gave him a good evaluation, but his evaluation contained many fewer superlatives in the additional comments section than did the black woman's.

Only when he left, did it dawn on me: I had been unfair to both of these candidates. My biases had totally directed my behavior, and my behavior had influenced the quality of the interview and the candidates' experiences in the interview. I saw the black woman and, without knowing her, loved her. Why did I love her? Hmmm? Is it really that hard to figure out? I love myself. She was a black woman—I am a black woman. She played softball; I was the center for my college basketball team. She attended Wellesley; I went to Barnard. Da-dah! Are you getting the picture? I assessed her based on my own attributes. She showed up looking like me, and I added the rest:

> She is a female athlete; so she must be disciplined. Discipline is
> an important characteristic for a good attorney. She attended an
> all women's college; she must be a feminist. This firm needs more
> feminists. If she had made it this far as a black woman, she must be
> really smart and resilient; she must have worked hard. She deserves
> this opportunity.

On the flip side with the white male candidate, if I uncovered my implicit bias, it sounded a little like this:

> He's one of those golden boys: golf, the military. He's probably formal,
> a conservative. Inflexible and serious and likes to follow the rules.
> Probably bossy, especially with women; doesn't have much use for
> diversity.

If I had asked more probing questions, I might have confirmed my assumptions about the black female candidate; after all, she did have great grades and credentials. It is also possible that I would have discovered that she came from means, had never overcome a single obstacle, was forced to go to her mother's alma mater, and sat on the bench most of her softball career because she regularly failed to show up for practice on time! If I had been a fairer interviewer, the white male candidate may have been my first choice for a drinking buddy, but I don't know that. When I realized how different the two interviews had been, I was feeling really bad until I realized that he was going to see Tom next, the head of the department who was white and male, loved golf, and was partial to men who served in the military. He was part of Tom's group! I realized that he would be just fine. In fact, I was reminded there were many more "Toms" in the firm than there were people like me.

Most fair-minded people know when they are struggling with a candidate and feel uncomfortable, but they don't always notice how easy it is when they are interviewing someone from their group or how they may be favoring them. In-group favoritism is a huge problem for racial inclusion if those doing the hiring, mentoring, and promoting are mostly white. The authors of the *Harvard Business Review* article write,

> In-Group Favoritism is tenacious when membership confers clear advantage, as it does, for instance, among whites and other dominant social groups. . . . Thus for a wide array of managerial tasks—from hiring, firing, and promoting, to contracting services and forming partnerships—qualified minority candidates are subtly and unconsciously discriminated against, sometimes simply because they are in the minority: There are not enough of them to counter the propensity for in-group favoritism in the majority.[9]

Again, this dance move not only undermines an organization's goals for inclusion but also hampers its ability to develop talent and enhance the organization's overall goals. If managers decide to mentor and invest in only particular individuals, to give them certain high-profile tasks, the chances to speak at a meeting, or to attend a conference, they are not utilizing others who may be just as capable and deserving. As individuals are underutilized, they become less capable of performing well on behalf of the organization, or they leave. On the next page are ways to avoid In-Group Favoritism.

The problem with all of the old dance moves—In-Group Favoritism, the One-Mistake Rule, Sloppy Sentimentalism, Guilt by Association, and the Prince Syndrome—is that the underlying motivation for and the impact of these behaviors are hidden to the white dance partner. Often the black person can see them, but if the white person doesn't notice his own biases, it is hard for the black person to overcome them. For sure, there are things that black people can do and have done to increase the likelihood of their success in the workplace. There are also ways, unfortunately, that some black people behave that are complicit with these old dance moves.[10] *However, even if the black person is competent and works hard, he still may not be chosen to lead the department if the white decision maker, based on In-Group Favoritism, decides to choose someone whom he sees as more like himself.*

No matter how smart a person is, she will make a mistake. However, if she is black and her manager is operating unconsciously on the One-Mistake Rule, she is not going to be able to get other projects to develop and advance. Worse yet, if her manager is a Sloppy Sentimentalist, it could be years before she finds out that this mistake is a problem and that she has no chance to advance in her area unless she transfers departments or leaves the company all together. If she leaves or even flounders, some new, unsuspecting black woman whom the organization was thrilled to hire as evidence of its untiring commitment to diversity, may have to contend with the Guilt by Association

---

New Moves to Avoid In-Group Favoritism

⇨ In the case of interviews, ask more job-related questions so that you are inquiring about the person's experiences and capabilities; rely less on your gut—your gut is full of biases.

⇨ If you don't know about entries on the resume, don't ignore those things (associations, articles, group memberships) because they are unfamiliar to you; inquire about them.

⇨ Notice your discomfort and/or ease—these are clues that you may be prone to bias for or against the person.

⇨ The authors of the *Harvard Business Review* article mentioned above suggest:

  • Be aware of your biases for your group and against others.

  • When trying to decide who to choose for an opportunity, always consult the full list of names of possible candidates and choose from that list. Don't use your mental short list; it is already biased.

  • Make it a point to rotate opportunity in a group or team—don't allow the same person to dominate.

  • Stay vigilant.

---

dance. She will be left wondering why some people don't want to work with her or hold her tiniest mistake against her.

One Big Move: Decide to Be Responsible for the Success of a Black Person

We can all try to find ways to counter the biases that we have discussed in this chapter. However, if you are the head of a department, a manager, CEO, chairman of a board, director, managing director, general counsel, or have any other influential role in your organization, you can do even more than counter these biases. You can reverse their impact. You can use your influence to make it possible for a talented black person to advance to the leadership ranks of your organization. Some people refer to it as sponsoring or championing or using one's gravitas to ensure a person's advancement. No matter what you call it, the idea is to put your weight, attention, time, resources, and reputation behind a person to help them navigate to the top. Most people, especially people of color and those from underrepresented groups, who make it to high-ranking positions, have done so with the active support and intervention of someone white above them. Here are some of the things white leaders do when they decide to invest in the career of a black person:

⇨ Help the black person strategize about his career and map out a plan.

⇨ Identify and provide challenging and career-defining assignments and opportunities.

⇨ Provide advice when needed about how to address misperceptions, disappointments, and biases that may be negatively affecting the black person's career.

⇨ Make introductions to others who can help enhance the person's career.

⇨ Ensure that the person is recognized for his contributions and are fairly compensated.

⇨ Give the person opportunities that increase his visibility.

⇨ Develop a personal as well as professional relationship with the person.

⇨ If the person is about to be passed over for a promotion, advocate for the promotion and, if necessary, use the bargaining chips you have to make it happen.

⇨ If the person makes a mistake in an otherwise stellar career, stand up for the person and remind people of the contributions the person has made.

⇨ Look behind practices, policies, and criteria for promotion and advancement to see if they unfairly disadvantage black people in any way; if they do, change them so that the person of color can bring their best to the position and thrive.

These are big moves, but some of you are in the position to make them. I see some white people working consciously in this way, but not enough. If white leaders are not willing to take on this responsibility, the old behaviors will persist, and organizations will fail to capitalize on the talents, perspectives, and networks of the many people they have already hired in the name of diversity. These individuals will continue to leave, exhausted and, in some cases, believing they were not given an equal opportunity to succeed on their own merits. If we are serious about becoming more creative, innovative and global enterprises that are attuned to and able to take advantage of the changing world around us, we have to build inclusive environments where people's contributions are not hindered by bias. What I am talking about is not impossible, once we decide to be intentional.

Endnotes

1. David A. Thomas & John J. Gabarro, BREAKING THROUGH: THE MAKING OF MINORITY EXECUTIVES IN CORPORATE AMERICA (Harvard Business School Press 1999).

2. Interview with Dr. David Thomas, Cambridge, MA, Apr. 13, 2011.

3. Affirmative action was established by President Johnson in 1965 to fight discrimination in employment, education, and business. Even though the Civil Rights laws made discrimination illegal, Affirmative Action was developed to provide opportunities for minorities, initially for federal contractors. Affirmative action was designed to remedy past discrimination based on race, color, or national origin and later gender and to limit existing discrimination. *See* www.naacp.org/ and for affirmative action http://plato.stanford.edu/entries/affirmative-action/and http://en.wikipedia.org/wiki/Affirmative_action (last accessed Apr. 18, 2011).

4. I first became of aware of this term when I was reading about the work of the black psychologist and educator, Kenneth B. Clark, who is most widely known for the black doll test—when presented with the choice of a white doll or black doll, most black girls chose the white doll. K. B. Clark & M. P. Clark, *Racial Identification and Preference in Negro Children.* In T. M. Newcomb & E. L. Hartley, READINGS IN SOCIAL PSYCHOLOGY (Holt, Rinehart & Winston 1947); K. B. Clark, *Effect of Prejudice and Discrimination on Personality Development,* FACT FINDING REPORT MID-CENTURY WHITE HOUSE CONFERENCE ON CHILDREN AND YOUTH, Children's Bureau—Federal Security Agency 1950 (mimeograph). *See also* Kiri Davis. (Director). A Girl Like Me Video (2005) http://www.youtube.com/watch?v=rjy9q8VekmE&feature=related (last accessed Apr. 18, 2011).

5. Valerie Batts, MODERN RACISM: NEW MELODY FOR THE SAME OLD TUNES (Episcopal Divinity School 1998).

6. E. A. Plant, E. A., P. G. Devine, W. T. Cox, C. J. Columb, S. L. Miller, J. Goplen, & B. M. Peruche, *The Obama Effect: Decreasing Implicit Prejudice and Stereotyping,* J. EXP. SOC. PSYCHOLOGY 45 (2009) 961-4; T. Jacobs, On Race, "Obama Effect" Cuts Two Ways, Miller-McCune.com (2009), accessed Feb. 8, 2011, http://www.miller-mccune.com/blogs/news-blog/on-race-obama-effect-cutstwo-ways-3942/; S. Lebrecht, L. Pierce , et al., *Perceptual Other-Race Training Reduces Implicit Racial Bias,* PLoS ONE 4 (2009).

7. M. Banaji, M. Bazerman, & D. Chugh, *How (Un)ethical Are You?" On Point*, Harvard Business Review at 3 (Dec. 1, 2003).

8. *Id.*, 5-6.

9. *Id.*, 6.

10. Dr. Valerie Batts's concept of Modern Bias asserts that there are unconsciously biased behaviors that white people (non-target group) engage in, and there are corresponding behaviors that black people (target group) use to cope with these white behaviors, in order to survive in institutions and a society where they are not in the power position. However, when the coping strategies of black people become habitual—the way they respond at all times to modern biased behavior from whites—these behaviors can be rooted in internalized biases rather than survival. The target group has begun to internalize the negative assumptions about themselves and is acting in a way that assumes that the individuals in the group do not have the power to do anything to change their fate. These reciprocal behaviors are like a dance of sorts—between the non-target and target groups—that never goes anywhere and maintains the status quo. *Supra*, note 5 in this chapter.

12

The Warm-Up Is Over—Now for the Big Dance Move: Biasproofing Your Organization's Systems

Dance Lessons for this Chapter:

☑ How to analyze your work allocation systems and other systems for bias

☑ How neutral systems can have a disproportionately negative impact on black people in your organization

☑ How race and gender can compound barriers to success faced by the general population

☑ Why paying attention to race is not special treatment—it is the only fair thing to do

☑ General and race-conscious solutions to biasproof your systems and remove barriers to the success of black people in your organization

In the previous chapters, we have talked about the important steps that you can take to expand your self-awareness and to appreciate black culture, history, and experiences as well as your own. We've discussed ways to: check and correct for your implicit biases, to explore white and other forms of unearned advantage, to discontinue using the Deadly Habits, and the old dance moves that work against inclusion. We also considered small ways to send messages of respect and inclusion to the black people with whom you interact where you live and work. When white people are proactive in these ways, it can make a difference for their own well-being and personal growth and for the sense of belonging and connection that black people feel in their personal and professional relationships. At work, these actions enhance team production; heighten morale; increase innovation; and allow all people, especially black people, to become part of the mainstream of the enterprise and contribute their best. Although the steps that individuals take are necessary and important, I want to turn our attention now to the big steps that organizations can take to ensure racial inclusion and equal opportunity.

To foster more racially inclusive organizations, as I mentioned in the last chapter, we need more white individuals—particularly those with influence within their institutions—to give more conscious and intentional support to black people and other underrepresented groups. Again, black people are completely capable of doing great work and, of course, they must take a great deal of responsibility for creating their own success, but the most difficult issues black people confront in our society and our institutions are not intentional racial prejudices of individuals or the insensitive and unconscious comments of naïve offenders.

> *The most stubborn impediments to racial equity and fair opportunity are embedded in the way an organization structures work opportunity, decides upon compensation, chooses its leaders, and evaluates and promotes its talent.*

The greatest obstacles for black people to surmount are structural; the different cultural lens (Chapter Seven), the biases of individuals (Chapter Eight), and the old dance moves (Chapter Eleven) are all built into the bones and struts of our society and its institutions. The most stubborn impediments to racial equity and fair opportunity are embedded in the way an organization structures work opportunity, decides upon compensation, chooses its leaders, and evaluates and promotes its talent. All these areas are decided upon by those in charge. For inclusion to grow to include and support people of every background, the architects and builders of major institutions in our society, who are mostly white, have to be willing to examine their systems and structures and the thinking behind them. Many of our organizations still carry systems that were formed based on an exclusivity that favored the dominant groups and purposefully excluded others. *These systems were never designed to include everyone.* So perhaps our thinking has changed, but our ways of doing things don't necessarily reflect that. A true commitment to inclusion will require us to change how we do the things we do: how we hire, compensate, reward, promote, evaluate, distribute opportunities, mentor and communicate.

Biasproof Your Organization's Systems and Practices— You Are Not "Doing Something Special"; You Are Doing Something Equitable

When I first explain to clients how their recruitment, evaluation, work allocation, orientation, compensation, promotion, and other systems may be biased, they find it hard to accept. They insist that they would never discriminate against a black person, a woman, someone who is disabled, or anyone else. They worry that I am accusing them of purposely constructing practices to make it more difficult for black people and other underrepresented groups to succeed. I believe them. I know they are good and kind people who are adverse to racism and any kind of discrimination. I do not believe that they have designed processes to impede the progress of blacks, other people of color, women, and LGBT attorneys, and yet the impact of their systems on these populations is the same as if they had.

I know, however, that if they don't do something to minimize the effect of these systems on these populations, they are never going to have real inclusion. They worry that doing something different for people of color, for example, would be unfair to others, but this is because they fail to appreciate that their present systems are doing something different and unfair to people of color. Making changes to these systems is not "doing something special." It is doing something equitable because you recognize that your systems are operating in a way that is unfair to those who are different.

As we have seen, my clients, despite being willing to expend great resources to recruit and train people of color, seem unable to retain and/ or advance most of them. They often conclude that their failure to retain racial and ethnic diversity is due to individual circumstances and often the person of color is seen as mostly responsible for the problem. They ignore the pattern or the possibility that all these individual failures point to a problem with their systems for which they would need to take responsibility and change. I was working with one white partner on a diversity task force who explained it this way: *"It's like you had a mixed race high school that had been operating for 80 years and it never graduated a black student. At some point you have to ask yourself if there is something wrong with that high school." Much of my work has been convincing clients that it's not their students; there is something wrong with their school.*

> Making changes to these systems is not "doing something special." It is doing something equitable because you recognize that your systems are operating in a way that is unfair to those who are different.

There is another explanation that some firms offer to explain their failure to retain people of color. I call it the "universal hell" rationale or the "I'm not sure this is a race (substitute gender/sexual orientation) problem" defense. The two arguments amount to the same thing. The explanation goes this way: law firms are terrible places to work for everybody. Firms do an awful job of mentoring and developing everyone, and the system is set up to get rid of most folks eventually anyway. It has nothing to do with race. Therefore, the fact that the racial/ethnic mix of the ownership ranks in firms hasn't changed much after all these years is not a race problem.

This is almost like saying, "People of color are better off not working and becoming successful in law firms. In fact, they are the lucky ones." This reasoning seems strangely defeatist coming from individuals who pride themselves on excellence and never meeting a challenge they couldn't overcome. As fair and meritocratic or as equitably terrible as you believe your institution to be, it is imperative that leaders be willing to unpack their systems to determine how they function with regard to the groups of people the organization is trying to include. Without that examination, we will have to keep having the "something special" argument, which is sometimes coupled with the worry about stigmatizing people of color. The revolving door of talent and lack of advancement by people of color is its own stigma. Also, if we are open and honest about the unintentionally unfair barriers the systems have posed, stigma will not be a problem.

So the big step that I am recommending in this chapter is bias proofing our systems. It is a huge step, because it goes to the heart of the enterprise and it involves change. Our organizations will never reflect our deeply held values of fairness and equality or experience the many benefits that inclusion can bring, unless we account and adjust for how the organizations' practices can hinder black people and non-majority groups from getting into the flow of the party, the lifeblood of the business.

Case Study: Law Firm A

To make more concrete what biasproofing entails, I would like us to look at a type of law firm that I have worked with over the years. By using this example, I hope we can examine a particular system within a context, dig into the analysis, and consider solutions that will be helpful to you and your organization. Even though it is based on a law firm structure, many points will be applicable to any professional organization.

Law Firm A is a large (around 750 attorneys), prestigious, very profitable firm with offices all over the country; its largest offices are in big cities on the east and west coasts. It also has offices in Beijing, London, and Munich. It just celebrated its seventy-fifth year and is well known for its excellent lawyers and for hiring the best and brightest students from the country's most elite law schools.

Firm A is fiercely committed to increasing its diversity. It was one of the first firms to sign on to the bar association's statement of commitment to diversity goals in the various cities in which it operates. In past years, it has scored well on the many diversity rankings that grade firms based on the aggregate number of female attorneys, LGBT attorneys, and attorneys of color. The firm has some of the most progressive policies when it comes to flextime, parental leave, antidiscrimination, and same-sex partner benefits. The firm's partners of color have won awards for their leadership roles in legal organizations outside the firm. The firm itself has received various awards for diversity. The Diversity Committee has focused a great deal on recruitment and has been able to increase the percentage of women and people of color in its incoming associate classes. The managing partner is a nice person and believes in diversity. So, according to some measures, Firm A is making progress.

But when we look at the indicia regarding inclusion, there is another story to tell. Although 15% of its partners are women, none of them, not even the senior women, are among the most highly compensated partners in the firm. Partners of color (Asian, black, Hispanic, multiracial, Native American) constitute only 5% of the partnership. However, only one of them is black. In the past, the firm had two other black partners; one is retired now, and the other left several years ago to become the general counsel at one of the firm's smaller corporate clients. Despite all the rankings and awards, there are complaints from female attorneys that culminated in a memo to management from their women's initiatives committee. An admonition from a black general counsel of a large client dissatisfied with the lack of racial diversity on her matters and persistent attrition among the firm's black and female attorneys has caused firm management to launch a comprehensive diversity initiative. The firm, like most firms, doesn't like consultants that much, but, over the years, they have hired various diversity consultants to facilitate awareness trainings and to advise the Diversity Committee about programs and strategies. The chair of the committee decided it was time to reach out for professional help to assist the firm with the comprehensive initiative; they interviewed several diversity consultants, and that's where the VMCG team and I enter.

When we begin our work with Firm A, we are informed that the partners on the Diversity Committee have asked to look at the utilization rates of women and people of color, especially black attorneys, as compared to those of white males within each practice group. The hours of full-time women and attorneys of color are significantly lower than the hours of their white and male counterparts. Not every woman is working fewer hours than all men and not every individual white person has more billable hours than every person of color, but there is a pattern of lower hours for women and people of color in every practice group. A historical analysis suggests this has been true for several years, and it has worsened in the economic downturn.

The work allocation system for its lawyers might be described as a modified free market system. This means that when work comes in from a client, a senior attorney, most likely a partner, goes looking for an associate to do the work. Associates are also looking for work, so they are free to go to senior attorneys and let them know that they are available for assignments and the type of work in which they are interested. There is a work coordinator in each practice group to whom associates go if they cannot find work. The coordinator usually has the less desirable work projects, which, nevertheless, still need to be done. If, for whatever reason, a senior attorney can't find an associate to do her work, the senior attorney can also consult the coordinator. Mostly this type of free market system runs one way—it is designed to give senior attorneys a choice about whom they use to do their work.

Firm A has always had this type of work distribution system and sees it as the best and most efficient way to train its associates and produce timely, quality work for its clients. It is aware that some firms have more centralized assignment systems where all client work that comes in the door goes first to an assigning partner. That partner looks broadly at the pool of associates, their hours, their prior experience, and developmental goals and makes assignments to associates accordingly. However, Firm A believes that its system provides senior attorneys with the flexibility and autonomy they need to satisfy their clients. It also believes that when associates have to go out into the market and find work, this builds entrepreneurial skills, which are the very skills necessary for lawyers to be successful in Firm A's environment.

We continue our work with Firm A, conducting focus groups and interviews with their women and people of color. In these meetings, participants tell us what the statistics have borne out—they are receiving less work and being utilized less frequently than many of their male and white peers. Among the attorneys of color, more black associates report a lack of work for longer periods of time. The associates of color and women associates are very concerned, because they know that their success in the firm begins with demonstrating productivity and commitment. Especially in the earlier years, productivity and commitment are measured by the number of hours they work. They also know that when they have lower hours each month, senior attorneys will assume that there is a performance problem. So it is a bit of a vicious circle. They need more hours so they can get more hours. They worry that they are falling behind their peers developmentally. They feel that there is no one whom they can really go to, to help them change this situation. The coordinator is not helpful because she has no power to insist a senior attorney work with a particular associate.

Firm A's formal mentor program is hit or miss as to whether mentors are engaged and helpful. The associates interviewed have some good relationships with senior attorneys, but many have not made a connection with a senior attorney who has taken them under his or her wing. They share various stories about insensitive remarks and exclusionary behavior by white senior attorneys. They also discuss the discomfort they feel doing what they think it takes to get work based on their culture and upbringing; how some white males seem to become the "go to" people in their groups; and how senior attorneys seem to be less comfortable with them. They rarely report any of these experiences to leaders or administrators (except the diversity manager) at Firm A because they don't think, for the most part, the behavior is intentional. They believe nothing can be done, or they worry that complaining will make it harder for them to get work in the future.

When we begin to discuss this issue, the first reaction by some firm leaders is what might be called, "blame the victim." Either the individuals with lower hours are not talented enough, or they just don't have what it takes to succeed at the firm. The unspoken assumptions are based in the cultural value of rugged individualism. If you are a star, you will be noticed, and the best people don't need any assistance getting work. Talent speaks for itself, which is why some people get work and others don't. Everyone at the firm has an opportunity to succeed on their own merit. *This analysis makes sense until you consider that the firm's way of allocating work can be influenced by implicit biases and the old dance moves that follow.* In addition, we can see that succeeding in this system is harder for the female attorneys and attorneys of color who are operating from a different set of cultural norms than those who have the power to allocate work. We can see almost immediately that Firm A has a work allocation system that is neutral on its face but is disadvantaging many of the people of color and women and making it less possible for them to thrive.

> *We can see almost immediately that Firm A has a work allocation system that is neutral on its face but is disadvantaging many of the people of color and women and making it less possible for them to thrive.*

We invite Firm A to use a diagnostic tool that we developed to analyze if certain groups are being unfairly hampered by what appears to be an impartial process. The tool is designed to help organizations examine and correct for the harmful impact of any institutional system, process, or policy (formal or informal) on racial minorities, women, members of the LGBT community, and other underrepresented groups. The tool has four steps:

Biasproofing Tool:

⇨ STEP ONE: What is the goal of the system/practices and why is it important to the organization and the employee?

⇨ STEP TWO: What are the barriers that make it hard to achieve the goals of the system/practice?

⇨ STEP THREE: Are there ways in which these barriers are compounded or made more difficult by race (or any other group variable being analyzed)? Are there additional barriers for racial (or other) minorities?

⇨ STEP FOUR: What do we need to do to improve this system/practice so that it addresses or minimizes these additional barriers? How do we make it a level playing field?

We work with Firm A to answer the above questions regarding its work allocation process by bringing together the firm's leaders (managing partner, management committee, leaders of the largest practice groups), the Diversity Committee chair, and the diversity manager. Firm A, like most firms, can answer Steps 1 and 2 easily, and yet these are important questions to spend a little time contemplating. The answers are key because they remind the firm's leaders why they have created the system in the first place. *They offer insights about the weaknesses in the system that affect all individuals, not just those who are underrepresented.* Step 3 is very difficult to answer without a keen awareness of the many issues we have discussed in the book thus far (implicit bias, diversity lens, cultural differences, etc.). Once you really grasp and believe what you learn from Step 3, Step 4 is really about identifying new ways to shore up the firm's practices and systems and solutions targeted at the unique issues that blacks and other underrepresented groups encounter in these systems. Part of Step 4 also includes how to create incentives and accountability to encourage the changes needed to better achieve the systems goals.

> Once you really grasp and believe what you learn from Step 3, Step 4 is really about identifying new ways to shore up the firm's practices and systems and solutions targeted at the unique issues that blacks and other underrepresented groups encounter in these systems.

Biasproofing System—Work Allocation

Step 1: What is the goal of the work allocation system and why is it important that the organization have a fair and effective system for distributing work?

1. Produce quality work for clients in an efficient manner so the firm will continue to be well-regarded and financially prosperous.
2. Allow associates to get the necessary experience to develop professionally.
3. Expose associates to different partners and working styles, both for the associate's growth and out of fairness to the associates.
4. Expose associates to client relationships and client development.
5. Challenge, stimulate, and motivate associates so they will want to stay at the firm and work hard.
6. Keep from overworking associates and experiencing the attrition that results.
7. Share the development of associates equally among partners
8. Encourage entrepreneurial skills.
9. Help the firm develop its entire associate population so there is less wasting of the investment that has gone into the hiring and the formal training of associates.

Step 2: What are the barriers to having a fair and effective way of distributing work?

1. Partners want the associates they want.
2. Once a partner trains an associate on a matter or has introduced the client to a certain associate, the partner wants to use that associate again.
3. Partners have a lot of pressure for productivity and feel they can't afford to bring associates up to speed; recently clients have been saying that they don't want to pay for junior associates' time.

4. Some partners don't want to work with associates to help them understand expectations, what an assignment entails, or what the associate needs to do to improve the work product.
5. Partners prefer self-starters and move their work to those who appear to get out of the blocks earlier.
6. The squeaky wheel (associate) gets the grease (plum assignments).
7. Partners may also have some concerns about client satisfaction—clients may want to work with the same associate with whom they have built a relationship or they may have concerns about the efficiency or using various associates.
8. Some associates lack the understanding or the initiative to make the system work.
9. Not all associates are the same with regard to their skills level and rate of development.
10. A highly leveraged firm produces a high volume of uninteresting (but profitable) work that has to be done, so some associates have to do the less interesting work.

As you can see, the list of barriers is long, which means that even with the general population, the system fails to accomplish many of its stated goals.

Now, let's work on Step 3. As I mentioned, I think it is the hardest for our clients. Often, when we get to this part of the analysis, the group gets quiet. So we might say something like, "So the firm has all these barriers that everyone is facing; what else would you be worried about if you were a person of color or a woman? Would you be more worried about any of those barriers if you were in one of these groups? If so, why?" Since we are meeting with the firm's leaders, there are very few people of color or females in the room. Here is where a white male partner who has done some of the work that we discussed in the prior chapters can really help. This is exactly the point where having tried on another's lens and life experience, and having paid attention to those who are not the fish in water, is invaluable. If the white male partners in the room have not taken these individual steps, it will be hard to make connections from Step 2 to Step 3.

Step 3 challenges managers and partners to recognize that there may be more barriers for particular groups to overcome and forces them to acknowledge white male privilege. It also causes leaders to evaluate whether the firm is operating as a pure meritocracy—whether difference is making a difference with regard to who has access to opportunity. This realization is sometimes new to many and hard to process, so I have created a very detailed answer to take you through Step 3. You may notice that just as the barriers overlap and influence each other (e.g., "Partners want who they want" and "Partners prefer self-starters"), so do the issues that emerge as we answer the questions in Step 3. In a workshop setting, all these complex ideas can be put in the room and discussed in a way that underscores the dynamics that play out as different groups enter and try to succeed in a system. I have attempted to detail some of the interplay below; however, the written format creates some limitations. I have also added after each barrier, steps that firms are taking to address these unique barriers attorneys of color encounter.

Step 3: Are there ways in which the general barriers to having a fair and effective work allocation system are compounded or made more difficult by race or ethnicity? Are there additional barriers for racial and ethnic minorities?

As mentioned, the general barriers affect all associates, but now let's look more closely at some of these barriers to see how they may have a different and more difficult impact on black associates and other associates of color.

> **General Barrier 1 and 2:** Start with the idea that in a free market system, not only do "partners want the associates they want," but they usually get them. And the second barrier follows: "Once a partner trains an associate on a matter or has introduced the client to a certain associate, the partner wants to use that associate again." It sounds like a neutral barrier (a potential problem for all associates who want work) until you consider what we have learned from the Implicit Association Test about unconscious biases with regard to black people, and the impact these biases have on behavior without our even knowing it—particularly when we are in stressful situations. A majority of the senior attorneys at Firm A are white males who look through their own personal diversity lens for the "best and the brightest." When it comes to going out to shop for talent on the open market, can you see how the implicit biases and old dance moves that follow them could make it harder for black associates to be sought out for work by a senior white attorney? This attorney can choose to work with any associate he wants; there are many white associates and few black associates. If he is unconsciously regarding the black associate down the hall from him, based on the poor performance of some other black associate he's worked with in the past (Guilt by Association), he might not select a black associate, even though he knows nothing about her work. He perceives that associate as a risk. His process for bypassing her will be invisible to him because it involves no intention or animus. Once he has chosen someone else and trains that associate, he keeps going back to that associate, and now he has a rationale (time and client relationship) to keep doing so. If the senior attorney gets beyond Guilt by Association and chooses an associate of color, but still harbors negative stereotypes about her intellectual capacity, he may go to her for a simple or low-risk matter, but not a cutting-edge transaction with a big client on a long-term project. This decision means she might be chosen for some work but would end up with fewer hours and less experience with complicated matters. This puts her at a disadvantage as compared to her white male peers, who do not have to overcome these initial negative presumptions.

One imperative step for all firms is to make sure that all their senior attorneys participate in inclusion training so they can be made aware of unconscious bias. These workshops are best done in small groups so there is ample time for discussion. Also, many firms look at the number of billable hours of black associates and other attorneys of color across firms and practice groups, and they talk with individual partners at the end of the year about their utilization of attorneys of color to help them become more conscious of ways they may be inadvertently overlooking these attorneys.

General Barriers 1 and 2 (cont'd): A white senior attorney making decisions about whom she wants to work with may also be influenced by how comfortable she is with black people. This is where In-Group Favoritism, one of the biases we discussed in Chapter Eleven, can enter and make it more difficult for black men and women to get work in a free market system or any assignment system. White male and female senior attorneys may have a harder time seeing black women and men as part of their group—so these associates might not be on the top of the list of "who the partner wants." Recall that In-Group Favoritism is the tendency to favor people who are like you. It is not that you have biases *against*, as much as you have biases *for* certain groups. If we are talking about associates still in their first three years at a firm, there are probably many people qualified for the junior associate work, so who is chosen? Commonalities may give the associate a connection and access to a first opportunity to prove herself or himself to a senior attorney. If he does a good job, then there will be more work for him. Since most senior attorneys are white men, people of color may be disadvantaged early in their careers.

To deal with In-Group Favoritism, we have advised our clients to create more centralized work allocation systems for their junior attorneys so they can have an equal opportunity to be utilized and prove themselves. Some organizations pay close attention to making sure that their black associates get solid first assignments with an inclusive senior manager.

Also when it comes to In-Group Favoritism and discomfort with difference, women of color have told me they believe some white men are uncomfortable relating to them as women and don't feel comfortable with them as a racial minority. They explain how men of color can connect with other white males around sports, and how white women don't have the racial barrier. Theirs, however, is a double barrier. We have learned that biases don't just stay in our heads; we act on them. Therefore, it is very possible that discomfort and a lack of identification will impact whom a senior white male partner chooses to work with, how he works with them, and how interested he is to work with them again.

Several firms we advise have created interest groups or events to stimulate cross-cultural or cross-gender connections and to break through stereotypical barriers. Partners and associates are able to learn more about their common interests and hobbies and begin participating in activities together based upon them. One firm has started a Women of Color task force and initiative to address some of the double barriers women of color face.

General Barrier 3: Partners have a great deal of pressure for productivity and feel they can't afford the time to bring associates up to speed (including clients that don't want to pay for junior associates' time). This barrier, as well as some of the others, concern time.

Time is of the essence in a law firm. It seems to matter the most because it is how lawyers make their money. If a white partner harbors an unconscious belief that black associates are not as smart as others, he will assume the associate will not be as quick or accurate with work. We already mentioned that he might pass the associate by, but what if he begins working with the associate for some reason and his negative biases trigger "stereotype threat" in the black associate—the concern by the black associate that his performance will be viewed through a negative stereotype. As we learned, stereotype threat creates anxiety, depressing the black associate's performance and making him less efficient. A longer response time by the associate means that it will be harder for him to get repeat business from this partner. If he is slower turning in an assignment because he wants it to be perfect, the research on stereotype threat suggests the associate will make more mistakes. If the white partner then engages in the "One-Mistake Rule," he may decide not to work with the black associate again. Worse than that, he may tell others, or he may decide to avoid working with any other black associate. The associate's position in the market will be weakened. Since he may already be laboring under negative biases, he may be written off more quickly and not given a second chance to redeem himself.

Some firms are training their partners how to mentor across differences and how to demonstrate high expectations for black attorneys while being supportive of their development. Firms are also finding numerous ways to encourage attorneys of color: to clarify the partner's expectations and timelines and find support from mentors and firm administrators.

General Barrier 4: "Some partners don't want to work with associates to help them understand expectations, what an assignment entails, or what the associate needs to do to improve the work product." This barrier in its essence is based on time as well. However, it also brings into focus how reluctant some senior lawyers are to develop associates, including giving them the feedback they need to improve their performance. Attorneys seem to hate giving anyone critical feedback, but racial and ethnic differences can compound this reluctance. Sometimes a white senior attorney withholds feedback from a black associate because he is still doing the Sloppy Sentimentalism dance; he wants the associate to do well, but he assumes the associate can't do better. Other times, the senior attorney is concerned that he will be accused of being "racist" or "sexist." The problem, of course, is that without critical feedback, the black associate is less likely to know what he should do to meet the senior attorney's requirements. If his performance isn't up to standard or if he isn't advancing, he will not be able to get more challenging assignments.

Some black associates tell me the first thing they tell their white supervisors is, "Please let me know if I am doing something wrong, or need to do something differently; I can deal with it. I am not going to get upset, I just want to be able to develop and give you what you need." The work of establishing competencies by levels and benchmarking the skills associates should be mastering is also extremely useful for helping associates to understand what is expected of them. It is important that partners are trained about evaluating associates on these competencies, as well as how to give constructive feedback across difference.

General Barriers 5 and 6: Who doesn't prefer "self-starters"? Partners have also admitted to me that work goes to the "squeaky wheels" in a free market system. So how might black people be affected more negatively by these issues? What I have discovered is that some people, including many people of color, do not understand the ins and outs of the law firm and business worlds when they first enter the workplace. They don't know how important it is to develop relationships with senior people to ensure that there is someone looking out for them when it comes to getting work, talking them up, and protecting them. This is true for many young people, despite their race, who are new to the workplace. However, I believe there are survival strategies that many people of color have employed prior to entering the corporate arena, that do not serve them as well, once they arrive. They believe if they keep their heads down and do good work, they will be rewarded with more opportunity. They are less strategic about which senior attorneys they choose to cultivate relationships with and from whom to get work. When they discover that relationship building with the right people in senior positions is essential to success, they find it much harder to develop these kinds of relationships, because senior white attorneys are uncomfortable with them and/or the attorneys of color don't enjoy and know how to relate to the senior white attorneys.

Several firms have boot camps for their attorneys of color before and after they start at the firm that are designed to give them information about the unwritten rules and how to navigate the firm culture. These sessions are well received and appreciated by black attorneys since sometimes they have few natural mentors and role models available to observe or to give them this information informally. Affinity (or employee resource) groups also dispense valuable information in this regard.

General Barrier 7: Client satisfaction is the hallmark of any successful law firm. However, what if clients have some of the same biases we've discussed? If a senior attorney knows his clients are biased, how does that impact which associate she selects for the project? What impact does it have on how the client interacts with (or chooses not to interact with) the associate? Some senior attorneys tell me that they would work with anyone, but they are concerned about a certain associate's "fit" with their clients. I accept that this is a real challenge. I also wonder sometimes if it is really the partner's own biases getting in the way. Some partners will speak up and confront clients when their clients have preferences that run against historically marginalized groups, but many do not. Of course, nowadays, more clients ask their law firms to present diverse teams of lawyers for their projects, and more diversity is represented in the client base than in the past. However, the law firm is functioning within a client world where the clients are still mostly white males who bring their biases about race, gender, sexual orientation, socioeconomic class, and so forth with them. This is another reason why people of color and women may not be a first choice for staffing or have limited utilization. I have been really impressed with the leadership of most of the firms that I work with regarding how well they confront client bias once it has been brought to their attention—the issue, of course, is getting that information from the partners and associates. On the other hand, I have been disappointed by how some individual partners fail to respond to these issues.

Addressing a problem of client bias is important. However, the proactive step is to require partners to think consciously about how they introduce and promote black associates and partners to their clients and how they publish the good work of black attorneys working on the client's deals.

General Barrier 8: Another major difference that impacts how well black women and men, and people of color generally, fare in a free market system depends on the cultural differences, values, and worldviews that we talked about in Chapter Six, when we learned the BASICS of cultural competence. All cultures are valid. However, often the cultural norms of the firm seem to clash with the cultural values and patterns of some people of color. It is true, as I mentioned above, that many people of color are new to this environment and don't understand how to maneuver within it. A work allocation system that requires a person to go from office to office, person to person, asking for work obviously worked well for attorneys who are now senior, but it can be intimidating and may put them at a disadvantage. When we listened to people in the focus groups at Firm A, they expressed sentiments I have heard many times and I have experienced myself. Many people of color come from cultures where respect for elders, being deferential, humble, and working hard but not "showing off" are expected norms. This goes back to Peggy McIntosh's list of Thirteen Deadly Habits and the "Instead Behaviors" in Chapter Nine. Many senior attorneys have become successful by being the Knower and acting on the more dominating behaviors, whereas many black people, especially women, have been trained to act according to the "Instead Behaviors." It is less natural for many people of color to be the squeaky wheels, to confront senior people to ask for work, to be assertive over and over again when work has not been forthcoming, and to be forceful about why they should get certain work. Their reluctance is often interpreted as a lack of initiative. When they are assertive and still do not get work, sometimes due to the biases we have been discussing, it makes it more difficult for them to keep operating in a way that was already somewhat uncomfortable for them. They are surprised when they learn in their evaluations that senior attorneys expect them to challenge the ideas of their supervisors and to speak up in meetings to clients. They tell me how uncomfortable they are blowing their own horns in order to prove that they are capable of taking on certain opportunities. This works against them in a free market system. Even when they know the rules of the game and change how they operate, it is exhausting because it is not their natural way of being. Also, they may be less successful at work attempting to adapt their behaviors than they would be if allowed to demonstrate their competencies in ways that come more easily to them.

One firm we consult to has undertaken a reverse mentoring program, where associates of color are the mentors to senior attorneys who volunteer to be mentored regarding racial and ethnic issues. This helps white attorneys appreciate different cultural values and patterns and find ways to support the person of color to develop a strategy for success that works for him or her.

General Barriers 9 and 10: In my experience, I have seen these barriers have a troubling impact on black attorneys. It is almost as if all the other barriers fold into these. Black attorneys are often presumed to have lesser skills and a slower rate of development. Sometimes it is true because their preparation before entering the firm was inadequate. However, often their skills are solid, but because they are new to the environment and how things work, they get a slower start. In addition, if they are contending with implicit biases and old dance moves are present, they get less work and fall behind as a result. What I often see is black attorneys getting assigned to high-volume, uninteresting work and getting stuck there. There are many reasons for this: the predilection of some black associates to put their heads down and work hard, their discomfort with being the squeaky wheel or aggressive with senior people about getting other work, and their lack of sophistication about how the systems work and how to maneuver through them—all the issues that we have set out above. Their hours are fine, but their development begins to lag, so when they look up and are finally able to remove themselves from this work, they are far behind classmates who got the opportunity to work on other types of matters. This issue greatly adds to the attrition of black associates. Either they leave because they are so disheartened by the situation and their prospects for making up the gap that has developed in their professional development or they are asked to leave because of this lagging development.

Firms need to monitor not just hours, but the type of work that black associates are doing. It is also important to have professional development administrators, diversity professionals, training personnel, and practice group leaders working together to monitor and address these issues.

Step 4: What do we need to do to improve the work allocation system so that it addresses or minimizes these additional barriers? How do we make a level playing field?

After learning about the many unique issues confronting both people of color, especially black associates, and how race (and gender) can create barriers to success, Firm A decided to work to find ways to minimize the bias within their present system. Its leaders didn't think it could successfully convince enough of its partners to move to a centralized assignment process. It would just be too countercultural. They also knew that centralized systems can be subject to many of the same issues, especially if the assignment partners are not powerful enough to insist that partners submit to the established system. Here are some of the steps that we agreed to take to correct for the bias, build more comfort and connections with senior attorneys, and support the development of their attorneys of color. Some of the changes are generally aimed at the system and, as such, help all attorneys more fairly. Other measures are directly race and gender conscious solutions.

General Solutions

⇨ Educate and get buy-in from senior attorneys on the goals of the work allocation system—require all departments/practice groups to address the issue.

⇨ Consider different allocation systems for different levels of attorneys—consider a more centralized system for first to third year associates.

⇨ Develop benchmarks and competencies for associates—train partners and associates how to use these tools.

⇨ Make sure department heads/practice group leaders and professional development staff know what work attorneys have and for whom they have worked.

⇨ Follow up after evaluations to make sure attorneys receive the right work.

⇨ Utilize self-evaluations and individual development plans to help associates, mentors, and partners to stay on track and remain accountable.

⇨ Provide training to all attorneys on how to work well with others who may have different communication styles.

⇨ Conduct inclusion and anti-bias training for all attorneys, especially department heads/practice group leaders and other firm leaders. Include biasproofing framework in these workshops.

Race and Gender—Conscious Solutions

⇨ Make sure department leaders and diversity/professional development personnel monitor work assignments and hours of attorneys of color and provide counseling advice for attorneys of color seeking work.

⇨ Conduct formal training for attorneys of color about how to be successful at the firm.

⇨ Build relationships between clients and attorneys of color: introductions, observations, mentoring, etc.

⇨ Require group heads to periodically report on their plans for and success with developing women and people of color.

⇨ Evaluate senior attorneys regarding how well they utilize associates, promote inclusion and work across differences.

⇨ Identify high performers of color and support their development.

⇨ Decide on the conditions for supporting attorneys of color who are underperforming.

⇨ Integrate diversity metrics into the practice group business plan.

⇨ Provide associates of color with strong mentors who can advocate for them.

⇨ Focus on getting work to junior attorneys where diversity is concentrated—don't wait for the "cream to rise to the top."

⇨ Support affinity group work: social, career, and professional development activities.

⇨ Provide one-on-one coaching for associates of color to increase their success and for senior attorneys to enhance their crosscultural and inclusion skills.

Firm A is still working on implementing these ideas. As you can see, the solutions have implications for other firm systems such as professional development, evaluation, and mentoring practices. You will also notice that these changes address the issues on four levels: personal, interpersonal, organizational, and cultural. The firm has taken steps to address general issues, including the need to have its partners recommit to the purpose and need for a fair work allocation system. In addition, the firm is giving all associates tools to measure and advocate for their own progress with benchmarks, competencies, work plans, and self-evaluations. It has instituted some checks and balances to detect and reduce biases by insisting on awareness training and increasing monitoring and evaluating performance by senior attorneys in these areas.

They have given practice group leaders the responsibility of making sure that work is moving around to all associates and that all attorneys of color are progressing within their practice groups. Most importantly, they have decided to support programs and initiatives specifically focused on people of color because they are able to see the unique and unfair disadvantages people of color encounter and how these issues can negatively affect those attorneys and the firm's bottom line.

Sometimes Cutting In Is the Right Move: Using Your Privilege to Interrupt Bias

Dance Lessons for this Chapter:

☑ What interrupting bias is and is not
☑ Eight techniques for interrupting bias
☑ Practice interrupting bias
☑ The cost of silence
☑ How to be an ally

In Chapter Twelve, we worked hard to analyze how bias within the systems in our organizations may be hindering the success of black people and other individuals from historically underrepresented groups. Admittedly, it is a big job to tackle. I know that not all of you are in the position to change the way your organization operates. However, in this chapter, I want to offer you one of the most important dances in the ballroom of inclusion. It is a step that anyone can do, anytime, anywhere. It is the work of standing up against racism, be it unconscious or otherwise, by finding a way to interrupt it.

In Chapter Ten, where we examined white privilege and other forms of unearned advantage, I mentioned that the benefit of recognizing your privilege is that you can use it to make a difference for those who are being targeted for exclusion. When you decide to use your privilege in this way, it is called "being an ally." In this context, allies defend, stand up for, and support those different from themselves. The ally comes from the point of view of being related and connected to those who are in the disadvantaged group. What affects the disadvantaged group affects the ally. Their fates are linked.

Standing up and interrupting is not easy. Once you notice that you are in the in-group or the one-up group, you may not want to act in a way that could jeopardize that status. If we use our power to help others, will we lose what we have come to enjoy, those benefits that are hidden from us and those that are not? For example, if, as an American, I advocate for immigrants, will I lose some of the privileges that come with being born in America? As a Protestant, if I want to create inclusion for Jews and Muslims, does that mean I have to give up the pretty lights and trees in the lobby of my office building or have to treat my high holidays as vacation days like many of those in the religious minorities have to do in many institutions?

Sometimes, we are reluctant to stand up because we see how people in the target groups are treated, and we fear we will suffer ourselves if we intervene. When you think about it, it is a privilege in itself to see a person being treated unfairly and not have to do anything about it because you are in the nontarget group. The "isms" (e.g., racism, sexism, elitism) only work if one group is "up" and the other group is "down." Even though we don't believe in systems of power and unearned privileges that are dominated by certain groups, they persist because, on some level, visible or not, we know that it is better to be in some groups than others.

A very funny white comedian, Louis C.K., performs a stand-up routine about being white, in which he talks about how good it is to be white. Below is a portion of the piece that he performed live. As most comedians do, he's peppered the piece with a few expletives. The words in the parentheses are my attempt to keep it clean. You can see the whole monologue on YouTube at http://www.youtube.com/watch?v=TG4f9zR5yzY. It is much funnier than anything you could read.[1]

> I love being white. I really do. Seriously, if you are not white, you are missing out because this (thing) is thoroughly good. But let me be clear, by the way: I am not saying that white people are better; I'm saying that being white is clearly better. Who could even argue? If it was an option, I would re-up every year: "Oh yeah, I'll take white again. Absolutely. I've been enjoying that. I'm going to stick with white, thank you." Here's how great it is to be white. I can get in a time machine and go to any time and it would be (absolutely) awesome when I get there. That is exclusively a white privilege. Black people can't (mess) with time machines. A Black guy in a time machine is like, "Hey, anything before 1980, no thank you; I don't want to go." But I can go to any time—the year 2. I don't even know what was happening then, but I know when I get there, "Welcome, we have a table right here for you, sir."

So being white has its advantages. The question is, "If, by circumstances not under your control, you landed in the white group, are you going to use your privilege to dismantle the racism that is giving you unearned advantages, or are you going to do nothing, which means that racism persists?"

The thought of breaking down unfair systems is less frightening when I am reminded of the idea Peggy McIntosh talks about seeing privilege as a bank account that you can spend on behalf of justice. She explains that the bank account of privilege will get refilled for a long time before it is eventually depleted.[2] If we are successful in closing the account completely, that just means that there will be a new balance that reflects our fuller humanity, and everyone will be better off. So when it comes to using white privilege to dismantle racism, my

> The question is, "If, by circumstances not under your control, you landed in the white group, are you going to use your privilege to dismantle the racism that is giving you unearned advantages, or are you going to do nothing, which means that racism persists?"

suggestion is to start small by focusing on our interpersonal relationships and looking at the everyday places where we are in advantaged positions. It is here where we can interrupt the biases that disadvantage people in our communities and workplaces and thereby erode these larger systems.

What Interrupting Bias Means

One day, early in the morning, my colleague and I were preparing for an "Interrupting Bias" workshop in a client's office when a woman who had participated in the previous day's workshop came to speak to us. Her words made my day. She told us that she really liked the workshop because she felt she had come away with something that she could actually do about the situations she found herself in and she had witnessed around her. Before, she explained, she had felt helpless, but now she felt like, "This is something I can do."

So what is the "This"? The idea of interrupting bias is that you are standing up against the "ism" and using your privilege to do so. First, you have to notice that you are witnessing or experiencing some type of bias, bigotry, or discriminatory or offensive behavior against a target group member. That is why we spent a good deal of time on awareness in this book. Awareness, as I have said, is a lifetime journey, so you can always know more; but just thinking about these issues for any period of time raises your antennae for bias. The second step is to find a way to stop the behavior from continuing so the perpetrator notices the error. This can begin to alleviate the burden of the offended party. You can also interrupt bias without anyone from the target group being in the room.

Interrupting Is about Engaging

An effective method for interrupting bias is staying engaged with the offender so she has an opportunity to understand what was troubling about what she did. It is also an attempt to keep the person from going "underground" with her behavior. When some people are made to feel ashamed of their behavior and don't have a chance to discuss the incident or their intent, they get hurt and harbor more negative feelings about the group they offended. The feelings and thinking that belie the offensive actions don't go away, so the person continues to think the same way and to behave the same way, but only in the company of those whom they believe have similar thinking and behavior.

Of course, there may be situations that are so blatantly offensive that it should be confronted without concern as to whether you can engage the offender. However, in the new millennium in our country, so much of what people say and do, especially with regard to race, is not blatant; it is racism that is more nuanced and unconscious. It might be harder as a white person to notice the more subtle forms of racism. However, if you think that some behavior may be coming from an unconscious or cloaked racism but are not sure, it is even more important to keep the conversation going so you can gain a better understanding of what the person actually meant by what he said or did. Sometimes, you might also find that the person was coming from a very innocent place, or you were mistaken about what she meant. Other times, you will discover that racism is impacting the behavior, and your conversation allows you to correct the misinformation from which the behavior stems. If an incident happens between people who work together, the best thing about keeping people engaged even when conflicts or uncomfortable situations arise is that you are modeling a behavior that will help the community as a whole learn how to have difficult conversations about race and other issues of difference.

Interrupting Bias Is Not about Changing People

When participants in my workshops are discussing one of the characters in a hypothetical situation who has said or done something outrageously offensive, they tell me, "You can't change people at this stage of the game. Some people are beyond hope." First of all, I maintain that it is not our place to decide who is beyond hope. My experience is that one just never knows. Sometimes, we start a workshop, and a participant can be really difficult. She will question everything the facilitator presents or spend all her time looking at her BlackBerry. Then, at the end of the session, she will come to us and say, "I thought that this was going to be simplistic and boring, but I really learned a great deal." So let's not give up on people too soon. I know you know what I am going to say by now, but I will say it anyway. All of us are on a journey, and you just never know where a person is when you encounter her.

Second, interrupting bias is not about teaching, retraining, or changing the mind of the perpetrator. People might be changed through the process, but that isn't your focus at the moment you are interrupting. What you are trying to do is to stop the troubling behavior and get people to think, to pause. Maybe your interruption keeps an unfair policy from being passed, prevents someone's promotion from being denied, or helps the offended party hang in there because he knows he is not alone. There are also places and times where the situation needs to go beyond interrupting—where the appropriate response to a situation is to teach and to talk to a person in depth about racism and racist behaviors or to bring a committee or community together to discuss a particular issue. However, those situations take planning and training and openness and willingness on the behalf of all the participants. Interrupting is a skill you can learn now and do now without convening a group or digesting all the materials I recommended in Chapter Six or A Resource Guide for Dance Partners in the appendix.

Let's take a quick look at an example of a microinequity that needs an interruption:

> George is a black senior partner, and Sam is a white mid-level associate. The two of them have been working together for several months on a matter that is finally coming to a close. George has a very successful practice, and Sam is enjoying working with and learning from George. One day, George and Sam travel to a client's office for a meeting. When they arrive at the front desk together, they are greeted by Jill, a white receptionist. George explains that they are there to see the client for a closing. Jill seems a little confused, ignores him, and directs her questions and responses to Sam. Even after Sam refers the questions back to George, Jill only looks at Sam.

In this situation, Sam has the privilege as the nontarget group person, and George is the target group person as race is the variable that is driving the biased behavior. Do you know what you would do if you were Sam? Would you let it slide? Would you want to crawl under the couch in the reception area? Or would you hope and pray that the client's assistant comes out and rescues you?

If Sam is a practiced interrupter, he might think of the following things to say:

⇨ "I think you might want to direct your questions to my partner."

⇨ "I wish I could answer your questions, but I am just the lowly associate here; why don't you direct your questions to the man in charge?"

⇨ "I know I am the more attractive (or the most distinguished looking) one here, but George is the one with all the power. You better talk to him."

⇨ "Boy, it's fun to be mistaken for the partner, as long as I don't have to make any decisions."

⇨ "Wait till I tell them back at the office that someone thought I was the partner."

⇨ "Oh George, I'm not sure she understands that you are the partner."

In this scenario, George is free to intervene on his own behalf. He also has the privilege of status as a partner who is talking to a staff person; because of elitism, staff members are often in the target position. The person in the one-down group may be totally capable and may even prefer to handle the situation himself, and he can also quite effectively use the same interrupting techniques described above to stop the behavior. However, there are several good reasons why it is helpful for the people in the privileged position to learn to interrupt bias. Below are some of the reasons why Sam's interruption is so valuable and more likely to help Jill notice that quite unconsciously she is acting in a racially biased manner.

Reasons Why Your Privilege Helps Interrupt Bias against Target Group Members

If you are the person in the privileged (nontarget) position:

⇨ You are usually not assumed to be too sensitive or having a personal axe to grind. George, as a black male partner, doesn't want to be perceived as weak or angry. Sam's interruption means that George doesn't have to fight off these assumptions at the same time that he is trying to correct for the one that has created the present awkward moment.

⇨ Your intervention often carries more authority by virtue of your privileged status. George is already being considered as not as good as Sam. When Sam speaks, the receptionist will give his opinion more weight than she would give George's opinion (until she realizes her mistake, and then she will be in the target position as compared to George because of his status as a partner).

⇨ Your comments may be easier for the offender to hear because you are perceived as a member of the same nontarget group. Sam's intervention means that a white person is correcting another white person about racial bias. If the receptionist is like many white people, she would have a harder time being confronted by George, a black person.

⇨ You are doing some of the work as the privileged person, allowing the target group person to take a rest from having to deal with many of these issues. George would love to take a break from the many microaggressions that he has confronted over time. Sam is giving him a gift.

⇨ You are preventing the target group member from saying something that might subject him to retaliation and put opportunities and relationships at risk. If the receptionist's comment were the last straw for George, then when Sam interrupts, George could calm down and collect himself. If George were to lose it there in the reception area, it would create a huge scene and he would risk his reputation with his clients. There are few white people who would find this behavior acceptable because most really don't understand the numerous daily indignities that many black men suffer.

⇨ You are more likely to hear and witness biased behavior against a target group because the offender will assume he or she is safe to commit this behavior when no member of that group is present. Biased behavior is still a problem even when the target group isn't present. If this behavior is not interrupted, it can grow, persist, and contaminate others and the larger community.

⇨ You are able to play an important role in correcting distasteful and uncomfortable situations. Sam is not left standing beside his partner feeling bad for this accomplished black man and feeling guilty for being the one who gets the receptionist's respect just because he is white. His ability to interrupt gets him beyond paralysis to action—action that is far more satisfying than apologizing to the target group person about someone's offensive behavior after everything is over.

Again, Sam is not trying to give Jill a big lesson on racial stereotyping; his job is to just make it stop. The statements he uses will get Jill to apologize to George and begin speaking to him instead of Sam. George may be mildly annoyed or angry depending on what kind of day he is having, but can you imagine how he feels when he sees that Sam knows how to deal with the situation? It is such a welcome relief for George. Sam feels useful rather than mortified. Jill has been given a clue that she needs to examine her assumptions. Best of all, the situation turns from something unpleasant to a bright spot in the day for George and Sam, and there is a real possibility for a deeper and more authentic connection between the two.

Techniques You Can Use to Interrupt Bias

Below, I have included a number of techniques and approaches I use to interrupt bias.[3] I want to share them with you and also invite you to think of other options you could use or might already use.

1. *Use a tone of voice that is welcoming and nonjudgmental.* Shame, blame, and attack may get people to stop, but you want to keep the relationships and the possibility for conversation if you can. You want to decrease defensiveness with your comments, not increase it.

2. *Treat the person with respect.* Remember that all of us have something to learn and that there are undoubtedly things we have said that demonstrate our own bias, "isms" and lack of awareness. Do not speak from a place of superiority.

3. *Give attention to the person who is making the remark.* Sometimes bigoted behavior is a cry for HELP or an indication that a person is feeling bad about him- or herself or a hurtful experience that he or she may have had. If you can, engage the person in a nonaccusatory way and listen to what he or she is feeling.

4. *Use humor or a light touch.* This is a great tool because it relaxes people and allows them to access the playful side of themselves—this opens them to possibly considering their behavior.

- "Come with me to the twenty-first century, Lewis. I think we use a different word now."
- "That's the silliest thing I have ever heard."
- "Come on, you are kidding, right?"
- "You want to try that again?"
- "Laurie, we're going to pretend we didn't hear (see) that."
- "You'll have to forgive John; he just climbed out from under a rock this morning."

5. *Try your best not to be mean.* Jokes don't work if they are biting and accusatory. Oops—maybe the last bullet point above violates that rule. You could probably get away with it if the people in the situation are friends. Harsh comments can stop the behavior, but people feel ashamed. Sometimes such comments can cause people to come back with worse behavior. Also, biting sarcasm doesn't keep people connected in a positive way. Sometimes, using facial expressions of shock or confusion or saying phrases like "Awkward!" or "Really?" can work.

6. *Ask a question.*
   - "Why do you say that?"
   - "What happened?"
   - "Are you sure you aren't expecting more from him than you are from other candidates (managers, teachers, board members)?"
   - "Do we have all the information we need? Where did we get this information from?"
   - "Didn't we approach this whole question differently when Diane was up for promotion?"
   - "What do you think the impact of our decision will be on the others who work full-time (who live out of the district, who have different cultural values)?"
   - "I wonder if we are being too hasty."

7. *Explain why the comment is troubling to you.* Use an "I" statement. If you use a statement about yourself, you are speaking about your own experience, and it isn't about pointing fingers. If it is a true statement that comes from your heart, it has the power and credibility that often opens the hearts and minds of others.
   - "I feel hurt (It pains me) when I hear ___."
   - "I really worry that we will never make any progress on racial diversity if we don't ___."
   - "As a Jew, when I see ___, I get angry because it reminds me of ___."
   - "I don't know how to feel when I see ___. On the one hand, I understand ___. On the other hand, my hope is that ___."

8. *Offer a different point of view.*
   - "Really? I have always had a wonderful experience with ___."
   - "If you look at it that way, yes. However, have you ever considered viewing it this way? Suppose ___."
   - "Do you want to know what I think about ___? I think back to five years ago, when we were in this room, and I was so proud that we ___, and now ___."
   - "I know Marianne; I've worked with her; I think she possesses ___."
   - "I lived in ____ for ten years and never experienced what you are worried about."

- "We should really do more research if we are going to go this way."
- "I'm not sure I agree with you there."
- "But look at Lisa and Gary; that hasn't been true for them."

9. *Practice.* It is hard to know how to respond in the moment unless you practice interventions. The more you practice, the more you gain the confidence that you can make a difference. You find ways that work best for you.

Of course, what method will work best in a situation depends on the context—the relationships, the history, the timing, the extent of the bias, the audience. Sometimes you can use humor or ask a question and follow with a different opinion. So the techniques can be combined. However, I never find interruption easy or comfortable. It would always be easier, if not comfortable, to do nothing.

Practice, Practice, Practice

Okay, now that you have the techniques under your belt, it's time to practice our dance steps! Read the situations below and think about what you could do to interrupt the bias in the example below:

> A small group of white managers and their supervisees, including a new black employee who recently moved to the city, are talking together at a diversity reception. The black employee is the only black person in their division. One of the managers in the group asks the young black man where he decided to live. When the new employee answers with the name of a mostly black urban neighborhood, the manager remarks, "Really? Aren't you scared to live there?" (EEK! GAFFE!!!) The circle grows a little quiet, and the black employee responds by talking about how much he appreciates his short commute to the office.

First, let's analyze the situation briefly:

⇨   What is the bias about?
⇨   Who is in the privileged (nontarget) and target group positions?
⇨   What could you say if you were in the group of white people who heard the comment?
⇨   What if nothing is said?
⇨   What is the possible impact on the new black employee? What might he be thinking and feeling about the other white managers? Might he have the same attitude toward his white peers?

Often, in a situation like this, there are people in the cluster who feel the same way as the manager but who just wouldn't ask the question. There are others who are utterly horrified and can't believe that this manager is about to reverse all the work that the diversity committee has done in the last year to increase the number of black employees. Most of the time, someone will try to change the subject, or folks will find a convenient excuse to walk away. The black person is upset but has just come to this company and doesn't want to be unpleasant or overreact, so he is gracious and says, "The commute works really well for me and my family."

Since we have committed to standing up, let's think about how we could do things differently:

⇨ Could you offer a different opinion about the neighborhood? "My sister/friend lives there and loves it." Or "There is a fabulous new restaurant that I heard about. I would love to check it out one day. Let's talk about getting our families together for dinner once you get settled."

⇨ Could you ask the manager about the meaning of the comment? "X, what are you asking? I am sure that they wouldn't have moved there if they felt unsafe."

⇨ What if you asked the manager in a curious, rather than accusatory tone, "X, have you ever spent any time there?"

⇨ How about a little humor. "Don't worry, we have diversity training coming up this fall, right, X?" (with a nice tone, a smile, and maybe a nice comforting hand on the back).

⇨ Or perhaps you could be bold and say, "You know, I have to admit, I haven't spent much time in that part of town. You know how some of us white folks can be; we rarely venture outside of our own neighborhoods. Can you tell us more about the neighborhood? What attracted you to it?"

As you can see, standing up in these situations is not easy, and getting the right nonjudgmental tone is quite difficult. There are different power relationships in this cluster, so the supervisees have their own target group status to consider, which may cause them to feel that there is nothing they can do. There is more risk for them to try to interrupt, but that doesn't mean they are off the hook. When you commit to taking a stand, you are committing to some risk. The supervisees can make some of those statements above and others that will help the situation without going very far out on the limb. Your success with interrupting has so much to do with your attitude and tone when you make the interrupting statement or question. Remember Techniques 1 and 2 about tone and treat the person with respect.

The best way I can remember to do this is to try to recall how I would want someone to talk to me if I had made an unconscious blunder like this. As I mentioned, many of us have the same bias; we just know not to say it. The secret here is to know that each of us somewhere in our nontarget roles has made an offensive remark as bad as or worse than this. So, if we can remember to go easy on each other, we might stay engaged and really learn about our biases and keep vigilant about them.

The Cost of Silence

When I ask people if they would say anything in the above situation, many people say no. They explain that the manager is not a malicious person, and they don't want to embarrass the black person. As white employees, they would worry about whether saying something to the manager would negatively affect their jobs. So there are many real concerns about interrupting, but I think one thing we want to remember is something we talked about in Chapter Five when we learned the S-A-M-E dance: *Don't hide behind your intent; impact is important.* Even if we can agree that the manager had no ill intent, the negative impact is easy to see. Instead of the black employee feeling included, he feels "other" and "less than." I can imagine that he is wondering, after the interaction, if this is going to be a place where he can thrive and build connections and networks now that people know where he lives. If people are afraid of his neighborhood, what other stereotypes are they harboring? It wouldn't be unreasonable for him to be worried about racism affecting his opportunities there. If no one speaks up, the black employee might believe that the statement of the manager is the thinking of everyone at the company. He will probably share the incident with other black individuals, and word of mouth may make it harder for the manager, the division, or the company to attract other black employees.

If there are other white employees or managers there who are sensitive to these issues or have loved ones who are black or live in the neighborhood, they may be insulted and concerned about what the comment means about the manager's attitude toward others from different backgrounds. *We rarely appreciate the impact that silence can have. It keeps in place the status quo and often retards the progress that has been made.* If we are not actively anti biased, we are passively allowing bias to persist.

What if you were there and you spoke up? The black employee would not feel alone and would know that there were some like-minded people at his workplace. The black employee might conclude that the manager is the aberration and not the norm. When the black employee related the story at a friend's dinner party, he would be reporting the offensive comment, as well as how you responded positively. The situation would then serve to attract rather than repel other black employees and other employees from backgrounds that are underrepresented at the organization.

Let's practice with one more situation:

> The hiring committee is meeting to decide on candidates for the fall. All of the committee's members are white except for Marilyn, who is black and who recently joined the committee. She is considered an up-and-coming superstar and is well respected. The discussion turns to Nelson Jordan, a black candidate who received high marks from those who interviewed him—his credentials are very good and meet the hiring criteria. One committee member, Noah, says, "Why don't we put him on the 'maybe' pile for now?" Then Noah turns to Marilyn with a smile and continues, "If we're going to hire a diversity candidate, we need another one who is as fantastic as Marilyn here is. Remember the mistake we made with that Jackie woman [referring to a black woman] whom we hired a couple years ago? She lasted no time." Another committee member, Cameron, counters, "I think we should hire Nelson. He would be good for diversity; our numbers have really gone down."

So, first let's do the analysis. Do you see the bias or "isms"? If not, go back to Chapter Eleven and review the five old dance moves. There are many unconscious biases operating here, but clearly Noah is doing the old Prince Syndrome move and Marilyn is the prince(ess) in this scenario. Unfortunately, it is also easy to see that

Mr. Jordan's candidacy is being negatively impacted by the Guilt by Association dance. Cameron is like many people who have a sincere desire to see more racial diversity in his organization, but he doesn't understand that focusing only on the numbers is not the way to get there.

> ⇨ Who is in the privileged position in this situation?
> ⇨ What might the impact be on Marilyn? Will the other committee members be affected? What will be the ramifications for Nelson?
> ⇨ If you were a member of this committee, what could you say at this moment?

You may find it helpful to go back and look at the techniques on page 160–162. Here are some possibilities, and I welcome you to come up with others:

Techniques 1, 2, 3, and 6
The quickest, safest way here is to ask an open-ended question in a nonjudgmental tone of voice. It is an important first step. The offenders' answers will offer more clarity about what their intentions were, and that simple act of reflection may already begin to shift their perspectives:

> ⇨ "Can we stop for a minute? Can you tell me more about what you mean by what you said, Noah? How about you, Cameron?"

Once they each explain more, you can ask follow-up questions to draw them out further. For example, you might ask, "What gave you that impression?" There will then be opportunities to move to other kinds of intervention, like those listed below.

Technique 4
You might try humor or a light touch:

> ⇨ "Hmmm . . . I'm not sure this committee has time to review the whole list of white people who haven't done well here over the years! If we took the time to go over those names, next we might have to start putting all the qualified white candidates on the 'maybe' pile!"
> ⇨ Or, depending on how well you know Noah, "It's back to diversity training for you, my friend!"

Technique 7
You could try communicating about why the comments troubled you personally:

> ⇨ "This conversation is very disturbing to me. We have a great candidate here, and yet there are statements being made that seem like new versions of old roadblocks. I don't hear us making this type of comment when white candidates are discussed."

Technique 8
You could offer a different opinion:

> ⇨ "I am not sure it is fair to compare this candidate to Marilyn or Jackie. He meets our standards, and he seems like a great candidate. Why wouldn't we hire him?"
> ⇨ To Cameron, you might offer your point of view this way: "Are you saying Nelson is a strong candidate, and it would be great if we could have such a talented

person who would also bring more racial diversity to our organization?" Here, you are leading him in a good direction, without focusing on what was "wrong" with his comment.

⇨ "Actually, I think Jackie was great, but the firm didn't provide the support she needed." (Try such a tactic if this is what you believe.). This comment will likely lead to a longer discussion of how to support new employees of color.

⇨ You could even try lifting the conversation away from Noah and Cameron and redefining the moment as a learning opportunity for the entire committee. This could sound something like this: "Noah, Cameron, I have to really thank you. You've brought to the forefront an issue that I've been thinking about for a while. Before we make any more decisions, I think it would be very important for us as a committee to spend some time talking about our perceptions with regard to race, and how our firm's diversity goals should impact our hiring process."

Here are a few things I would recommend you not say:

⇨ "Well, Marilyn, you're black. What do you think of Nelson?" Or, "What do you think of Noah's comments?" You want to give Marilyn some space. She can speak if she wishes.

⇨ "You know, Noah, I always thought you were a racist, and Cameron, your token-ism isn't that much better!" Labeling them this way will probably make them defensive, create a tense situation for everyone, and make it harder for the committee to talk about the issues.

⇨ "Well, Noah, I've heard you joined the firm because your father played golf with the manager partner. Isn't that the oldest form of affirmative action around?" If you insult Noah personally, he will not want to reevaluate his beliefs about race; in fact, it might make him dig into his position.

Interrupting Later Can Work Too

I know that it feels really difficult to say something in meetings or in a group when biased behavior happens. There are just so many relationships to worry about, and your personality might be such that you find it hard to speak up in a group no matter what you have to say. Also, you may be so shocked, hurt, or confused by behavior, even when it is a one-on-one situation, that you don't know what to say. I have to remind people that they are not always going to be able to find the right tone or comment to interrupt the behavior in the moment, especially if they are concerned about embarrassing the perpetrator or if there is a power differential between them and the offending party. That's okay. You can go back and bring the subject up with the person or group responsible for the behavior when you have your wits about you, have cooled off, and have thought of a constructive way to approach the issue.

So, anyone in the diversity reception can go to the manager who made the comment about the employee's neighborhood, and members of the hiring committee can go to the two members who commented on Nelson's candidacy. They can go the next day or sometime that week and say something like, "I'd like to talk with you about ___. I was worried about how Y (black employee/Marilyn) may have felt about a comment you made." Sometimes, the offenders will not remember an incident well or their remarks, and you will have to describe the situation. They will often feel bad and defend their comments or intent. However, sometimes they will say, "I know. I was mortified once it came out, but I didn't know what to say once I had put my foot in my mouth." Either way, you are free to try the interrupting steps, including why the comment is troubling to you. You can share the possible impact of the situation on the other people who heard the comment, the overall work and morale of the division or committee, and the organization's objectives. Of course, the downside of waiting until later is that the black person and the other white people who were present are not there to see the intervention.

One thing you might do is advise the perpetrator to apologize to the offended parties. You might also decide after the incident to have a conversation with the black person and possibly with the others who were there. So as not to lead with your assumptions about another person, you could say, "I don't know what you thought about X's comment, but personally I was offended by it, and I actually plan to talk to X later about it." Wait to hear what they have to say. I can imagine that the black individuals in the two situations above might tell you not to worry about it and advise you not to say anything further. However, if you can explain to them why this is a problem for you as a white person, they may appreciate your willingness to approach the perpetrator and to make the future intervention.

There is one other step you should take if the behavior is egregious and occurs at work. You will need to follow the organization's antidiscrimination grievance policy and reporting protocols. Human resource personnel are trained to investigate and correct the offender and protect the offended party. Sometimes, even with egregious behavior, the black person who is a target of the behavior may not want to report it. You can try to be there to listen to him, including his anger about racism. This is another way to use your privilege to be supportive. Work with the black person to find an agreeable solution to the problem. Often, when you can be there for him or her as an active listener, the person will find the resolve to either confront the perpetrator him- or herself or to seek institutional help.

More on Practice

I want to say more about the last step PRACTICE. When we were learning about white privilege and other forms of unearned advantage, we discussed how hard it is to see our own privilege; so, of course it is quite a task for us to detect the bias, remember our privileged position, and then try to use our unearned status to stop the bias.

There are times when the situation happens so quickly that you don't see it; or you see it, you know something isn't right, but you don't know exactly why. The idea is not that you don a cape with a WP (white privilege) on it and capture every misconduct, racist behavior, or unconscious offender. Give yourself credit every time you notice racism and every time you think of something to say but don't quite get it out of your mouth until after the situation has passed.

Having said that, it's time to practice the art of interrupting. Begin to practice interrupting in low-risk situations. I used to tell people to practice on their families because you hear and see biased behavior all the time at the holiday table or on vacation. I figure that these are people you know and who love you. If you tell them that they are being biased, what are they going to do? Fire you? Well, some people tell me, "Yes, my family would." Clearly, all people are different and come from different backgrounds and react in different ways. But if you think about who is sitting around the family table when Uncle Joe starts going on about "those people," you might decide to take the risk. The young and the impressionable and the future of your family are there listening intently to what the grown-ups are saying. If we don't interrupt at that table or take those kids aside afterward, Uncle Joe's thinking may become theirs. Remember, Uncle Joe is just saying out loud the racist messages that most of us caught. If we are not actively antibias, we become passively so and are thus part of perpetuating it. Give yourself credit every time you notice racism, and every time you think of something to say but don't quite get it out of your mouth until after the situation has passed.

My next recommendation would be to practice with strangers who have no power over your life. I travel a lot and I take a lot of taxis. When I am talking to a driver who starts going on about a particular group, I use my kindest or most comic self and say things like,

> "Oh you don't really believe that, do you?"
> "Wow, really, that hasn't been my experience. When I visited my friend in that country, I felt very welcomed."
> "Really? Now, is that fair? What if I said that about (his group)?"
> "We don't use that term anymore."
> "You're kidding me, right? You can't believe that."

Here's the thing that I know. Maybe I won't change the driver's mind; that's not my job. However, at least I have done something to make him stop and perhaps think, if only during our cab ride. Of course, I am hoping it spills over to his other interactions with his patrons. When I do it, I feel like I have helped myself, because if he is saying these things about other groups, I can only imagine what he might say about my group. I am hopefully doing something for the group he was insulting, and I am doing my best to dismantle a tiny part of the system.

Sometimes being a good ally is about stepping forward even when you don't know the person, as I have done with my taxi drivers. Sometimes, it's about standing behind and encouraging a person to move forward. Other times, it is about looking out for possible issues that may be damaging if not addressed in a certain way. My white friends, who have been incredible allies to me, often volunteer support that I didn't even know I needed; but because I trusted them and their motivations, I accepted their help. Black people are rarely at the table in most boardrooms or management committee meetings, but white people of goodwill are. We desperately need white people to stand up and say, "Why are we insisting that Joe spend another year proving himself when we didn't require that of every other candidate?" or "Have we thought about the implication that this decision has on black kids in our school?" or "As a white person who believes deeply in racial justice, I have to tell you that statement concerns me because ___."

Mark Warren, in his book *Fire in the Heart: How White Activists Embrace Racial Justice*, questions even the use of the word "ally" because he believes white antiracists are simply fighting racism. They are not fighting for racial minorities. They are really fighting for themselves, for their vision of a better society, and for their humanity.[4] I certainly believe that I am fighting for myself when I am in the nontarget position and see a friend, colleague, or stranger in the target group encountering mistreatment and injustice. I have discovered that to be a good ally, I have to keep working at being useful and effective—staying connected, paying attention to issues impacting them directly, and keeping up with changing language and terminology. I have to constantly watch for the privilege that keeps me from seeing how my reality may be very different than theirs. When Proposition 8 passed, overturning same-sex marriage in California on the same night that President Obama won the presidency, I had to be reminded by my gay friend who had voted for the president that it wasn't a universally happy day. So I find myself doing the same work that I am asking you to do: trying to stay self-aware and getting information I don't know and skills I don't have. I go to trainings, read books, ask questions, and, most of all, build and solidify relationships. I am motivated to make others' lives more livable, but I am also clear, especially as a member of a target group myself, that I have a stake in their safety and just treatment. I think the famous statement of the German theologian, Pastor Martin Niemöller says it all:

First they came for the Jews and I did not speak out—because I was not
a Jew.
Then they came for the communists and I did not speak out—because I
was not a communist.
Then they came for the trade unionists and I did not speak out—because
I was not a trade unionist.
Then they came for me—and there was no one left to speak out for me.[5]

Endnotes

1. Louis C.K. (2008, November 27). Louis CK Being White, Youtube.com, http://www.youtube.com/watch?v=TG4f9zR5yzY (from a comedy DVD titled, Louis C.K. "Chewed Up") (accessed Feb. 13, 2011).

2. McIntosh, P., *White Privilege: Unpacking the Invisible Knapsack*, 12 (1998). McIntosh, P., *White Privilege and Male Privilege: A Personal Account of Coming to See Correspondences through Work in Women's Studies*, 12 (1998).

3. This list was adapted from the National Coalition Building Institute, www.ncbi.org (last accessed Feb. 12, 2011).

4. The National Coalition Building Institute (NCBI) is an international, nonprofit leadership training organization based in Washington, D.C. Since 1984, NCBI has worked to eliminate racism and all other forms of prejudice and discrimination throughout the world.

5. Mark Warren, Fire in the Heart: How White Activists Embrace Racial Justice 16–17 (Oxford Univ. Press 2010). Mark Warren discusses the two ways in which whites oppose racism: (1) the coalition model, which focuses on shared interests (where whites are not truly supporting racial justice, but merely aligning themselves with those with common goals); and (2) the altruistic model, which accepts that whites' interests are normally in competition with those of people of color but that they will act against their own interests for altruistic reasons.

6. Text and historical analysis available at http://www.history.ucsb.edu/faculty/marcuse/niem.htm (last accessed Apr. 14, 2011).

Conclusion

First of all, thank you. Thanks to all of you who decided to take this journey with me. I am humbled that you have allowed me to be your dancing instructor through some difficult and challenging steps. Whether you began in the Aware and Ready to Dance, the Cool Moves But Still in Need of School, or the Oh, Was That Your Foot? stage, I am hopeful that you found the journey worthwhile and have emerged farther along the path. The optimist in me hopes that even if you were in the I'm Not Dancing stage and somehow decided to read this book anyway, you are no longer rooted there. The point is, whatever stage you were in before, you have already gone from well-meaning to well-doing. You have been willing to open your heart and mind and to assess your actions and those of the institutions and communities to which you belong. You have listened, often cringing I'm sure, to the stories of the many micro-aggressions and exclusions that black people have endured. You have encountered self-awareness, assignments, and admonitions. You have learned skills and taken stands. You are to be congratulated.

If you don't believe me, let me remind you where you have been.

We started by acknowledging that being nice and having good intentions is not enough to bridge the racial gap that still exists between black and white people in this country. We need action, and we need the initiation of that action to come from you, white people who are the owners and hosts of so many of our society's institutions.

We experiencedthe need for the end of the diversity dance—with the focus on bringing in and counting up the numbers of racial and ethnic faces—and we decided that the better dance these days is called Inclusion. This dance requires white people who are committed to racial equality to learn new information and new skills and to unlearn some old dance moves. Removing the legal barriers was important; black people have been invited in, but if we want to see true meritocracy, fairness, and equality, we have to move our focus and our efforts in step with the new dance of inclusion.

We learned that we are *both* the same *and* different. We share many basic human needs across race, culture, and experiences; yet, we may understand and approach our common basic needs differently. We also started digging into some of our differences and seeing how they can enrich our personal lives and the bottom lines of our organizations if we learn how to cultivate inclusive environments. After doing some of the cultural exercises in this book, you may have come into contact with your own sense of "otherness," how you have learned to "cover" it, and how you want to walk more fully in it and make more space for others to do the same.

We accepted that perfection and pretending to know are the enemies of building inclusion in our workplaces and of genuine and deep relationships between black and white people. We learned that we need to develop a social intelligence that helps us pay attention to the messages we send about who is included in our communities and organizations. There are many small processes and steps that we can take to deepen and expand our relationships and opportunities across race.

We tried to get comfortable with making mistakes in the dance of inclusion and seeing that they are part of the process. We fall down, but we get back up following the S-A-M-E dance steps and the BASICS of cultural competence when we are not sure about what's at play in our cross-racial interactions.

As we peered through the diversity lens at who we are and where we have been, we realized that there is more than one way to see things and that there are some things we appear to be missing or misconstruing. We discovered that black people, just like white people, have different experiences and worldviews that shape the way they celebrate, work, approach life, and interpret situations. I encouraged you to take advantage of opportunities where you can learn more about how black people experience the world; their history, which is intricately linked to those of other races; and the pieces of contemporary black culture that are often hidden from most white viewers. Also check out A Resource Guide for Dance Partners list in the appendix for more books, conferences, movies and documentaries that can expand your awareness.

We challenged our denial about biases, so now we are in a better position to use our explicit beliefs about justice and equality to correct for our implicit biases and automatic responses. Peggy McIntosh reminded us to look at the Thirteen Deadly Habits that reinforce dominance and superiority and prevent blacks and other historically marginalized groups from bringing their best to the workplace. We discovered the Instead Behaviors, which can help us create a better work environment for everyone.

I imagine that it might have been difficult to hear that there are also at least five old dance moves that are damaging to black people's careers in majority white institutions! Painful, yes, but nobody wants to be caught doing the same dances that their fathers and mothers used to do. Now that you know you have biases because you are human and that the five old dances are more visible, we have alternative steps that will help us better notice and correct for them. I also gave those of you who are ready and willing to do it one big move to consider: Decide to be responsible for the success of a black person!

I asked you to look more closely at your organization and how its neutral systems can put black people and other traditionally underrepresented people at a disadvantage. I reminded you that you can't get change without changing. Cultures and practices in an organization have to be examined and revised if you want to reap the benefits of difference. The biasproofing framework and exercise I offered can be used with any kind of system, formal or informal, at work, at your place of worship, at your kids' schools, and anywhere else you want to promote racial inclusion or inclusion of any group that has been underrepresented.

As if that wasn't enough, you bravely opened your eyes to "whiteness," "white privilege," and other forms of unearned advantages and the systems that created and support them. You did the line dance of opportunity and considered your own group privilege and the connections between your target and nontarget identities. Seeing yourself as a group member can be hard, but I asked you to reckon with the idea that an invisible system of racism (and other "isms") favoring your group and disadvantaging blacks is in full operation even when you, as an individual, aren't mistreating any particular black person. Once we learned that doing nothing keeps racism and other systems of exclusion and oppression alive and well, you committed with me to stand up, to do more to interrupt bias when you see it, and to be allies to black people.

Do you see what I mean? You have been amazing!

I know that it has all been a great deal to digest, but as I said earlier when we started this journey together, it takes a lifetime. That, of course, is no excuse not to start. People of all backgrounds have a great deal at stake here. Of course, like any successful endeavor, it is a two-way street. There are awareness (of self and others), skills, and actions to which black people have to commit as well if we are going to be successful at building communities of inclusion and overcoming racism in our country and our organizations. The majority of black people are true believers in the American dream, and they are working hard at achieving it, but they will never get there alone. It is time for us to seek true collaboration—a partnership of well-meaning, justice-seeking people who are willing to do the work on themselves and with others to build true friendship, a fair society, and a richer culture. Let's keep dancing!

Join us for more discussion; to access more resources for the journey; and to share your questions, strategies, and successes for racial inclusion and equity at www.movingdiversityforward.com.

A Note on the Typography

Text for this book was set in ITC Cushing Std, a contemporary typeface designed by Vincent Pacella in 1982. J. Stearns Cushing designed the typeface Cushing No. 2 for American Type Founders in 1897 and the Cushing name was given to a variety of other loosely related faces released by ATF. International Typeface Corporation licensed the Cushing typefaces and Pacella redrew them into a consistent family. ITC Cushing has linear serifs that are a revision of the original sloping serifs.

The book was designed and composed by Lachina Publishing Services in Cleveland, Ohio.

Printed and bound by Thomson Reuters, Eagan, Minnesota.

Appendix A
A Resource Guide for Dance Partners

Throughout this book, I have mentioned various books, articles, events, and websites that can help enrich your journey and enhance your dance moves as you take an active stand for racial and ethnic inclusion and understanding, especially with regard to black people.

Below are some additional resources that promise to broaden your knowledge and awareness, change your attitudes, and enhance your skills in relating across racial and ethnic differences. This is just my short list. You may want to ask members of a broad spectrum of races and ethnicities for suggested resources to expand your understanding of the history, diverse life experiences, and perspectives regarding race. Perhaps you will make your own list after exploring these works and as you follow what resonates with you.

Books and Articles

Nonfiction

General/Historical

This book describes what court-ordered school desegregation in Boston meant to black and working-class white families.

> J. Anthony Lukas, Common Ground: A Turbulent Decade in the Life of Three American Families (Knopf 1986).

This account gives the inside story of the first black female candidate for assistant attorney general, whose nomination was withdrawn by the Clinton administration after a right-wing attack.

> Lani Guinier, Lift Every Voice: Turning a Civil Rights Injustice into a New Vision of Social Justice (Simon & Schuster 1998).

This piece challenges what we think are objective notions of meritocracy and why people succeed (stars are developed, not just born).

> MALCOLM GLADWELL, OUTLIERS: THE STORY OF SUCCESS (Little Brown & Co. 2008).

This work reveals the surprising history of race and racism in our country.

> NELL IRVING PAINTER, THE HISTORY OF WHITE PEOPLE (W.W. Norton & Co. 2010).

Two quite recent contributions brilliantly explore the journey of black people in twentieth-century America and how historical and contemporary racism manifest in our judicial system and result in unequal treatment of blacks.

> MICHELLE ALEXANDER, THE NEW JIM CROW: MASS INCARCERATION IN THE AGE OF COLOR-BLINDNESS (Perseus Books 2010).
>
> ISABEL WILKERSON, THE WARMTH OF OTHER SUNS: THE EPIC STORY OF AMERICA'S GREAT MIGRATION (Random House 2010).

Faith Connections

These volumes helped me to understand the connections between my faith in God, responsibility to community, and the struggle for equality and freedom.

> JAMES H. CONE, A BLACK THEOLOGY OF LIBERATION (Lippincott 1970).
>
> DR. MARTIN LUTHER KING JR., STRENGTH TO LOVE (Harper & Row 1963).
>
> DR. MARTIN LUTHER KING JR., WHERE DO WE GO FROM HERE: CHAOS OR COMMUNITY? (Beacon 1968).

Memoirs

They made me angry, they made me cry, and they also made me appreciate the complexity of the black experience. With love and dedication, black families endure great hardship in hopes that their children will survive and have better lives.

> TA-NEHESI COATES, THE BEAUTIFUL STRUGGLE: A FATHER, TWO SONS AND AN UNLIKELY ROAD TO MANHOOD (Spiegel & Grau 2009).
>
> JAMES MCBRIDE, THE COLOR OF WATER: A BLACK MAN'S TRIBUTE TO HIS WHITE MOTHER (Riverhead Books 1996).
>
> NATHAN MCCALL, MAKES ME WANT TO HOLLER: A YOUNG BLACK MAN IN AMERICA (Vintage 1994).

Research/Academic

This publication clearly articulates how we all have a racial identity, how it develops, and how racism operates and affects all of us.

> BEVERLY DANIEL TATUM, "WHY ARE ALL THE BLACK KIDS SITTING TOGETHER IN THE CAFETERIA": A PSYCHOLOGIST EXPLAINS THE DEVELOPMENT OF RACIAL IDENTITY (Basic Books 1997).

This book explains the dynamic of oppression and strengthened my desire to liberate myself and others.

> Paulo Freire, Pedagogy of the Oppressed (Continuum Int'l Publ'g Group 1970).

The following clearly document the barriers to and provide solutions for creating more inclusive workplaces where people of color and other underrepresented groups can thrive.

> Ida O. Abbott & Rita S. Boags, Minority Corporate Counsel Ass'n, Mentoring Across Differences: A Guide to Cross-Gender and Cross-Race Mentoring (Dec. 2003).
>
> Am. Bar Ass'n Comm'n on Women in the Profession, Visible Invisibility: Women of Color in Law Firms (Oct. 2006).
>
> Minority Corporate Counsel Ass'n, The Myth of the Meritocracy: A Report on the Bridges and Barriers to Success in Large Law Firms (MCCA 2003).
>
> David A. Thomas, *The Truth About Mentoring Minorities: Race Matters*, Harv. Bus. Rev. (Apr. 2001).
>
> David A. Thomas & Robin J. Ely, *Making Differences Matter: A New Paradigm for Managing Diversity*, 28 Harv. Bus. Rev. (Sept. /Oct. 1996).

Fiction

The complexity of racism endured by black people throughout the world—including the anger, confusion, pain, resilience, humor, and faith that spring from those life experiences—has inspired brilliant fiction. These are just some of the novels, poems, and plays that evoke the richness and depth of the culture.

> Maya Angelou, I Know Why the Caged Bird Sings (Random House 1969).
>
> James Baldwin, Go Tell It on the Mountain (Doubleday 1963).
>
> Octavia E. Butler, Kindred (Doubleday 1979).
>
> Ralph Ellison, Invisible Man (Random House 1947).
>
> Zora Neale Hurston, Their Eyes Were Watching God (Lippincott 1937).
>
> Harper Lee, To Kill a Mockingbird (Lippincott 1960).
>
> Toni Morrison, The Bluest Eye (Holt, Rinehart & Winston 1970).
>
> Alan Paton, Cry the Beloved Country (Scribner 1948).
>
> Zadie Smith, White Teeth: A Novel (Random House 2000).
>
> Kathryn Stockett, The Help (Penguin 2009).
>
> Alice Walker, The Color Purple (Harcourt Brace Jovanovich 1982).
>
> Richard Wright, Native Son (Harper & Bros. 1940).

There are many inspirational writings (essays, books, and poems) by the prolific Langston Hughes and Audre Lorde. A few are noted below.

> Langston Hughes, *I, Too, Sing America, in* The Life of Langston Hughes: Vol. I: 1902-1941, I, Too, Sing America (Oxford Univ. Press, 2d ed. 2002).
>
> Langston Hughes, Let America Be America Again (George Brazillern 2005).
>
> Audre Lorde, *The Master's Tools Will Never Dismantle the Master's House, in* Sister Outsider: Essays and Speeches (Crossing Press 1984).
>
> Audre Lorde, *Who Said It Was Simple?, in* A Land Where Other People Live (Broadside Press 1973).

Documentaries and Training Videos

My clients and I found the following informative and instructive films worthwhile and a refreshing contrast to many hokey training videos in circulation.

This documentary chronicles the stark contrast between how blacks and whites viewed the death of a poor, young black woman hit by a truck crossing a busy street by a suburban mall outside Buffalo. Members of the black community blamed her death on racism, while the white community saw it as an unfortunate accident.

> *Nightline: The Color Line and the Bus Line* (ABC television broadcast Nov. 1999). For an analysis of this documentary and classroom exercises, see *Analysis: The Color Line and the Bus Line*, Authentic Voice, http://www.theauthenticvoice. org/TeachersGuide_ColorLine.html.

This documentary recounts the profound lesson that Ms. Jane Elliot teaches to her all-white third-grade class in Riceville, Iowa. She divides the class by blue and brown eye color, giving one group superior status and the other inferior status, designated by a collar they must wear. The next school day, the groups reverse status. When in the superior group, the children are happy and outgoing and act as if they are better than their classmates in the inferior group. Members of the "out" group are withdrawn, frustrated, and angry and perform poorly. At the fourteen-year anniversary of the experiment, her grown students returned to watch the recording of themselves and discussed how deeply the experience affected them.

> *Frontline: A Class Divided: Then and Now* (PBS television broadcast 1987), http://www.pbs.org/wgbh/pages/frontline/shows/divided/etc/view.html? autoplay; *see also* William Peters, A Class Divided (Yale Univ. Press 1987).

This is an incredibly well-done fourteen-hour television series that captures the black Civil Rights movement from the viewpoints of the many women and men who fought to end legalized discrimination. The sound track is also amazing as it captures so much of the rich soul music from the '60s and '70s, as well as the freedom songs and hymns of the movement.

> *American Experience: Eyes on the Prize: America's Civil Rights Movement 1954– 1985* (PBS television broadcast 1987), http://www.pbs.org/wgbh/amex/eyesontheprize/about/index.html.

The newest PBS documentary on our racial history chronicles the 1961 Freedom Rides that started with a courageous band and grew to more than 400 black and white men and women who defied Jim Crow laws by boarding buses and trains and sitting together throughout the South. Despite violence and imprisonment over six months, the courage of the Freedom Riders forced the U.S. government to pass laws ending segregation on public trains and buses.

> *American Experience: Freedom Riders* (PBS television broadcast 2011), http:// www.pbs.org/wgbh/americanexperience/freedomriders/.

This film is a three-part series that includes interviews with scientists, historians, psychologists, etc., defining what race is and its implications for society today. The documentary explains how race is not biological and illustrates how race and racism have been perpetuated in our country through structures, policies, and laws that continue to influence the life outcomes of groups based on racial differences. This well-drafted website includes great quizzes, facts, maps, and other information to broaden understanding and awareness.

>*Race: The Power of an Illusion* (PBS television broadcast 2003), http://www. pbs.org/race/000_General/000_00-Home.htm.

This riveting documentary shows a gathering of eight North American men, two African Americans, two Latinos, two Asian Americans, and two Caucasians at a retreat convened by the director to talk about race relations. The discussion goes deep and becomes quite emotional. By the end of the weekend session, it is clear that the group has had a life-changing experience.

>*The Color of Fear* (USA television broadcast 1994).

Journalist Elvis Mitchell interviews twenty-two black leaders ranging from athletes like Kareem Abdul Jabbar and Serena Williams to political leaders such as Colin Powell and Massachusetts Governor Deval Patrick to actor Laurence Fishburne, activist Angela Davis, and artist Kara Walker. Fresh insights are revealed as the interviews move from personal challenges and triumphs to broader repercussions and struggles.

>*The Black List: Volumes One and Two* (HBO television broadcast 2008).

Movies and Shows

I already shared some of my favorite movies in Chapter Six. Below are some of those as well as some other movies and plays. I offer these films and plays because they really resonated with me as a black person. In particular, I found them moving because they capture the complexity of the historical and social context in which black and white people find themselves. They also demonstrate the subtlety, pervasiveness, unfairness, and resistance to change of structural racism and how white people are not the only ones who learn it. Some of these films are sad and distressing because they explain the self-destructive, isolated, hardened, and nihilistic behavior we sometimes witness within the black community. But they also score entertainment points and make me marvel all over again at how funny, talented, creative, loving, and resilient black people are.

>Boyz n the Hood (Columbia 1991).
>Bird (Warner Bros. 1988) (1989 Academy Awards Best Sound for this biography of Charlie Parker).
>The Color Purple (Warner Bros. 1985).
>Crash (Lion's Gate 2004) (2006 Academy Awards Best Picture).
>Do the Right Thing (Universal 1989).
>The Great Debaters (Metro-Goldwyn-Mayer 2007).
>Imitation of Life (Universal 1959).
>In the Heat of the Night (United Artists 1967) (1967 Academy Awards Best Picture; Best Actor, Rod Steiger; and three others).
>Lady Sings the Blues (Paramount 1972).
>Love and Basketball (New Line Cinema 2000).

LOVE JONES (New Line Cinema 1997).

MALCOLM X (40 Acres & a Mule 1992) (1993 Academy Awards Best Actor nominee, Denzel Washington).

A RAISIN IN THE SUN (Columbia 1961) (ABC aired a remake in 2008).

A SOLDIER'S STORY (Columbia 1984).

SOMETHING NEW (Focus Features 2006).

AUGUST WILSON, FENCES (1983).

AUGUST WILSON, TWO TRAINS RUNNING (1991).

Books My White Friends Recommend

While writing this book, I asked my white friends and colleagues to share with me the books that had opened their minds and expanded their awareness about race and racial issues. The following are some that they suggested.

W. E. B. DU BOIS, THE SOULS OF BLACK FOLK (A.C. McClurg & Co. 1903).

ATUL GAWANDE, THE CHECKLIST MANIFESTO (Metropolitan 2009).

ALEX HALEY, AUTOBIOGRAPHY OF MALCOLM X (Grove Press 1965).

MARTIN LUTHER KING JR., LETTER FROM BIRMINGHAM JAIL 1963 (Harper Collins 1994).

PAUL KIVEL, UPROOTING RACISM: HOW WHITE PEOPLE CAN WORK FOR RACIAL JUSTICE (Quarry Press 2002).

GERHARD E. LENSKI, POWER AND PRIVILEGE: A THEORY OF SOCIAL STRATIFICATION (McGraw Hill 1966).

GREGORY MICHIE, SEE YOU WHEN WE GET THERE: TEACHING FOR CHANGE IN URBAN SCHOOLS (Teachers Coll. Press 2004).

ESMERALDA SANTIAGO, WHEN I WAS PUERTO RICAN (Vintage 1994).

JOSÉ SARAMAGO, BLINDNESS: A NOVEL (Houghton Mifflin Harcourt 1998).

PIRI THOMAS, IN THESE MEAN STREETS (Knopf 1967).

CORNEL WEST, RACE MATTERS (Beacon 1993).

Resources to Explore White Identity and Help Become an Ally to People of Color

In Chapter Six, I referred to various resources for exploring white racial identity. Below are some of those as well as additional books, articles, and websites that can help you increase your awareness about whiteness and how to use your understanding to be an ally to black people and other people of color.

DR. OMI OSUN JONI L. JONES, 6 RULES FOR ALLIES (video Feb. 2010) (luncheon address at a conference at University of Texas at Austin), http://www.blip .tv/file/3252101.

JAY SMOOTH, HOW TO TELL PEOPLE THEY SOUND RACIST (video 2008), www .illdoctrine.com.

SHELLY TOCHLUK, WITNESSING WHITENESS: THE NEED TO TALK ABOUT RACE AND HOW TO DO IT (Rowman & Littlefield Educ. 2007).

Stephanie M. Wildman & Adrienne D. Davis, *Making Systems of Privilege Visible, in* Privilege Revealed: How Invisible Preference Undermines America (Stephanie Wildman ed., N.Y. Univ. 1996).

Tim Wise, White Like Me: Reflections on Race from a Privileged Son (Soft Skull Press 2004).

Conferences, Events, Trainings, and Websites

Throughout the book, I mentioned organizations and trainings in which you could participate if you want to join with others who are also on the journey of self-awareness and skill building. I have included them below as well as added others.

This annual conference brings together students, teachers, social workers, and nonprofit staffers from thirty-five states and several foreign countries to examine and challenge concepts of privilege and oppression and offer solutions and team-building strategies to work toward a more equitable world. It is a program of the Matrix Center for Advancement of Social Equity and Inclusion at the University of Colorado.

White Privilege Conference (WPC), www.whiteprivilegeconference.com.

Since 1970, the YWCA's one imperative asks members to use their collective power to eliminate racism. In recent years, it has brought people together from all walks of life throughout the country to raise awareness that racism still exists and how it hurts everyone. Individual YWCAs invite groups from schools, businesses, nonprofits, and government agencies to take a stand. They provide ideas for activities and guides for discussions for gatherings ranging from small groups to large rallies; and they help organize the events at work, in neighborhoods, and in other settings.

YWCA, Stand Against Racism, http://www.standagainstracism.org/.

This organization offers training, prejudice-reducing workshops, and publications such as Welcoming Diversity and a free download of Principles into Practice: Strengthening Leadership for a Diverse Society (2003). NCBI recently sponsored a great step-by-step guide to help individuals and groups to effect sustainable multicultural change in their organizations and communities: Cherie Brown & George J. Mazza, Leading Diverse Communities: A How-To Guide for Moving from Healing into Action (Jossey-Bass 2004).

National Coalition Building Institute (NCBI), http://ncbi.org/.

This four-day workshop offers strategies for participants to identify personal prejudice and misinformation, recognize institutional and systemic discrimination, change racially dysfunctional behavior, promote understanding of the impact of discrimination on individuals, and incorporate relevant current problems into their examination of multicultural issues.

Visions Inc., http://www.visions-inc.org/.

This nonprofit organization in Boston, Massachusetts, promotes racial justice and equity. It was formed in 1968 as a white-led organization purposely focused on what it calls the "white problem," i.e., white systematic racism and unearned privilege enjoyed by white Americans. It sponsors open forums, discussions, and events to raise awareness regarding white racism and to support the communities of color that are negatively impacted by such racism. It has an extensive resource center that can be accessed online.

Community Change, Inc. (CCI), http://www.communitychangeinc.org.

Appendix B
Lifetime Benefits of Being a Working Class White Person in the Early 21st Century
by Chip Smith

(See note at end for key to abbreviations.)

Heritage

*246 million acres of **land** distributed to white homesteaders during the 19th Century (only .3%
were black),* affecting about one quarter of today's population [BC, 3]

*Trillions in **accumulated earnings differences** favoring white people, as a result of slavery,
segregation and contemporary discrimination* [BC, 3]

*Effects of Federal Housing Administration and Veterans Administration **redlining and home
loan restrictions**, from the 1930s through the 1960s favoring white homeowners' asset
building* [SFC, 2; HC, 190]

*Effects of GI Bill after World War II favoring white **employment advancement*** [HC, 190]

*White people's **inheritances**:*

> *3.6 times the likelihood of **receiving an inheritance**:* 28% of white families vs. 7.7%
> for African Americans [2004, UFE, 17]

> *4 times greater **parental median net worth*** (assets minus debts): $198,700 (w) vs.
> $47,000 (A) [2004, UFE, 17]

At *birth*

*Less than half the chance of **dying as an infant**:* 5.7 per 1,000 live births (w) vs. 14.0 (A)
[2001, WIR, 103]; just under half the rate (n) [2003, APH]

*Greater **life expectancy**:*

> *male:* 74.8 years (w) vs. 68.2 years (A) [2003, APH]

> *female:* 80.0 years (w) vs. 74.9 years (A) [2003, APH]

Reprinted with permission from Chip Smith, from *The Cost of Privilege: Taking On the System of White Supremacy and Racism*
(Fayetteville, NC: Camino Press, 2007).

Youth

*Less than half the chance of **growing up in poverty**:* 14.3% of children (w) vs. 34.1 %(A) and 29.7% (L) [2003, SWA, 319]

*About half the chance of growing up in a family that is **"asset poor"**:* 26% (w) vs. 52% (A) and 54% (L) [1999, HC, 40]

*If arrested, twice as likely to be **processed as a juvenile**, and not as an adult:* 66% (w) vs. 31% (A) [2000, MM, 6]

*When **arrested the first time**, one ninth the chance of being sent to juvenile prison:* compared to African Americans [2000, MM, 6]

*When arrested **on a drug charge**, 1/48th the chance of being sent to juvenile prison:* compared to African Americans [2000, MM, 6]

*Overall less likely to be **held in juvenile jails** or placed in **adult prisons**:* compared to the African American youth, who make up 44% and 58% of the youth in these facilities, while being about 15% of the youth population [2000, MM, 6]

*Spend less time in prison for **violent offenses**:* 193 days on average (w) vs. 254 (A) and 305 (L) [2000, MM, 6]

*Less likely to be **under correctional supervision**:* 1 in 15 young males (w) vs. 1 in 3 (A) and 1 in 10 (L) [2003, MM, 5]

Education

*Higher chance of **completing high school**:* 88.7% (w) vs. 79.2% (A) [2002, WIR, 214]

*More likely to **attend a racially segregated school**:* percentage of students of own race at their school, on average, 80% (w) vs. a little over 50% (A and L, taken together) [2001, HC, 143]

More likely as a white student to: [HC, 144-145]

> *begin school **without a "cognitive skills" gap***
>
> *attend a **higher quality school***
>
> *be taught by **higher paid teachers***
>
> *be tracked into a **higher-level ability grouping***
>
> *have more access to **special program** opportunities*
>
> *have more access to **technology***
>
> *have **more money spent** on you, both as capital investment and operating costs*
>
> *have **questions on the SATs** favor you:* "every question chosen to appear on every SAT in the past ten years has favored whites over blacks" [2003, *Nation*, 24]

College

*More likely to **complete four or more years** of college:* 29.4% (w) vs. 17.2% (A), as percent of the group's adult population [2002, WIR, 103]

*More than a third more likely to **graduate in six years**:* 59% (w) vs. 37 % (A), as percent of group entering college [1998, BP, 6]

*More likely to have a **professor of your own race**:* compared to African Americans, who are 11.1% of students and 5% of faculty [1998, BP, 6]

*One third the chance of being a **victim of a hate crime** on campus:* compared to African Americans [2000, BP, 4]

Employment and unemployment

Less likely to be **unemployed**: 4.8% (w), 10.9% (A), 6.8% (L) [2004, SWA, 222]

Less likely to hold a **low-wage job**: white people are 58.4% of low-wage workers and 69.6% of the overall population, or 58.4% / 69.6% (w) vs. 14% / 11.2 % (A) and 21.9% / 13.4 %(L) [2003, SWA, 341]

More likely to be **interviewed and hired** *by someone of your own race* [COOS, 60]

Less likely to be subjected to **special hiring tests** [COOS, 60]

(Benefits of being a working class white person, continued)

More likely to **use computers** *at work:* 51.3% (w) vs. 39.9% (A) [1997, SWA, 211]

More **favorable employment position**, *shown by smaller gain from unionization:* 13.8% wage premium when unionized (w) vs. 20.9% (A) and 23.2% (L) [2003, SWA, 191]

Have a greater chance at **higher paying jobs** *in:*   [1999, COOS, 55-59]

    advertising: <2% African American

    largest law firms: .01% African American [1990]

    media: TV writers, movies, publishing houses, news reporters, and editors

or in **positions** *as:*

    sales representatives

    engineers

    magazine staff, including "liberal" or left media like *The Nation* or *Rolling Stone*

    police

    firefighters: <2% African American

During a recession **less likely to lose**:

    your **job**: job loss from 2001-2003, 1.9% (w) vs. 3.4% (A) [2003, SWA, 251]

    a **long-tenure job**: during 2001-2003 recession, 5.6% (w) vs. 7.3% (A) [CEPR, 4]

Much less likely to be a **target of racial harassment** *on the job* [2000, BW]

Income and poverty

Bring home more **income** *in a year:*

    about 40% higher median family income: $55,768 (w) vs. $34,369 (A) and $34,272 (L) [2003, SWA, 48]

    higher women's hourly wage: $12.94 (w) vs. $11.14 (A) and $9.75 (L) [2003, SWA, 167]

    higher men's hourly wage: $16.82 (w) vs. $12.23 (A) and $10.67 (L) [2003, SWA, 167]

Be cushioned against **income loss** *during recessions:* -1.7% average income loss from 2001 to 2003 (w) vs. -3.5 % (A) [WIR, 96]

Less than half as likely to:

    be **poor**: 10.5% (w) vs. 24.4% (A) and 22.5% (L) [2003, SWA, 316]; 8% (w) vs. 26% (n) [2001, WIR, 42]

    experience **food hardship**: 17.1% (w) vs. 37.6% (A) and 43.7% (L) [2002, REEW, 3]

    experience **housing hardship**: 10.0% (w) vs. 23.5% (A) and 19.6% (L) [2002, REEW, 3]

Housing and homelessness

Less likely to be **homeless***:* white people are 35% of the homeless and 70% of the overall population, or 35% / 70% (w) vs. 50% / 12% (A), 12% / 12% (L), and 2% / <1% (n) [2001, CL, 26]

More likely to be offered: [1995-1997, COOS, 39]

> *lower* **rents**
>
> *more* **incentives**
>
> *more* **choices***:* "60 to 90 percent of housing units shown to whites are not made available to blacks"

More likely to **own your own home***:* 72.1% (w) vs. 48.1% (A) and 46.7% (L) [2003, SWA, 295]

More likely to have **help from your family** *to make down payment:* 46% (w) vs. 12% (A) [1991-1995, HC, 113]

Half as likely to be **turned down** *for a mortgage or home improvement loan* [2004, UL]

Pay a lower **interest rate** *on your mortgage:* 8.12% (w) vs. 8.44% (A) [1999, HC, 111]

Have more **equity** *in your home:* median $58,000 (w) vs. $40,000 (A) [1994, HC, 109]

Less likely to live by a **toxic waste** *dump* [1999, EF, 2]

More likely to live in a **segregated** *community* [2003, BCGI, 4]

Have the value of your house **secured by segregation** *and threatened by integration* [HC, 121]

Have your home be more **highly valued** *on the market:* by 22% compared to African American homeowners [2001, HC, 121]

Household wealth and asset poverty

Ten times as much **wealth** (assets minus debts):

> *median household:* $106,400 (w) vs. $10,700 (A) [2001, SWA, 285]
>
> *single woman headed household:* $56,590 (w) vs. $5,700 (A) and $3,900 (L) [2001, WIR, 65]

Twice as likely to own **stocks, bonds or mutual funds** [BCGI, 5]

Have more than 5 times the **savings** *in IRAs, thrifts, and future pensions:* $63,506 (w) vs. $11,890 (A) and $9,904 (L) [2001, WIR, 14]

Less than half the likelihood of:

> *living in a household with* **debts** *equal to or greater than your assets:* 13.1% (w) vs. 30.9% (A) [2001, SWA, 285]
>
> *being* **asset poor***:* 25% (w) vs. 54% (A) [1999, HC, 39]
>
> *having* **trouble paying** *rent or mortgage* [BCGI, 5]

Greater **ability to bounce back** *from economic recession:* between 1996 and 2002, wealth up 17% (w), down 22% (A), back to original level (L) [BC, 1]

(Benefits of being a working class white person, continued)

Health

More likely to:

> *be in* **good health***:* 92% (w), 86% (A), 87% (L), 83% (n) [2003, APH]
>
> *have* **health insurance***:* 88.3% (w), 79.8% (A), 67.6% (L) [2002, APH]
>
> *have a* **regular doctor***:* 80% (w), 67% (A), a little over 50% (L) [2003, APH]

be able to **choose your medical provider**: 84% (w), just over 70% (A and L) [2003, APH]

see a **doctor of your own race**: compared to African Americans and Latinos, who make up >25% of the population but have just 11% of medical school graduates [2005, GDN]

receive **higher quality** health care [2002, HA, 314]

If insured:

one third the chance of having **public insurance**, like Medicaid, which some doctors refuse to accept [2002, APH]

50% more likely to **receive authorization** for an emergency room visit: compared to African Americans [2002, APH]

Less likely to:

have **trouble communicating** with your doctor: 16% (w), 23% (A), 33% (L), 27% (API) [2003, APH]

suffer from **hypertension and diabetes**: compared to African Americans [2000, LH]

die from **coronary disease, stroke, prostate, and breast cancer**: compared to African Americans [2002, HA, 313]

Half the likelihood of dying from **diabetes**: compared to Native Americans and Latinos [2003, APH]

One-sixth the chance of being the victim of a **homicide**: compared to African Americans [2003, APH]

One-seventh the chance of dying from **AIDS**: compared to African Americans [2003, APH]

Justice system

Less chance of **going to jail**: 160 out of 100,000 residents of the same race (w) vs. 765 (A) and 262 (L) [2004, BJS]

Much less chance of:

being stopped by police as a result of **racial profiling** [1999, AI]

being subjected to **"police brutality, unjustified shootings and deaths in custody"** [1999, AI]

being sentenced to **death and executed** [2003, AI2]

Half as likely to be **stopped and searched** for drugs, if a white male, while twice as likely to have drugs when searched [2002, TW, 13]

Far less chance of going to prison for a **drug charge**: compared to African Americans, who are 14% of drug users, 35% of drug arrests, 55% of drug convictions, and 75% of those sent to prison on drug charges [2003, MM, 5]

Serve a year **less time** on average when convicted: compared to African Americans [Debt, 214]

Elections

Less likely to be **disenfranchised**: in 23 states more than 10% of African American males cannot vote; in AL and FL the number is above 30%; and in MI, VA, and NM it is about 25% [2003, MM, 6]

More likely to have **your own race vote for you** if you run for office [2001, BCGI, 80]

Retirement

*Have more than 5 times the **retirement and pension assets:*** average value $65,411 (w) vs. $12,247 (A) and $10,206 (L) [2001, UFE, 18]

*Less likely to have **retirement income** under half your current income:* 25.4% (w) vs. 40.0% (A or L) [2001, SWA, 297]

Letters in parentheses signify (w) = white, (A) = African American, (L) = Latino, (n) = native, (API) = Asian/Pacific Islander Year, source, and page number of data are in brackets.

Abbreviations are as follows, with full citations listed in the bibliography: AI= Amnesty International, 1999; AI2=Amnesty International, 2003; APH=American Public Health Association; BC=*Black Commentator*; BCGI=*Breaking the Code of Good Intentions*, Bush; BJS=Bureau of Justice Statistics; BP=BlackPressUSA, Edney; BW=*BusinessWeek*, Bernstein; CEPR=Center for Economic and Policy Research, Schmitt; CL=*ColorLines*, Talvi; COOS=*By the Color of Our Skin*, Steinhorn and Diggs-Brown; EF=Earth First, Schweizer; GDN=*Greater Diversity News*, Curry; HA=*Health Affairs*, Lavizzo-Mourey; HC=*Hidden Cost of Being African American*, Shapiro; LH=Leslie Harris; MM=Manning Marable, "Abolishing American Apartheid, Root and Branch"; *Nation*, Rosner; REEW="Race, Ethnicity, and Economic Well-Being," Finegold and Wherry; SFC=*San Francisco Chronicle*, Adelman; SWA=*State of Working America*, Mishel; TW=Tim Wise, "White Racism in the Present Era"; UFE=United for a Fair Economy, Leondar-Wright, et. al.; UL=Urban League, Ferguson; WIR=*Wealth Inequality Reader*, Collins, et. al.

'Asset poverty results when household wealth (assets minus debts) is insufficient to maintain the family at the poverty line for three months ($4,175 in 1999) when no income is coming in.

Index